SRA
Reading Mastery
Signature Edition

Textbook A

Siegfried Engelmann
Jean Osborn
Steve Osborn
Leslie Zoref

McGraw Hill **SRA**

Columbus, Ohio

Acknowledgments
Grateful acknowledgment is given to the following publishers and copyright owners for permissions granted to reprint selections from their publications. All possible care has been taken to trace ownership and secure permission for each selection included. In case of any errors or omissions, the Publisher will be pleased to make suitable acknowledgments in future editions.

The Estate of Eleanor Clymer
"The Spider, The Cave, and the Pottery Bowl" Eleanor Clymer. Used by permission.

HarperCollins
"Mrs. Dunn's Lovely, Lovely Farm" from THE WITCH OF FOURTH STREET AND OTHER STORIES by Myron Levoy. COPYRIGHT © 1972 MYRON LEVOY. Used by permission of HarperCollins Children's Publishing.

Penguin Group (USA)
"The Doughnuts", from HOMER PRICE by Robert McCloskey, copyright 1943, renewed © 1971 by Robert McCloskey. Used by permission of Viking Penguin, A Division of Penguin Young Readers Group, A Member of Penguin Group (USA) Inc., 345 Hudson Street, New York, NY 10014. All rights reserved.

Illustration Credits
Meg Aubrey, Doris Ettinger, Kate Flanagan, Greg Harris, Holly Jones, Jane Kendall, Deborah Maze, Robert McCloskey

Photo Credits
193, © Photodisc; **290,** © Chris Hellier/Corbis; **320,** © Corbis.

SRAonline.com

Table of Contents

Skilled Hands

Your life is in your hands. With just ten fingers, two palms, and a little help from the rest of your body, you can do almost anything. You can build, fix, write, paint, catch, throw, and hold.

In this unit, you will meet many different characters—young and old, male and female, ancient and modern. Yet, despite their differences, they all depend on their hands to help them solve problems, meet challenges, and find happiness. To begin their stories, use your fingers to turn the page.

1

A WORD LISTS

1
Hard Words
1. freight
2. chauffeur
3. recipe
4. receipt
5. Odyssey

2
Character Names
1. Athena
2. Hermes
3. Homer
4. Odysseus
5. Ulysses
6. Zeus

3
Word Practice
1. advertise
2. advertising
3. improve
4. improvements

4
New Vocabulary
1. box social
2. up-and-coming
3. unkindly disposed
4. for a spell
5. advanced
6. batter
7. chauffeur
8. receipt

B VOCABULARY DEFINITIONS

1. **box social**—A *box social* is a fund-raising event where box lunches are sold to the highest bidders.
2. **up-and-coming**—Something that is becoming popular is *up and coming.* A singer who is becoming popular is an up-and-coming singer.
3. **unkindly disposed**—When you are *unkindly disposed* toward something, you don't like it.
4. **for a spell**—*For a spell* is another way of saying "for a while."
5. **advanced**—When something is ahead, it is *advanced.* If somebody has ideas that are ahead of other people's ideas, that person has advanced ideas.

6. **batter**—Doughnuts, pancakes, and similar foods are made from *batter.* When the batter is raw, it can be poured.
7. **chauffeur**—A *chauffeur* is a person who is paid to drive a car for somebody else.
8. **receipt**—*Receipt* is another word for *recipe.*

Life in the 1930s

The first story you will read is called "The Doughnuts." The story was written by Robert McCloskey, and it is set in the United States during the late 1930s.

The main character in the story is a boy named Homer Price. Homer is good at fixing machines and solving problems. He lives with his mother and his father near the small town of Centerburg, where his aunt and uncle own a lunchroom.

Looking for Work

During the 1930s, jobs were hard to find in the United States. Many unemployed people wandered from town to town looking for work. Some traveled by sneaking onto freight trains. This practice was called "riding the rods."

Sometimes store owners gave these travelers odd jobs. One job was to walk around wearing a "sandwich" sign that advertised the store. One half of the sign hung down the person's front side, and the other half hung down the back. The result looked like a walking sandwich, with the person in the middle.

Even though money was scarce during the 1930s, Americans still volunteered for the Red Cross. This organization, which still exists, helps the victims of fires, floods, and other disasters. In "The Doughnuts," Homer's mother gets together with other women to make clothing for the Red Cross.

Laborsaving Devices

Some Americans who lived during the 1930s believed that machines would help solve the country's problems. These people were particularly interested in machines that could make work easier. Such machines were called "laborsaving devices."

Because so many people were out of work, other Americans wondered why there was so much interest in laborsaving devices. They argued that laborsaving devices would just put more people out of work.

"The Doughnuts" makes fun of laborsaving devices by showing what can happen when one of these machines stops working properly.

The Doughnuts
by Robert McCloskey
Part 1

One Friday night in November Homer overheard his mother talking on the telephone to Aunt Agnes over in Centerburg. "I'll stop by with the car in about half an hour and we can go to the meeting together," she said, because tonight was the night the Ladies' Club was meeting to discuss plans for a box social and to knit and sew for the Red Cross.

"I think I'll come along and keep Uncle Ulysses company while you and Aunt Agnes are at the meeting," said Homer.

So after Homer had combed his hair and his mother had looked to see if she had her knitting instructions and the right size needles, they started for town.

Homer's Uncle Ulysses and Aunt Agnes have a very up and coming lunch room over in Centerburg, just across from the court house on the town square. Uncle Ulysses is a man with advanced ideas and a weakness for labor saving devices. He equipped the lunch room with automatic toasters, automatic coffee maker, automatic dish washer, and an automatic doughnut maker. All just the latest thing in labor saving devices. Aunt Agnes would throw up her hands and sigh every time Uncle Ulysses bought a new labor saving device. Sometimes she became unkindly disposed toward him for days and days. She was of the opin-

ion that Uncle Ulysses just frittered away his spare time over at the barber shop with the sheriff and the boys, so, what was the good of a labor saving device that gave you more time to fritter?

When Homer and his mother got to Centerburg they stopped at the lunch room, and after Aunt Agnes had come out and said, "My, how that boy does grow!" which was what she always said, she went off with Homer's mother in the car. Homer went into the lunch room and said, "Howdy, Uncle Ulysses!"

"Oh, hello, Homer. You're just in time," said Uncle Ulysses. "I've been going over this automatic doughnut machine, oiling the machinery and cleaning the works. . . wonderful things, these labor saving devices."

"Yep," agreed Homer, and he picked up a cloth and started polishing the metal trimmings while Uncle Ulysses tinkered with the inside workings.

"Opfwo-oof!!" sighed Uncle Ulysses and, "Look here, Homer, you've got a mechanical mind. See if you can find where these two pieces fit in. I'm going across to the barber shop for a spell, 'cause there's somethin' I've got to talk to the sheriff about. There won't be much business here until the double feature is over and I'll be back before then."◆

Then as Uncle Ulysses went out the door he said, "Uh, Homer, after you get the pieces in place, would you mind mixing up a batch of doughnut batter and putting it in the machine? You could turn the switch and make a few doughnuts to have on hand for the crowd after the movie . . . if you don't mind."

"O.K.," said Homer, "I'll take care of everything."

A few minutes later a customer came in and said, "Good evening, Bud."

Homer looked up from putting the last piece in the doughnut machine and said, "Good evening, Sir, what can I do for you?"

"Well, young feller, I'd like a cup o' coffee and some doughnuts," said the customer.

"I'm sorry, Mister, but we won't have any doughnuts for about half an hour, until I can mix some dough and start this machine. I could give you some very fine sugar rolls instead."

"Well, Bud, I'm in no real hurry so I'll just have a cup o' coffee and wait around a bit for the doughnuts. Fresh doughnuts are always worth waiting for is what I always say."

"O.K.," said Homer, and he drew a cup of coffee from Uncle Ulysses' super automatic coffee maker.

"Nice place you've got here," said the customer.

"Oh, yes," replied Homer, "this is a very up and coming lunch room with all the latest improvements."

"Yes," said the stranger, "must be a good business. I'm in business too. A traveling man in outdoor advertising. I'm a sandwich man, Mr. Gabby's my name."

"My name is Homer. I'm glad to meet you, Mr. Gabby. It must be a fine profession, traveling and advertising sandwiches." ★

"Oh no," said Mr. Gabby, "I don't advertise sandwiches, I just wear any kind of an ad, one sign on front and one sign on behind, this way . . . Like a sandwich. Ya know what I mean?"

"Oh, I see. That must be fun, and you travel too?" asked Homer as he got out the flour and the baking powder.

"Yeah, I ride the rods between jobs, on freight trains, ya know what I mean?"

"Yes, but isn't that dangerous?" asked Homer.

"Of course there's a certain amount a risk, but you take any method a travel these days, it's all dangerous. Ya know what I mean? Now take airplanes for instance . . ."

Just then a large shiny black car stopped in front of the lunch room and a chauffeur helped a lady out of the rear door. They both came inside and the lady smiled at Homer and said, "We've stopped for a light snack. Some doughnuts and coffee would be simply marvelous."

Then Homer said, "I'm sorry, Ma'm, but the doughnuts won't be ready until I make this batter and start Uncle Ulysses' doughnut machine."

"Well now aren't *you* a clever young man to know how to make *doughnuts*!"

"Well," blushed Homer, "I've really never done it before but I've got a receipt to follow."

"Now, young man, you simply must allow me to help. You know, I haven't made doughnuts for years, but I know the best receipt for doughnuts. It's marvelous, and we really must use it."

"But, Ma'm . . ." said Homer.

"Now just *wait* till you taste these doughnuts," said the lady. "Do you have an apron?" she asked, as she took off her fur coat and her rings and her jewelry and rolled up her sleeves. "Charles," she said to the chauffeur, "hand me that baking powder, that's right, and, young man, we'll need some nutmeg."

E COMPREHENSION

Write the answers.

1. During the 1930s, why were some Americans opposed to laborsaving devices?
2. Why do you think Uncle Ulysses liked laborsaving devices?
3. How did Aunt Agnes feel about laborsaving devices? Why did she feel that way?
4. How can you tell the lady is probably rich?
5. What do you think will happen with the lady's batter? Explain your answer.

F WRITING

How do you feel about laborsaving devices?

Write a paragraph that explains how you feel. Try to answer the following questions:

- What is good about laborsaving devices?
- What is bad about laborsaving devices?
- How do you feel about laborsaving devices?
- Why do you feel that way?

Make your paragraph at least forty words long.

A WORD LISTS

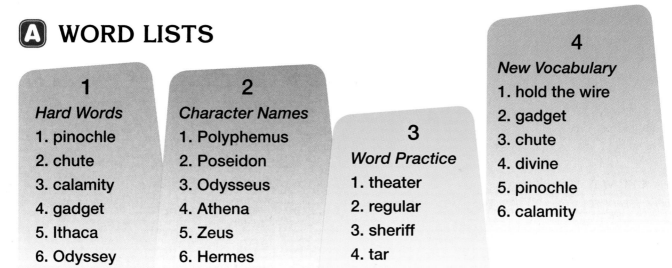

1

Hard Words
1. pinochle
2. chute
3. calamity
4. gadget
5. Ithaca
6. Odyssey

2

Character Names
1. Polyphemus
2. Poseidon
3. Odysseus
4. Athena
5. Zeus
6. Hermes

3

Word Practice
1. theater
2. regular
3. sheriff
4. tar
5. tarnation

4

New Vocabulary
1. hold the wire
2. gadget
3. chute
4. divine
5. pinochle
6. calamity

B VOCABULARY DEFINITIONS

1. **hold the wire**—*Hold the wire* is another way of saying "wait a minute" to somebody on the phone.
   - What's another way of saying *Wait a minute*?
2. **gadget**—A *gadget* is a device.
   - What's another way of saying *She invented a useful device*?
3. **chute**—A *chute* is a slide.
   - What's another way of saying *They shoveled coal into the slide*?
4. **divine**—*Divine* is another word for *marvelous*.
   - What's another way of saying *I had a marvelous time*?
5. **pinochle**—*Pinochle* is a card game played with a special deck of cards.
   - What is pinochle?
6. **calamity**—A *calamity* is a misfortune.
   - What's another way of saying *She suffered through misfortune after misfortune*?

The Doughnuts
Part 2

So Homer and the chauffeur stood by and handed things and cracked the eggs while the lady mixed and stirred. Mr. Gabby sat on his stool, sipped his coffee, and looked on with great interest.

"There!" said the lady when all of the ingredients were mixed. "Just *wait* till you taste these doughnuts!"

"It looks like an awful lot of batter," said Homer as he stood on a chair and poured it into the doughnut machine with the help of the chauffeur. "It's about *ten* times as much as Uncle Ulysses ever makes."

"But wait till you taste them!" said the lady with an eager look and a smile.

Homer got down from the chair and pushed a button on the machine marked, "Start." Rings of batter started dropping into the hot fat. After a ring of batter was cooked on one side an automatic gadget turned it over and the other side would cook. Then another automatic gadget gave the doughnut a little push and it rolled neatly down a little chute, all ready to eat.

"That's a simply *fascinating* machine," said the lady as she waited for the first doughnut to roll out.

"Here, young man, *you* must have the first one. Now isn't that just *too* delicious!? Isn't it simply marvelous?"

"Yes, Ma'm, it's very good," replied Homer as the lady handed doughnuts to Charles and to Mr. Gabby and asked if they didn't think they were simply divine doughnuts.

"It's an old family receipt!" said the lady with pride.

Homer poured some coffee for the lady and her chauffeur and for Mr. Gabby, and a glass of milk for himself. Then they all sat down at the lunch counter to enjoy another few doughnuts apiece.

"I'm so glad you enjoy my doughnuts," said the lady. "But now, Charles, we really must be going. If you will just take this apron, Homer, and put two dozen doughnuts in a bag to take along, we'll be on our way. And, Charles, don't forget to pay the young man." She rolled down her sleeves and put on her jewelry, then Charles managed to get her into her big fur coat.

"Good night, young man, I haven't had so much fun in years. I *really* haven't!" said the lady, as she went out the door and into the big shiny car.

"Those are sure good doughnuts," said Mr. Gabby as the car moved off.

"You bet!" said Homer. Then he and Mr. Gabby stood and watched the automatic doughnut machine make doughnuts.

After a few dozen more doughnuts had rolled down the little chute, Homer said, "I guess that's about enough doughnuts to sell to the after theater customers. I'd better turn the machine off for a while."

Homer pushed the button marked "Stop" and there was a little click, but nothing happened. The rings of batter kept right on dropping into the hot fat, and an automatic gadget kept right on turning them over, and another automatic gadget kept right on giving them a little push and the doughnuts kept right on rolling down the little chute, all ready to eat.

"That's funny," said Homer, "I'm sure that's the right button!" He pushed it again but the automatic doughnut maker kept right on making doughnuts.

"Well I guess I must have put one of those pieces in backwards," said Homer.

"Then it might stop if you pushed the button marked 'Start,'" said Mr. Gabby.

Homer did, and the doughnuts still kept rolling down the little chute, just as regular as a clock can tick.

"I guess we could sell a few more doughnuts," said Homer, "but I'd better telephone Uncle Ulysses over at the barber shop." Homer gave the number and while he waited for someone to answer he counted thirty-seven doughnuts roll down the little chute.

Finally someone answered "Hello! This is the sarber bhop, I mean the barber shop."

"Oh, hello, sheriff. This is Homer. Could I speak to Uncle Ulysses?"

"Well, he's playing pinochle right now," said the sheriff. "Anythin' I can tell 'im?" ◆

"Yes," said Homer. "I pushed the button marked *Stop* on the doughnut machine but the rings of batter keep right on dropping into the hot fat, and an automatic gadget keeps right on turning them over, and another automatic gadget keeps giving

them a little push, and the doughnuts keep right on rolling down the little chute! It won't stop!"

"O.K. Wold the hire, I mean, hold the wire and I'll tell 'im." Then Homer looked over his shoulder and counted another twenty-one doughnuts roll down the little chute, all ready to eat. Then the sheriff said, "He'll be right over . . . Just gotta finish this hand."

"That's good," said Homer. "G'by, sheriff."

The window was full of doughnuts by now so Homer and Mr. Gabby had to hustle around and start stacking them on plates and trays and lining them up on the counter.

"Sure are a lot of doughnuts!" said Homer.

"You bet!" said Mr. Gabby. "I lost count at twelve hundred and two and that was quite a while back." ★

People had begun to gather outside the lunch room window, and someone was saying, "There are almost as many doughnuts as there are people in Centerburg, and I wonder how in tarnation Ulysses thinks he can sell all of 'em!"

Every once in a while somebody would come inside and buy some, but while somebody bought two to eat and a dozen to take home, the machine made three dozen more.

By the time Uncle Ulysses and the sheriff arrived and pushed through the crowd, the lunch room was a calamity of doughnuts! Doughnuts in the window, doughnuts piled high on the shelves, doughnuts stacked on plates, doughnuts lined up twelve deep all along the counter, and doughnuts still rolling down the little chute, just as regular as a clock can tick.

"Hello, sheriff, hello, Uncle Ulysses, we're having a little trouble here," said Homer.

"Well, I'll be dunked!!" said Uncle Ulysses.

"Dernd ef you won't be when Aggy gits home," said the sheriff.

"Mighty fine doughnuts though. What'll you do with 'em all, Ulysses?"

Uncle Ulysses groaned and said, "What will Aggy say? We'll never sell 'em all."

D COMPREHENSION

Write the answers.
1. What two things did the machine do to the rings of batter after they dropped into the hot fat?
2. Why did Mr. Gabby think the machine might stop if Homer pushed the start button?
3. How can you tell that Uncle Ulysses wasn't a very hard worker?
4. How do you think Uncle Ulysses could sell all the doughnuts?
5. What might Aunt Agnes say to Uncle Ulysses when she finds out about the doughnuts?

E WRITING

Uncle Ulysses might try to sell the doughnuts by advertising them.
    Write a paragraph that advertises Homer's doughnuts. Be sure it answers the following questions:
  • How do they taste?
  • What ingredients are used?
  • How are they made?
  • Why should people buy them?
Make your paragraph at least forty words long.

3

Ⓐ WORD LISTS

1

Hard Words
1. skeptical
2. lyre
3. citizens
4. merchandise
5. trident
6. Ithaca
7. Iliad

2

Character Names
1. Penelope
2. Circe
3. Rupert
4. Poseidon
5. Polyphemus
6. Hermes
7. Zeus
8. Athena

3

Word Practice
1. pinochle
2. Odyssey
3. Odysseus
4. bracelet
5. suspicious

4

New Vocabulary
1. demand
2. create a market
3. enlarge
4. hire
5. citizens
6. merchandise
7. skeptical

Ⓑ VOCABULARY DEFINITIONS

1. **demand**—The *demand* for a product tells how many people want to buy that product. When the demand is high, many people want to buy the product.
   • What happens when the demand is low?
2. **create a market**—When you *create a market,* you create a demand.
   • What's another way of saying *She created a demand for small computers*?
3. **enlarge**—When you *enlarge* something, you make it bigger.
   • What's another way of saying *He made the circle bigger*?
4. **hire**—When you *hire* somebody, you give that person a job.
   • What's another way of saying *They gave the gardener a job*?

5. **citizens**—*Citizens* are people who live in a place. The people who live in Centerburg are the citizens of Centerburg.
   • What do we call the people who live in Springfield?
6. **merchandise**—When you *merchandise* a product, you carry out a plan for selling that product. When you carry out a plan for selling razors, you merchandise razors.
   • What are you doing when you carry out a plan for selling doughnuts?
7. **skeptical**—When you are suspicious about something, you are *skeptical* of that thing.
   • What's another way of saying *She was suspicious about his ability*?

The Doughnuts
Part 3

Then Mr. Gabby, who hadn't said anything for a long time, stopped piling doughnuts and said, "What you need is an advertising man. Ya know what I mean? You got the doughnuts, ya gotta create a market . . . Understand? . . . It's balancing the demand with the supply . . . That sort of thing."

"Yep!" said Homer. "Mr. Gabby's right. We have to enlarge our market. He's an advertising sandwich man, so if we hire him, he can walk up and down in front of the theater and get the customers."

"You're hired, Mr. Gabby!" said Uncle Ulysses.

Then everybody pitched in to paint the signs and to get Mr. Gabby sandwiched between. They painted "SALE ON DOUGHNUTS" in big letters on the window too.

Meanwhile the rings of batter kept right on dropping into the hot fat, and an automatic gadget kept right on turning them over, and another automatic gadget kept right on giving them a little push, and the doughnuts kept right on rolling down the little chute, just as regular as a clock can tick.

"I certainly hope this advertising works," said Uncle Ulysses, wagging his head. "Aggy'll certainly throw a fit if it don't."

The sheriff went outside to keep order, because there was quite a crowd by now—all looking at the doughnuts and guessing how many thousand there were, and watching new ones roll down the little chute, just as regular as a clock can tick. Homer and Uncle Ulysses kept stacking doughnuts. Once in a while somebody bought a few, but not very often.

Then Mr. Gabby came back and said, "Say, you know there's not much use o' me advertisin' at the theater. The show's all over, and besides almost everybody in town is out front watching that machine make doughnuts!"

"Zeus!" said Uncle Ulysses. "We must get rid of these doughnuts before Aggy gets here!"

"Looks like you will have ta hire a truck ta waul 'em ahay, I mean haul 'em away!!" said the sheriff who had just come in. Just then there was a noise and a shoving out front and the lady from the shiny black car and her chauffeur came pushing through the crowd and into the lunch room. ◆

"Oh, gracious!" she gasped, ignoring the doughnuts, "I've lost my diamond bracelet, and I know I left it here on the counter," she said, pointing to a place where the doughnuts were piled in stacks of two dozen.

"Yes, Ma'm, I guess you forgot it when you helped make the batter," said Homer.

Then they moved all the doughnuts around and looked for the diamond bracelet, but they couldn't find it anywhere. Meanwhile the doughnuts kept rolling down the little chute, just as regular as a clock can tick.

After they had looked all around the sheriff cast a suspicious eye on Mr. Gabby, but Homer said, "He's all right, sheriff, he didn't take it. He's a friend of mine."

Then the lady said, "I'll offer a reward of one hundred dollars for that bracelet! It really *must* be found! . . . it *really* must!"

"Now don't you worry, lady," said the sheriff. "I'll get your bracelet back!"

"Zeus! This is terrible!" said Uncle Ulysses. "First all of these doughnuts and then on top of all that, a lost diamond bracelet . . ."

Mr. Gabby tried to comfort him, and he said, "There's always a bright side. That machine'll probably run outta batter in an hour or two."

If Mr. Gabby hadn't been quick on his feet Uncle Ulysses would have knocked him down, sure as fate.

Then while the lady wrung her hands and said, "We must find it, we *must!*" and

Uncle Ulysses was moaning about what Aunt Agnes would say, and the sheriff was eyeing Mr. Gabby, Homer sat down and thought hard. ★

Before twenty more doughnuts could roll down the little chute he shouted, "SAY! I know where the bracelet is! It was lying here on the counter and got mixed up in the batter by mistake! The bracelet is cooked inside one of these doughnuts!"

"Why . . . I really believe you're right," said the lady through her tears. "Isn't that *amazing?* Simply *amazing!*"

"I'll be durn'd!" said the sheriff.

"OhH-h!" moaned Uncle Ulysses. "Now we have to break up all of these doughnuts to find it. Think of the *pieces!* Think of the *crumbs!* Think of what *Aggy* will say!"

"Nope," said Homer. "We won't have to break them up. I've got a plan."

So Homer and the advertising man took some cardboard and some paint and printed another sign. They put this sign in the window, and the sandwich man wore two more signs that said the same thing and walked around in the crowd out front.

FRESH DOUGHNUTS
2 FOR 5¢
~~$~~ WHILE THEY LAST
$100.00 PRIZE
FOR FINDING
A BRACELET
INSIDE A DOUGHNUT
P.S. YOU HAVE TO GIVE THE
BRACELET BACK

THEN . . . The doughnuts began to sell! *Everybody* wanted to buy doughnuts, *dozens* of doughnuts!

And that's not all. Everybody bought coffee to dunk the doughnuts in too. Those that didn't buy coffee bought milk or soda. It kept Homer and the lady and the chauffeur and Uncle Ulysses and the sheriff busy waiting on the people who wanted to buy doughnuts.

When all but the last couple of hundred doughnuts had been sold, Rupert Black shouted, "I GAWT IT!!" and sure enough . . . there was the diamond bracelet inside of his doughnut!

Then Rupert went home with a hundred dollars, the citizens of Centerburg went home full of doughnuts, the lady and her chauffeur drove off with the diamond bracelet, and Homer went home with his mother when she stopped by with Aunt Aggy.

As Homer went out of the door he heard Mr. Gabby say, "Neatest trick of merchandising I ever seen," and Aunt Aggy was looking skeptical while Uncle Ulysses was saying, "The rings of batter kept right on dropping into the hot fat, and the automatic gadget kept right on turning them over, and the other automatic gadget kept right on giving them a little push, and the doughnuts kept right on rolling down the little chute just as regular as a clock can tick—they just kept right on a comin', an' a comin', an' a comin', an' a comin'."

D VOCABULARY REVIEW

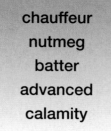

chauffeur

nutmeg

batter

advanced

calamity

For each item, write the correct word.
1. Another word for misfortune is ▆▆▆.
2. Something that has moved forward is ▆▆▆.
3. A person who is paid to drive a car for somebody else is a ▆▆▆.

E COMPREHENSION

Write the answers.
1. Before the lady came back to the lunchroom, how did Mr. Gabby market the doughnuts?
2. Why didn't his plan work?
3. How did the lady's bracelet get into one of the doughnuts?
4. After Homer found out about the bracelet, how did he market the doughnuts?
5. Why did his plan succeed?

F WRITING

What would you do if you won a hundred dollars?

Write a paragraph that explains what you would do. Try to answer the following questions:
- What are three things you would like to do?
- Which one of those things would you do?
- Why would you do that thing?

Make your paragraph at least forty words long.

A WORD LISTS

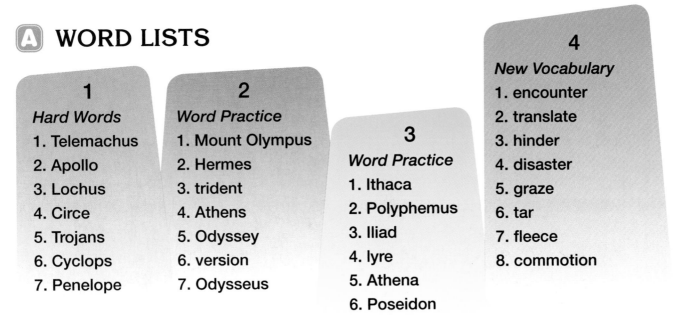

1
Hard Words
1. Telemachus
2. Apollo
3. Lochus
4. Circe
5. Trojans
6. Cyclops
7. Penelope

2
Word Practice
1. Mount Olympus
2. Hermes
3. trident
4. Athens
5. Odyssey
6. version
7. Odysseus

3
Word Practice
1. Ithaca
2. Polyphemus
3. Iliad
4. lyre
5. Athena
6. Poseidon

4
New Vocabulary
1. encounter
2. translate
3. hinder
4. disaster
5. graze
6. tar
7. fleece
8. commotion

B VOCABULARY DEFINITIONS

1. **encounter**—When you *encounter* something, you come into contact with that thing.
   - What's another way of saying *He came into contact with misfortune*?
2. **translate**—When you tell a story in another language, you *translate* the story into that language. If you tell an English story in German, you translate it into German.
   - What do you do if you tell a Japanese story in French?
3. **hinder**—Some of the people helped her, but others tried to *hinder* her.
   - What could *hinder* mean?
4. **disaster**—A horrible event is a *disaster.*
   - What's another way of saying *The flood was a horrible event*?
5. **graze**—When animals *graze,* they eat plants that are growing in the ground.
   - What do animals do when they graze?
6. **tar**—*Tar* is a hard black substance that turns into a sticky mass when it's heated.
   - What is tar?
7. **fleece**—The fur of a sheep is called *fleece.*
   - What do we call the fur of a sheep?
8. **commotion**—A *commotion* is a disturbance.
   - What's another way of saying *There was a great disturbance in the hall*?

Two Old Stories

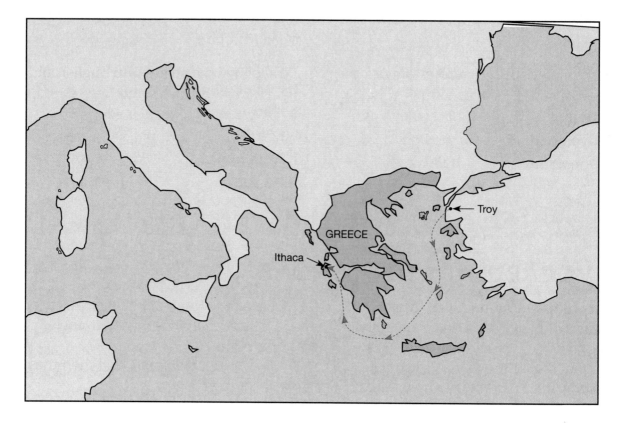

In the next lesson, you will begin reading *The Odyssey*, one of the oldest stories in the world. The story tells about Greek heroes who lived more than three thousand years ago. The story is fictional, but it describes real places and tells about people who may really have lived during that time.

The Iliad and *The Odyssey*

The story told in *The Odyssey* actually begins in another book, called *The Iliad*. That book tells about a war between Greece and the walled city of Troy, where the Trojans lived. This war lasted for ten years.

The war ended when the Greek army gave the Trojans a huge wooden horse and then pretended to leave. The horse actually contained some soldiers. When the Trojan army brought the horse into Troy, the Greek soldiers sneaked out of the horse and opened the gates of the city. Then the Greek army marched into Troy and conquered it.

The Greek army was made up of soldiers from different parts of Greece. Each part of Greece had its own king. One of the most important kings was Odysseus, who ruled over the island of Ithaca, off the west coast of Greece. Odysseus was one of the heroes of the Trojan War, and he was the one who thought up the trick with the horse.

The Iliad has many characters and many heroes. *The Odyssey* begins right after the Trojan War. It tells about Odysseus's long journey back to Ithaca and all the dangers he encounters. Unlike *The Iliad*, *The Odyssey* has only one main character, Odysseus. His name is almost the same as the title of the book.

Homer

The Iliad and *The Odyssey* were probably first told by a blind poet named Homer, who lived almost five hundred years after the Trojan War. Homer probably told his stories out loud to large groups of people. As he told his stories, he may have played a small musical instrument called a lyre, and he may even have sung the words of the story.

Some of the people who heard Homer learned the stories from him, and they continued to tell the stories after Homer died.

Another two hundred years went by before anyone wrote down the stories. Some of the storytellers may have changed Homer's words by that time, but we will never know for sure. What is remarkable is that the stories survived at all and that they remained so powerful.

The Iliad and *The Odyssey* were originally written in Greek, in the form of long poems. Over the years, many writers have translated the poems into English and other languages. Some writers have kept the stories as poems, and others have turned them into novels. You will read a translation of *The Odyssey* in the form of a novel. This translation is shorter than the original Greek version, and some of the parts have been left out, but the basic story remains the same. Someday you may want to read the complete *Odyssey*. Many people feel it's one of the greatest stories ever told.

Greek Gods and Goddesses

Odysseus is the main character in *The Odyssey*, but there are many other characters who appear in the story. Some of these

other characters are Greek gods. As you may know, the Greeks believed that the world was ruled by many gods. Here are the names of some of the gods and goddesses who appear in the story: Zeus, Poseidon, Hermes, and Athena. ◆

Zeus was the chief god. He lived in a palace on top of Mount Olympus, which is the highest mountain in Greece. He saw and knew everything. He controlled the sky, and he usually carried a lightning bolt in his hand. Zeus could give orders to all the other gods, but sometimes the other gods gave him trouble.

One of the gods who gave Zeus a lot of trouble was his brother, Poseidon, who ruled the sea. Poseidon had his own palace under the sea, and he could make storms and earthquakes. He carried a three-pointed staff called a trident, and he had a terrible temper. He once tried to overthrow Zeus, but he didn't succeed. Many Greeks were afraid of Poseidon because they believed he caused shipwrecks and other disasters. It wasn't a good idea to make him angry. ★

Hermes was the messenger god. He carried orders from Zeus to the other gods, and he could run as fast as the wind. He wore a round hat and winged sandals, and he carried a staff with snakes on it. He loved to play jokes on the other gods, but they all liked him.

Athena was the daughter of Zeus. She did many things. She protected people who were in danger and gave them courage. She was also the goddess of wisdom and of work. She showed people how to tame horses and how to make clothes. Many Greeks loved Athena, and the city of Athens is named after her.

Although the gods had many powers, they could not control the way people acted. In *The Odyssey*, some of the gods try to help Odysseus, and some try to hinder him. But none of the gods is able to control Odysseus's mind. He must face all the dangers by himself. That is why Odysseus is the main character in the book. The gods are important, but the story is really about Odysseus and his adventures.

D VOCABULARY REVIEW

freight

advanced

gadget

merchandise

skeptical

For each item, write the correct word.
1. When you are suspicious about something, you are ▆▆▆ of that thing.
2. When you carry out a plan for selling a product, you ▆▆▆ that product.
3. A device is a ▆▆▆.

E COMPREHENSION

Write the answers.
1. What parts of *The Odyssey* are not fictional?
2. Explain how the Greeks tricked the Trojans and won the war.
3. What are the main differences between *The Iliad* and *The Odyssey*?
4. Tell how Homer probably told *The Odyssey*.
5. What was one thing the gods could not control?

F WRITING

Which Greek god or goddess do you like best?

Write a paragraph that explains how you feel. Try to answer the following questions:
- What do you like about that god or goddess?
- Why do you like that god or goddess more than the others?

Make your paragraph at least forty words long.

5

Ⓐ WORD LISTS

1
Hard Words
1. Scylla
2. Calypso
3. Apollo
4. Telemachus
5. Lochus

2
Word Practice
1. Poseidon
2. dairy
3. Cyclops
4. lyre
5. Penelope

3
Word Practice
1. Athena
2. Circe
3. monstrous
4. Polyphemus

4
New Vocabulary
1. draw straws
2. fulfill
3. risk
4. bronze
5. pluck
6. depart
7. slay
8. mast

Ⓑ VOCABULARY DEFINITIONS

1. **draw straws**—When people *draw straws,* they pull pieces of straw out of a bundle. Whoever pulls out the shortest piece has to do a hard job.
   • Why do people draw straws?
2. **fulfill**—When something is *fulfilled,* that thing comes true. If a dream comes true, that dream is fulfilled.
   • What happens if a promise comes true?
3. **risk**—When you take a *risk,* you take a chance.
   • What's another way of saying *Race drivers take chances*?
4. **bronze**—*Bronze* is made by mixing copper with other metals.
   • How is bronze made?

5. **pluck**—When you *pluck* a plant from the ground, you quickly remove it from the ground.
   • What are you doing when you quickly remove a plant from the ground?
6. **depart**—When you *depart* from a place, you leave that place.
   • What's another way of saying *They left the building*?
7. **slay**—When you *slay* something, you kill it.
   • What's another way of saying *They will kill their enemies*?
8. **mast**—A *mast* is a large pole that holds up sails on a sailing ship.
   • What do we call a pole that holds up sails?

The Odyssey
*by Homer**

* Adapted for young readers

Chapter 1
The Cyclops

One day, more than three thousand years ago, the Greek king Odysseus sailed away from the battlefields of Troy to return to his home—the island of Ithaca. He had come to Troy with all the other Greek kings to fight a long and terrible war. The war had lasted for ten years, but the Greeks had finally won, and now they were all returning to Greece.

Odysseus commanded a large ship. The ship had a small sail, but most of its power came from the oars. Fifty-two men pulled on the oars while Odysseus steered. The ship had enough supplies for the journey to Ithaca, which Odysseus figured would take several weeks.

The ship sailed for two days without any problems. On the third day, a great storm arose and beat upon the craft. For ten days, the storm pushed the ship far to the west.

On the tenth day, the ship reached the land of the Cyclopes. These were giant men who had only one eye, set in the middle of their foreheads. They did not live in houses, but in caves among the hills. They had no king and no laws, and they kept great flocks of sheep. ◆

Odysseus did not know about the Cyclopes. He landed his ship and went to see what kind of people lived on the land. He found a large cave close to the sea, with vines growing on the rocky roof and a wall of rough stones built around a court in front. Odysseus took twelve men and went up to the cave. Nobody was there, but the cave had baskets full of cheese, pails full of milk, and lambs playing in their pens.

All seemed quiet and pleasant. The men wanted to take back to the ship as much cheese as they could carry, but Odysseus wished to see the owner of the cave. His men, making themselves at home, lit a fire far within the cave and toasted and ate the cheese.

Suddenly, a shadow thrown by the setting sun fell across the opening of the cave. A giant Cyclops named Polyphemus entered and threw down a dry trunk of a tree that he carried for firewood. Next he drove in his flock of sheep. He then picked up a huge flagstone and used it to block the cave opening. A hundred horses could not have dragged away that stone.

Polyphemus milked his sheep and put the milk in pails to drink at supper. Meanwhile, Odysseus and his men sat quietly and in great fear, for they were shut in a cave with a one-eyed giant, whose cheese they had been eating.

After Polyphemus had lit a fire, he happened to see the men, and he asked them who they were. Odysseus said they were Greeks who were wandering lost on the seas.

He asked Polyphemus to be kind to them in the name of their chief god, Zeus.

"We Cyclopes," said Polyphemus, "do not care for Zeus or the other gods on Mount Olympus. The only god we respect is my father, Poseidon. Where is your ship?"

Odysseus answered that his ship had been wrecked on the coast, which was not true, for he did not want Polyphemus to destroy the ship. At first, Polyphemus did not answer. Then he suddenly snatched up two of Odysseus's men. As he held them, he bragged about his power and said he was more powerful than any Greek. At last, he hurled the men into the back of the cave, where they fell and stumbled among the rocks. Both men were injured, but they were not killed. Polyphemus laughed, drank many pails of milk, and fell asleep.

Now Odysseus wanted to drive his sword into Polyphemus. But he remem-bered that even if he killed Polyphemus he could not move the huge stone that blocked the opening of the cave. So he sat down to think. He thought all night long, but he could not figure out how to escape.

In the morning Polyphemus drove out his sheep and again placed the great stone in front of the cave entrance. To him, the stone was as light as a feather. Then away he went, driving his flock to the green hills. ★

All day long, Odysseus explored the cave, looking for a weapon to use against Polyphemus. At last, he found a bowl of thick black tar. The tar gave Odysseus an idea, so he sat down to wait for the Cyclops to return.

Polyphemus came back at sunset and drove his flock into the cave. Then he put up his stone door and milked his sheep. He ate his dinner, drank several pails of milk,

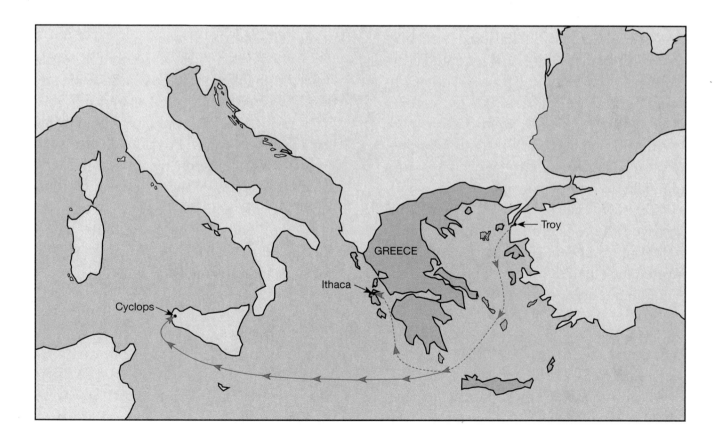

and became drowsy. Just before he fell asleep, he looked at Odysseus and asked him, "What is your name?"

"My name is Nobody," said Odysseus.

"Then I will kill Nobody after I kill the others," said Polyphemus. An instant later, he was sound asleep.

When all was quiet, Odysseus began heating the bowl of tar over the fire. The tar was soon boiling. Odysseus then crept up to Polyphemus while holding the bowl. When he reached the giant's eye, Odysseus ordered his men to make a loud commotion.

Startled by the racket, Polyphemus opened his eye. At that moment, Odysseus threw the hot tar into the eye. Polyphemus roared in pain and leaped to his feet. He shouted for help to the other Cyclopes who lived in neighboring caves.

"Who is troubling you?" they asked. "Why do you wake us from our sleep?"

Polyphemus answered, "Nobody has blinded me."

"Then if nobody is harming you, why are you calling for our help?" shouted a Cyclops. "If you are ill, call to your father Poseidon, the god of the sea."

So the Cyclopes all went back to bed, leaving Polyphemus to suffer alone. Odysseus was pleased to see how his cunning had deceived them.

The next morning, the blinded giant removed the rock from the cave entrance to let out his sheep. He sat in the doorway, stretching out his arms to make sure the men did not escape.

But Odysseus had a plan. He told each man to select a large sheep, get under the animal, and hold on to its fleece with his hands and feet. As the sheep went out through the doorway, Polyphemus felt them, but he did not know they were carrying the men.

"Dear sheep," he said to the biggest, which carried Odysseus, "you do not come out first as usual, but last, as if you were slow with sorrow for your master, whose eye Nobody has blinded!"

The sheep trotted out into the open country. The men stayed under the sheep until they were far from the cave. Then the men let go and ran down to the ship. Their comrades welcomed them back and began rowing quickly out to sea.

When the ship was a safe distance from shore, Odysseus shouted at Polyphemus and mocked him. The blinded giant picked up a huge boulder and threw it in the direction of the sound. But the boulder missed the ship.

Full of pride, Odysseus shouted to the giant, "If anyone asks who blinded you, say that it was Odysseus, king of Ithaca."

Hearing that, Polyphemus called to his father, the sea god Poseidon. The giant prayed that Odysseus would never reach Ithaca. Then Polyphemus threw another rock, but Odysseus was too far away.

Polyphemus could do nothing more, but Poseidon heard his son's prayer, and he began to plot against Odysseus.

E VOCABULARY REVIEW

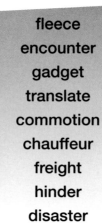

fleece

encounter

gadget

translate

commotion

chauffeur

freight

hinder

disaster

For each item, write the correct word.
1. When you come into contact with something, you ▆▆▆ that thing.
2. A terrible event is a ▆▆▆.
3. The fur of a sheep is called ▆▆▆.
4. Another word for *disturbance* is ▆▆▆.
5. When you tell a story in another language, you ▆▆▆ the story into that language.
6. Some of the people helped her, but others tried to ▆▆▆ her.

F COMPREHENSION

Write the answers.
1. Why did Odysseus and his men end up in the land of the Cyclopes?
2. When the men were in the cave with Polyphemus, why didn't Odysseus kill the Cyclops?
3. Why do you think Odysseus told Polyphemus that his name was Nobody?
4. Explain how the men escaped from the cave after Odysseus blinded Polyphemus.
5. Why do you think Odysseus finally told Polyphemus his real name?

G WRITING

Do you think Odysseus is a smart person?

Write a paragraph that explains how you feel. Try to answer the following questions:
- What smart things did Odysseus do in his adventure with Polyphemus?
- What things that were not smart did Odysseus do in those adventures?
- What could Odysseus have done differently?

Make your paragraph at least forty words long.

A WORD LISTS

1
Hard Words
1. cease
2. Ino
3. Sirens
4. Phacia
5. suitors
6. Calypso
7. hideous
8. Scylla
9. perish

2
Word Practice
1. Penelope
2. mermaid
3. companies
4. Lochus
5. wisdom
6. Apollo
7. Circe
8. Telemachus

3
New Vocabulary
1. hideous
2. perish
3. mist
4. sheltered
5. cease
6. deed
7. wallow
8. suitor

B VOCABULARY DEFINITIONS

1. **hideous**—When something is *hideous,* it is horrible or disgusting.
   • What's another way of saying *a horrible scene*?
2. **perish**—When something *perishes,* it dies.
   • What's another way of saying *Plants will die without water*?
3. **mist**—*Mist* is fine rain.
   • What is fine rain called?
4. **sheltered**—When something is *sheltered,* it is protected.
   • What's another way of saying *They lived in a protected spot*?
5. **cease**—When something *ceases,* it stops.
   • What's another way of saying *The rain stopped*?
6. **deed**—A *deed* is an action.
   • What's another way of saying *Her actions were admirable*?
7. **wallow**—When something *wallows,* it struggles in mud or water.
   • What's another way of saying *The ship struggled in the wild waters*?
8. **suitor**—A man who wants to marry a particular woman is that woman's *suitor.*
   • What do we call a man who wants to marry a particular woman?

Chapter 2
Circe

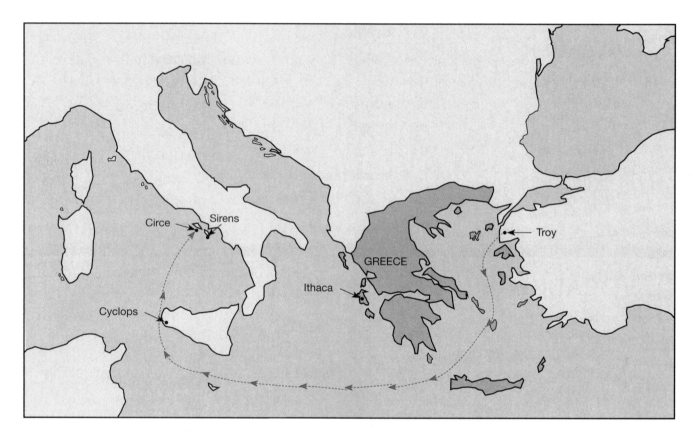

After Odysseus's ship left the land of the Cyclopes, a wicked wind from the south blew the ship north through a rough sea. The men guided the ship in that direction until they came to a small island, where they landed.

Unknown to the men, Circe the sorceress lived on the island. For two days, the men rested on the land near their ship, which they had anchored in a bay. On the third morning, Odysseus took his sword and spear and climbed to the top of a high hill. He saw smoke rising from the forest where Circe had her palace.

Odysseus thought of venturing through the forest and going to the palace, but it seemed better to return to his men and send some of them to explore the place. Since the adventure with Polyphemus, Odysseus did not care to take risks among unknown people. For all he knew, there might be man-eating giants on the island.

On the next morning, Odysseus divided his men into two companies. A sailor named Lochus led one company, and Odysseus led the other. They drew straws to decide who should go to the palace in the forest. Lochus lost, and weeping with fear, he led his twenty-five men away into the forest. Odysseus and the other twenty-six men waited by the ship.

That night, Lochus came back alone. He was weeping and full of sorrow. At last he told his story. "We came to a beautiful palace within the forest," he said. "Tame wolves and lions were walking around in front of the palace. They wagged their tails and jumped up like friendly dogs. My men stood in the doorway and heard a woman singing in a sweet voice. Then one of the men called to her, and she came out.

"She was a beautiful woman in a white robe covered with jewels and gold. Her name was Circe, she said. She opened the doors and asked the men to come in, which they did. But I hid myself and watched. I saw Circe and her maidens mix honey and milk for the men. When the men had drunk the milk, the sorceress touched them with her wand. All the men were changed into pigs, and Circe drove them out and shut them up in pens."

When Odysseus heard what had happened, he slung his sword-belt around his shoulders, seized his bow, and asked Lochus to go with him to Circe's palace. But Lochus was afraid, so Odysseus went alone through the woods. He soon met a handsome young man, who took his hand and said, "Odysseus, here is how you can free your friends from the great sorceress." ◆

The young man plucked a flower from the ground. The flower was as white as milk, but its roots were black. "Take this plant and keep it with you at all times," the young man said. "When Circe has made you drink her enchanted milk, the plant will protect you from her power. Then draw your sword and rush at her and make her swear she will not harm you with her magic."

No man could have known about that flower, but this handsome stranger was not a man. He was really the messenger god, Hermes.

After Hermes had departed, Odysseus went to the palace of Circe. She asked him to enter, seated him on a chair, and gave him the enchanted milk to drink. Then she touched him with her wand. But Odysseus drew his sword, and the sorceress fell at his feet with a great cry, saying, "You must be Odysseus of Ithaca, for the god Hermes has warned me about you. Come now, fear not; let us be friends."

Then the maidens of Circe came into the room. They threw covers of purple silk over the chairs, and they placed golden baskets on the silver tables. Meanwhile, Odysseus bathed himself. The maidens gave him new clothes and led him to the table and asked him to eat and drink. But he sat silently, neither eating nor drinking, in sorrow for his men. At last, Circe called the men out from the pen and removed the spell. The men were glad to see Odysseus, and they embraced him and wept for joy. A great feast followed.

Circe invited all the men to be her guests. She fed them well, and they stayed for several weeks. But the men missed their wives and children. When Odysseus was alone with the sorceress, he told her that his men were homesick and longed to return to Ithaca. Circe answered that Poseidon was angry because of the blinding of his son, Polyphemus, and would make Odysseus's voyage difficult. But if Odysseus's men were wise and did not slay and eat the sacred cattle of Apollo, they might all arrive home soon. At worst, Odysseus would lose only a few of his men.

The sorceress then gave Odysseus this warning in a solemn voice: "If the men are unwise, then only you, Odysseus, will arrive home, lonely and late. You will arrive on the ship of strangers, and you will find men eating your food and seeking to marry your wife, Penelope." ★

Circe then explained that even if Odysseus could get rid of these men, his troubles would not be ended. He would have to wander over the land as he had wandered over the water, carrying an oar on his shoulder, until he came to men who had never heard of the sea or of boats. If these men did not know what an oar was, then Odysseus must plant the oar in the ground and go home, where he would at last live in peace. She once more repeated, "Do not eat the sacred cattle of Apollo."

Circe then warned Odysseus of other dangers and showed him how he might escape them. He listened and remembered all she said, and then he bid her farewell. A short while later, Odysseus and his men set sail across the unknown seas.

To their joy, a strong wind blew from the north, driving the ship south. Presently the wind fell, and the sea was calm. Nearby, they saw a beautiful island from which came the sound of sweet singing. Odysseus knew who the singers were, for Circe had

told him. They were the Sirens—beautiful mermaids who were deadly to men. The Sirens sat and sang among flowers, but the flowers hid the bones of men who had listened to their singing. The singing had enchanted these men and carried their souls away. They had landed on the island and died of that strange music.

Odysseus wanted to hear the Sirens. He took a great piece of wax and cut it up into small pieces, which he gave to his men. Then he ordered his men to bind him tightly to the mast with ropes and told them not to unbind him until after they had passed the Sirens.

After Odysseus was bound to the mast, he ordered his men to soften the wax and place it in their ears so they would not hear the Sirens. When all this was done, the men sat down on the benches and pulled their oars. The ship rushed along and soon came near the island.

Odysseus heard the sweet singing of the Sirens. They seemed to offer him all knowledge and wisdom, which they knew he loved more than anything else in the world. He wanted to go to their island, and he begged his men to loosen his ropes. But the men could not hear him, and they rowed the ship past the island until the song of the Sirens faded away. Then they set Odysseus free and took the wax out of their ears.

VOCABULARY REVIEW

citizens
risk
chute
depart
hire
slay
fulfilled

For each item, write the correct word.
1. Another word for *kill* is ▬▬.
2. When you go from a place, you ▬▬ from that place.
3. When something comes true, that thing is ▬▬.
4. When you take a chance, you take a ▬▬.

E COMPREHENSION

Write the answers.
1. Why did Odysseus and Lochus draw straws?
2. Why do you think Hermes offered to help Odysseus?
3. Give at least two examples of Circe's magic powers.
4. Explain what happened to men who heard the Sirens singing.
5. Why do you think Odysseus wanted to hear their song?

F WRITING

Pretend you are one of the Sirens.
Write a paragraph that tells what you sing to Odysseus as he sails by. Try to answer the following questions:
• What do you offer him?
• How do you make your offer sound appealing?
Make your paragraph at least forty words long. If you want, you can arrange your sentences into a song.

A WORD LISTS

1

Hard Words
1. Phacia
2. perils
3. Ino
4. tunic

2

Word Practice
1. Calypso
2. Scylla
3. Telemachus
4. scale
5. scaly

3

New Vocabulary
1. in the midst
2. loom
3. cherish
4. perils
5. carpenter
6. lurk

B VOCABULARY DEFINITIONS

1. **in the midst**—When you're *in the midst* of something, you're in the middle of that thing.
   - What's another way of saying *They were in the middle of an argument*?
2. **loom**—A *loom* is a device used for weaving cloth.
   - What do we call a device used for weaving cloth?
3. **cherish**—When you *cherish* something, you value it.
   - What's another way of saying *They valued her friendship*?

4. **peril**—A *peril* is a danger.
   - What's another way of saying *She experienced many dangers*?
5. **carpenter**—A *carpenter* is a skilled person who makes things from wood.
   - What do we call a skilled person who makes things from wood?
6. **lurk**—When someone *lurks,* that person hides somewhere for an evil purpose.
   - What are people doing when they hide somewhere for an evil purpose?

Chapter 3
Calypso

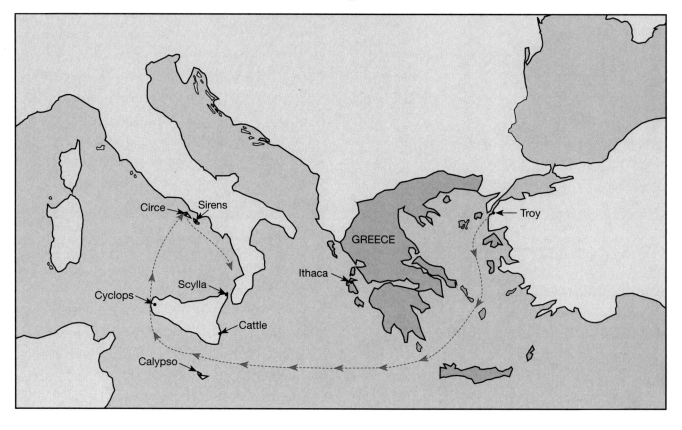

The ship continued to sail south after passing the Sirens. Soon the men heard the sea roaring and saw a great wave, over which hung a thick shining cloud of spray. They had drifted to a place where the sea narrowed between two high black cliffs.

In the narrows between those two cliffs, the sea ran like a rushing river. Afraid for their lives, the men stopped rowing. But Odysseus ordered them to grasp the oars again and row hard. Circe had warned him that the ship must go through these narrows. Odysseus directed the crew to steer near the cliff on the right and keep clear of the whirlpool and the cloud of spray on the left.

Within the cliff on the right was a deep cave, where a monster named Scylla lived, yelping with a shrill voice from her six hideous heads. Each head hung down from a long, thin, scaly neck. In each mouth were three rows of greedy teeth. Instead of arms, she had twelve long feelers with claws at the ends. Scylla would sit in her cave, fishing with her feelers for sharks and other large fish—and for men, if any sailed by.

Odysseus knew all this, for Circe had warned him. But he also knew that the whirlpool on the left side of the narrows would swallow up his whole ship, while Scylla might only catch a few of his men. For this reason, he told the men to steer close to Scylla's cliff. He did not tell them that Scylla lurked there, hidden in her deep cave.

Odysseus put on his armor, grasped two spears, and stood on the raised half-deck at the front of the ship, thinking that at least he would try to strike Scylla. Then the men rowed down the swift sea stream between the cliffs. The wave of the whirlpool rose, and then it fell and bubbled. As the men watched the whirlpool, Scylla suddenly reached out of her cave with all twelve feelers and grabbed six men. Odysseus watched helplessly as the men rose in the air and were devoured by Scylla's six heads.

Before Scylla could strike again, the ship swept through the roaring narrows and into the open sea. The men, weary and heavy of heart, bent over their oars and longed for rest.

The ship continued to sail south. The next day, it came to a beautiful island, and the men could hear the mooing of cows. These were the sacred cattle of Apollo. Thanks to Circe's warning, Odysseus knew that if his men killed and ate the cattle, they would all perish. So he told them about the warning and asked them to row past the island.

But Lochus was angry and said the men were tired and could row no farther. He wanted to eat and sleep comfortably on shore. When the crew heard Lochus, they shouted and said they would go no farther that day. Odysseus could not stop them. He could only make them swear not to touch the cattle of Apollo, to which the men agreed. So they went ashore, ate fish for supper, and fell asleep. ◆

In the night, a great storm arose. The clouds and driving mist blinded the face of the sea and the sky. For a whole month, the wild south wind hurled the waves onto the coast, and the ship could not go out to sea. Meanwhile, the crew ate all the food in the ship. They tried to catch fish and sea birds, but they caught only a few because the sea was so rough. Odysseus went alone to the top of a hill to pray to Zeus. Afterward, he found a sheltered cave and fell asleep.

While Odysseus was away, the crew decided to eat the sacred cattle, despite their promise. When their master awoke and came near the ship, he smelled the roast meat and realized what they had done. He warned the men, but they kept eating the cattle.

No disaster came that night or the next morning. The next day, Lochus laughed and told Odysseus, "Your warnings have no meaning. There is no danger here." For six days the crew ate the meat of Apollo's sacred cattle while the storm raged.

On the seventh day, the storm ceased, the wind fell, and the sun shone. Odysseus and his men set their sails and left the island, but their evil deed was punished. As soon as they were out of sight of land, a great thunderstorm arose. The wind howled and broke the mast, and the ship wallowed in great white waves.

Suddenly, lightning struck the ship in the center, breaking it in half. The two halves of the ship reeled and were soon swallowed by the enormous waves. All the men fell into the water, and all except one were drowned.

That one man was Odysseus. He managed to hang on to the broken mast while the north wind howled furiously.

The wind drifted him at last to the beach of an island, where the fairy Calypso lived. She found Odysseus nearly dead on the beach. She was kind to him and kept him in her cave. He lived there for nine long years, always desiring to leave and return to Ithaca and his wife, Penelope. But no ship of men ever came near the island, and Odysseus had no ship to sail and no men to row it. Calypso was kind and friendly, but Odysseus longed to see the houses of rocky Ithaca. ★

• • •

As the years went by, most of the people of Ithaca came to believe that Odysseus must be dead. Only his wife, Penelope, his son, Telemachus, and a few of his servants thought he was still alive.

With Odysseus gone, the people of Ithaca no longer had a king. Telemachus was too young to become the king, and Penelope was not allowed to take her husband's place. But any man who married Penelope could become the new king.

Many men wanted to marry Penelope, but she refused them all. After a while, these men decided to join together and stay at Odysseus's palace until Penelope agreed to marry one of them. They were called suitors, and there were more than a hundred of them. They did nothing but eat all day long, and nobody could stop them. They would never go away, they said, until Penelope chose one of them to be her husband and king of the island.

Year after year, Penelope kept hoping that Odysseus was still alive and would return soon. Telemachus hoped so, too, although he worried about what the suitors might do if Odysseus did return. They might kill Odysseus, and then Penelope would be forced to marry one of them.

The goddess of wisdom, Athena, learned of the trouble in Ithaca. She had always liked Odysseus, so she spoke to the chief god, Zeus, in his palace on Mount Olympus. She told Zeus how good, wise, and brave Odysseus was. Then she explained how Calypso was keeping Odysseus on her island while the suitors ate his food and tried to marry his wife.

After Athena had spoken, Zeus said, "I think Odysseus should return to Ithaca. But my brother Poseidon is still angry with Odysseus for blinding his son. I can order Calypso to release Odysseus, but I cannot control my brother. Odysseus will have to take his chances on the sea."

Athena answered, "It would be better for Odysseus to drown than for him to stay in Calypso's cave forever."

Zeus agreed, so he ordered Hermes, the messenger god, to fly to the island of Calypso on his winged sandals and set Odysseus free.

D VOCABULARY REVIEW

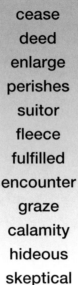

cease

deed

enlarge

perishes

suitor

fleece

fulfilled

encounter

graze

calamity

hideous

skeptical

For each item, write the correct word.
1. An action is a ▆▆▆.
2. When you stop, you ▆▆▆.
3. When something dies, it ▆▆▆.
4. When something is horrible or disgusting, it is ▆▆▆.
5. A man who wants to marry a particular woman is that woman's ▆▆▆.
6. A misfortune is a ▆▆▆.
7. When you come into contact with something, you ▆▆▆ that thing.
8. When you are suspicious of something, you are ▆▆▆ of that thing.
9. When something comes true, that thing is ▆▆▆.

E COMPREHENSION

Write the answers.
1. Why did Odysseus decide to sail by Scylla instead of the whirlpool?
2. Why did the men ignore Odysseus's warning about eating the cattle?
3. How did Odysseus feel about staying on Calypso's island?
4. Why did so many men want to marry Penelope?
5. What dangers do you think Odysseus will encounter if he leaves Calypso's island?

F WRITING

On each island Odysseus visited, he found a new kind of monster or person. Which island do you think is the most frightening?

Write a paragraph that explains your answer. Be sure the paragraph answers the following questions:
- What is on the island?
- What makes the island frightening?
- Why is the island more frightening than other islands?

Make your paragraph at least forty words long.

A WORD LISTS

1
Hard Words
1. Eumayus
2. Melanthius
3. tunic
4. farewell
5. Phacia
6. shadowy

2
Word Practice
1. Scylla
2. backwash
3. Ino
4. reins

3
New Vocabulary
1. canvas
2. launch
3. surf
4. savage
5. peer

B VOCABULARY DEFINITIONS

1. **canvas**—*Canvas* is a strong cloth used for sails.
   - What do we call a strong cloth used for sails?
2. **launch**—When you *launch* a ship, you put it into water.
   - What do you do when you put a ship into water?
3. **surf**—The *surf* is the waves near a shore.
   - What do we call the waves near a shore?
4. **savage**—When something is *savage,* it is wild and cruel. A wild and cruel beast is a savage beast.
   - What's another way of saying *a wild and cruel animal*?
5. **peer**—When you *peer* at something, you stare at that thing.
   - What's another way of saying *She stared at the waves*?

Chapter 4
The Princess

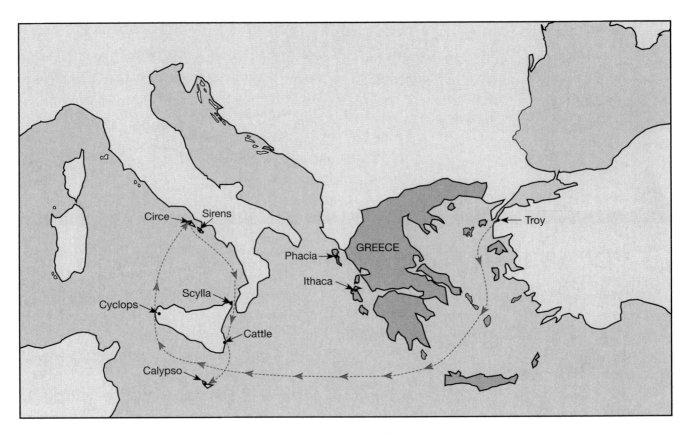

Hermes put on his golden sandals and flew to Calypso's island as swiftly as the wind. When he reached the island, he raced to Calypso's cave. A great fire was burning there, and the smell was enchanting. Calypso sang with a sweet voice as she sat before her loom.

Hermes went into the wide cave, and Calypso knew at once who he was. "Why have you come here?" she asked.

"Zeus sent me," answered Hermes. "He orders you to send Odysseus away as quickly as you can. The man must have a chance to return to Ithaca."

Calypso shuddered and said, "I saved Odysseus when he was all alone and clinging to a mast. Poseidon had crushed his swift ship in the midst of the dark sea. All the rest of his men were lost, but the wind and the waves brought him here. I have loved and cherished him, and I promised that I would never let him know death or age here. But I cannot disobey Zeus."

"Give Odysseus the tools to make a raft," said Hermes. "Then speed him upon his path."

Hermes left as quickly as he had come, and Calypso went to see Odysseus. She found him sitting on the shore with his eyes full of tears. Every day he sat on the beach, straining his soul with grief; through his tears, he gazed across the deep sea.

Calypso said to him, "Unfortunate man, sorrow no more on this island, nor let your good life waste away. I will send you home with all my heart. Rise up and cut long beams and make a wide raft, strong enough to carry you over the sea. I will give you bread and water and milk to keep hunger far away. I hope you will arrive unharmed in your own country, for Zeus has said it must be so."

Odysseus was glad and sad—glad the gods had thought of him but sad to think of crossing the wide seas alone. He said, "I have longed to go homeward and to see the day of my return. Even if Poseidon wrecks my raft in the dark sea, I will continue my journey. I have already suffered much, and I have survived perils of waves and war." ◆

The next day, Calypso brought carpenters' tools to Odysseus. He cut down trees and made a great raft with a mast and a sail. He finished in five days. Calypso loaded the raft with skins full of water, bags of flour, and many pleasant things to eat. Then she said farewell.

Odysseus went alone onto the wide sea, and Calypso returned to her own home. He might have lived in her cave forever, but he chose to live and die, if he could, with his wife, Penelope.

He sailed to the east, never seeing land or ship for seventeen days. On the eighteenth day, he spied the shadowy mountain peaks of an island. But now Poseidon saw him and remembered that Odysseus had blinded his son, Polyphemus. In anger, Poseidon raised a terrible storm. Great clouds raced across the sky. The winds broke the mast of the raft, and the waves dragged Odysseus deep into the sea. At last, he rose to the surface and climbed back onto the raft. The winds tossed the vessel like a feather.

The sea goddess, Ino, saw Odysseus and pitied him. Rising from the water, she threw a bright cloth to him, saying, "Wrap this cloth around your chest and throw off your clothes; then leap from the raft and swim. When you reach land, throw the cloth back into the sea and turn away your head."

Odysseus caught the cloth and wrapped it around his chest. Just after he had thrown off his clothes, the raft was torn apart by the waves. He leaped off and began to swim. Then the winds died, except for the south wind, which pushed Odysseus north for two days and two nights. On the third day, all was calm, and he drew near an island named Phacia.

Odysseus swam toward the island through a terrible surf that crashed and foamed on jagged rocks that could have broken all his bones. Three times he clutched a rock, and three times the backwash of the wave dragged him out to sea. Then he swam outside the breakers along the line of rocks, looking for a safe place to land. At last, he came to the mouth of a river. All was smooth here, with a sloping beach. His feet finally touched bottom.

He staggered out of the water and fainted as soon as he was on dry land. When he came to, he unwrapped the cloth of Ino and cast it into the sea. Then he fell back among the reeds of the river, cold and

starving. He crept between two thick olive trees that grew close together and made a shelter against the wind. There he covered himself with fallen dry leaves until he grew warm again. Then he fell into a deep sleep.

Meanwhile, the goddess Athena made herself invisible and visited the palace of the king of Phacia. After everyone was asleep, she gave a dream to the king's beautiful daughter. ★

In the dream, a girl came to the princess and said, "How could you be such a careless daughter? There are many beautiful garments in the house that need to be washed for your wedding day. Some of these are splendid outfits for your maiden friends.

Some are fine robes for boys and men. Let us travel to the river tomorrow to wash those garments."

When the princess awoke the next day, she remembered the dream and asked her father to lend her a wagon and mules to carry the clothes. She said nothing about her wedding, for though many young princes were in love with her, she was in love with none of them. Still, she felt a strong desire to wash the clothes. Servants piled them in the wagon and packed food in baskets. Then the princess took the reins and drove slowly to the river, followed by several maidens.

They came to a deep, clear pool in the river, and there they washed the clothes.

Then they laid the clothes out to dry in the sun and ate their meal.

When the young women had eaten, they began to play with a ball. The princess threw the ball at a friend who was running, but the young woman missed the ball, and it fell into the deep, swift river. All the young women screamed and laughed. The noise awakened Odysseus, who was in the olive grove nearby.

"Where am I?" he said to himself. "Can this be a country of fierce and savage men? I hear the sound of young women at play around me. Can they be maidens of the hilltops, rivers, and meadows?"

Because he had no clothes, Odysseus used a branch to hide his body. But his feet were bare, his face was wild with weariness and cold and hunger, and his hair and beard were matted and rough with salt water.

The young women, when they saw his face peering over the leaves of the branch, screamed and ran along the beach. But the princess was unafraid. Odysseus did not dare go near her. He spoke from a distance and said, "I beg you to be kind to me. Maybe you are a goddess. But if you are a woman, then your father is a happy man, for I have never seen a woman so fair. Have pity on me. I have been tossed here by the sea and have nothing. Give me something to put on and something to eat and show me the way to your city."

The princess said, "You do not look like a bad or foolish man. You are in a sorry state, but the gods give good luck to some and bad luck to others. You shall have clothing and food and everything you need. I will take you to the city, for I am the princess of this country."

(D) VOCABULARY REVIEW

mist
commotion
lurks
disaster
slay
hinder
skeptical
cease

For each item, write the correct word.
1. A terrible event is a ▬▬.
2. Some of the people helped her, but others tried to ▬▬ her.
3. Another word for *stop* is ▬▬.
4. When you are suspicious about something, you are ▬▬ about that thing.
5. Another word for *disturbance* is ▬▬.
6. When a person hides somewhere for an evil purpose, that person ▬▬.

E COMPREHENSION

Write the answers.

1. What do you think would have happened to Odysseus if he had stayed on Calypso's island?
2. What feelings did Odysseus have as he left Calypso's island? Why?
3. Explain what Odysseus had to do with Ino's cloth.
4. Athena could have given a dream to anybody. Why do you think she chose the princess?
5. Why were most of the young women frightened of Odysseus?

F WRITING

If you were Odysseus, would you have left Calypso's island?

Write a paragraph that explains your answer. Be sure the paragraph answers the following questions:

- What reasons would you have for staying?
- What reasons would you have for leaving?
- Which reasons are more important? Why?

Make your paragraph at least forty words long.

A WORD LISTS

1

Character Names
1. Antinous
2. Melanthius
3. Eumayus

2

New Vocabulary
1. flask
2. noble
3. minstrel

B VOCABULARY DEFINITIONS

1. **flask**—A *flask* is a kind of bottle.
   • What is a flask?
2. **noble**—A *noble* person is proud and brave.
   • What do we call a person who is proud and brave?

3. **minstrel**—*Minstrels* are entertainers. In ancient Greece, minstrels told stories, sang songs, and played the lyre.
   • What did minstrels do in ancient Greece?

Chapter 5
Phacia

The princess turned away from Odysseus and said to her friends, "Why do you run away when you see a man? No one comes here to do us harm, for the gods love us and take care of us. If someone in trouble comes here, we should help him. Give this man food and drink and let him wash in the river."

So the young women gave Odysseus a tunic to wear next to his skin and a cloak to wear over it. They led him down to the river and gave him a flask of olive oil to use after he had his bath. Then they left him alone.

Odysseus bathed in the river and washed the salt from his skin and his hair. Then he rubbed the olive oil on his body and put on the tunic and the cloak. Athena, who was still invisible, made him look taller than he was. She also made his hair grow thicker and darker.

When he was finished, Odysseus sat down on the seashore and waited. When the princess saw him, she said, "Surely, it is the gods who have brought this man here. When I first saw him, I thought he was handsome, but now he is so handsome that he seems more like a god than a man. I should be happy to have such a man for my husband. Perhaps he would be willing to stay in this country."

Then she turned to her friends and said, "Give the stranger food and drink."

Odysseus ate a great deal, for it was now the third day since the raft had been broken by the sea, and all the food and drink Calypso had given him had been lost. ◆

Then the princess told her friends to harness the mules and said to Odysseus, "Come with me, stranger, and I will take you to my father's house. But listen carefully and do as I tell you. As long as we are in the country, walk with my friends and keep close to the wagon. When we come to the city, stay outside the gates, for I do not wish the people to gossip about me. Every time I am seen with a man, people start rumors that I am going to marry him. I do not want people to see you and say, 'Who is this tall and handsome stranger that comes with the princess? Will he be her husband? Is he a god come down from heaven, or is he a man from a place over the seas? The princess is too proud, it seems, to marry one of us.'"

The princess continued, "Stay outside the city until you think I have arrived at my home. Then pass through the gate and ask for the king's palace. Anyone, even a child, can tell you the way, for there is not another house in the city like it."

Then she climbed into the wagon, touched the mules with the whip, and headed back to the city. The party arrived

at the city gate just as the sun was setting. Odysseus stayed outside the gate while the princess went on to the palace with her friends.

After waiting for some time, Odysseus walked through the gate and into the city, which stretched along the shore. He was amazed by the harbor full of ships and by the strength of the walls. The goddess Athena, disguised as a young woman, met him. She told him how to get to the palace and said that the queen was wise and kind and had great power in the city. ★

Odysseus thanked the young woman and walked off. He soon reached the palace, which had shining bronze walls. Within the palace were golden statues of young men holding torches. The gardens were full of fruit trees and were watered by streams that flowed from two fountains. Odysseus stood and wondered at the beauty of the gardens. Then he walked through the palace and knelt at the feet of the king and the queen. He begged them to send him in a ship to his own country.

The queen looked at Odysseus and saw that his clothes were from the palace. She asked him who he was and how he had obtained the clothes. He told her that he had been shipwrecked and that the princess had given him food and garments.

The queen said her daughter should have brought Odysseus straight to the palace, but he answered, "Do not blame your daughter. I am quite shy, and I was afraid you might not like to see your daughter coming home with a stranger."

The king said he would be happy to have his daughter marry a stranger as noble as Odysseus and would give him a house and whatever else he wanted. But Odysseus explained that he was already married and wanted to return home.

The king said a ship would be made ready for Odysseus to carry him home. He could tell that Odysseus, who had not yet told him his name, was a noble person, strong and wise.

Then they all went to their rooms, and Odysseus's room had a soft bed with purple blankets.

Ⓓ VOCABULARY REVIEW

peer
slay
launch
cherished
citizens
peril

For each item, write the correct word.
1. When you put a ship in the water, you ▬▬ it.
2. Another word for *danger* is ▬▬.
3. Something that is valued is ▬▬.
4. When you stare at something, you ▬▬ at that thing.

E COMPREHENSION

Write the answers.
1. Why do you think Athena changed the way Odysseus looked?
2. Why didn't the princess want to be seen with Odysseus?
3. What evidence shows that Phacia was a rich island?
4. Why did the king think Odysseus would make a good husband for the princess?
5. Do you think Odysseus's troubles are almost over? Why or why not?

F WRITING

Odysseus has visited several islands. Which island would you most like to visit?

Write a paragraph that explains your answer. Be sure the paragraph answers the following questions:
- What is on the island?
- Why would you like to visit the island?
- Why does that island interest you more than the others?

Make your paragraph at least forty words long.

Ⓐ WORD LISTS

1

Character Names
1. Argos
2. Antinous
3. Phacians
4. Eumayus
5. Melanthius

2

Word Practice
1. faithful
2. anchored
3. challenged

3

New Vocabulary
1. sow the seeds of doom
2. boar
3. lice
4. flee

Ⓑ VOCABULARY DEFINITIONS

1. **sow the seeds of doom**—When you *sow the seeds of doom* for somebody, you plan how to punish that person.
   - What's another way of saying *Odysseus planned how to punish the suitors*?
2. **boar**—A *boar* is a wild pig.
   - What's another way of saying *They hunted a wild pig*?

3. **lice**—*Lice* are small insects that live in the hair of people and other animals.
   - What are lice?
4. **flee**—When you *flee,* you run away from danger.
   - What's another way of saying *The boar will run away from the lion*?

Chapter 6
Ithaca

The next day, the king sent fifty-two men to prepare a ship for Odysseus. As the men worked, the king gave a feast for Odysseus in the palace.

During the feast, a minstrel sang about the Trojan War. Odysseus was so moved by the minstrel's song that he held his cloak before his face and wept. When the king saw Odysseus weeping, he suggested the guests go outside and amuse themselves with sports. The king's son asked Odysseus if he would join in, but the traveler answered that he was too sad. When the prince heard this, he said Odysseus was probably just a merchant and not a sportsman.

Odysseus was not pleased with this remark. He said that when he was young and happy, he was skilled in all sports, but now he was weak with war and wandering. Still, he would show what he could do. He seized a heavy weight, much heavier than any the Phacians used. Then he hurled it far beyond the farthest mark the Phacians had reached when throwing a lighter weight.

After that, Odysseus challenged any man to run a race with him or box with him or shoot at a mark with him. But no one dared accept his challenges.

The king sent for the minstrel again, and he sang a merry song. The young people danced and played ball, and the older ones brought gold and clothing for Odysseus. The king himself gave Odysseus a beautiful trunk and a great golden cup; and the queen carefully packed the other gifts in a chest.

Then the princess came up to Odysseus. She was sad, for she knew that Odysseus was already married. She said, "Farewell, and do not soon forget me in your own country."

"May the gods let me see my own country, dear princess," Odysseus answered. "I will think of you there, just as I think of the blessed gods, all my days."

Then everyone went back to the palace to continue the feast. The minstrel sang a song about the deeds of Odysseus at Troy, and again Odysseus wept. The king observed his tears and asked, "Did you lose a friend in the Trojan War?"

Odysseus said, "I am Odysseus of Ithaca, of whom your minstrel sings." ◆

The guests were amazed to discover they were in the presence of a hero. They were even more amazed when Odysseus told them the story of his adventures, from the day he left Troy till he arrived in Phacia. He spoke for a long time, and no one moved.

When Odysseus had finished his wonderful story, many other gifts were given to him. The gifts were carried on board the ship and stored there. Then Odysseus bid the queen farewell, saying, "Be happy until old age and death come to you, as they come to all. Be joyful in your house with your children and your people."

At last, Odysseus departed. He lay on the raised deck of the ship and slept soundly while the crew rowed south to Ithaca.

When Odysseus awoke, he found himself alone. The Phacians had landed the ship and carried him on shore as he slept. They had placed all his rich gifts under a tree, and then they had sailed away.

A morning mist hid the land, and Odysseus did not know his own island. He thought the Phacians had set him in a strange country, so he walked up and down sadly by the seashore. Here he met a young man with a spear in his hand.

"Tell me," said Odysseus, "what land is this, and what men dwell here?"

The young man said, "Truly, stranger, you know little, or you come from far away. This island is Ithaca, and it is known around the world."

Odysseus was glad indeed to learn he was home at last. But he did not know how the people of the island would treat him. So he did not say he was the king of the island. Instead, he said he was a merchant.

The young man asked Odysseus why he had come alone to Ithaca with great riches and yet did not know where he was. So Odysseus made up a story. He said his crew had been angry with him and had left him there while he was asleep and had given him enough riches to survive.

The young man laughed at Odysseus's story. Suddenly, he changed into the great goddess Athena. "How clever you are!" she said. "Yet, you did not know who I really was. But listen, much trouble lies before you. You must not let anyone know who you really are, for you have many powerful enemies." ★

"You never helped me in my dangers on the sea," said Odysseus. "Are you now making fun of me, or is this really my own country?"

"I could not quarrel with my uncle Poseidon," answered Athena. "He is still angry with you for the blinding of Polyphemus. But come, you shall see that this is really Ithaca."

Athena scattered the morning mist, and Odysseus saw the island he knew so well. He knelt down and kissed the dear earth of his own country. Then Athena helped him hide all his gold and other presents in a cave. Afterward, she told him how to get rid of the suitors, who would certainly kill him if they knew who he was.

Athena began her plan by disguising Odysseus. She made his skin seem wrinkled, his hair thin, and his eyes dull. She gave him dirty rags for clothes. She also gave him a staff and a bag to hold scraps of food. Not a man or a woman in Ithaca would know that this humble beggar was really Odysseus.

The goddess told Odysseus to go across the island to visit Eumayus, a faithful old servant who herded pigs. Odysseus would stay there while Athena went to get Odysseus's son, Telemachus. The young man was now twenty years old and would be a great help to Odysseus.

Athena disappeared, and Odysseus climbed the hills that lay between the cave and the farm where Eumayus lived. When Odysseus reached the farmhouse, Eumayus was sitting alone in front of his door, mak-

ing himself a pair of shoes from the skin of an ox. He was an honest man. He was fond of Penelope and Telemachus, and he hated the proud suitors.

When Odysseus came near Eumayus's house, four great dogs rushed out and barked at him. They would have bitten him, but Eumayus ran up and pulled them back. He did not recognize Odysseus, but he took him into his house, gave him food and drink, and told him all about the greed and pride of the suitors.

Odysseus then made up a long story to explain who he was. He said he was a Phacian who had fought at Troy and had later been shipwrecked. He reported that Odysseus was alive and would soon return to Ithaca.

Eumayus did not believe this tale, but he gave Odysseus a good dinner of his own pork. Then Odysseus amused Eumayus with stories about the Trojan War until it was bedtime.

VOCABULARY REVIEW

bronze
minstrel
noble
savage
risk
cherished

For each item, write the correct word.
1. A person who lived at the same time as Odysseus and told stories, sang songs, and played the lyre was called a ▄▄▄.
2 Somebody who is proud and brave is ▄▄▄.
3. Things that are wild and cruel are ▄▄▄.
4. Something that is valued is ▄▄▄.

E COMPREHENSION

Write the answers.
1. Why did Odysseus weep when he heard the minstrel's song?
2. Why didn't any of the Phacians accept Odysseus's challenges at sports?
3. When Odysseus landed on Ithaca, why didn't he tell Athena who he was?
4. Describe Odysseus's appearance after Athena disguised him.
5. How do you think Odysseus will get rid of the suitors?

F WRITING

Pretend you are Odysseus telling his story to the Phacians.
  Pick your favorite part of his story and then tell it as Odysseus would have.
  Start your story with the word *I*. Try to answer the following questions in your story:
  • Where were you?
  • What happened?
  • Why did you do what you did?
Make your story at least eighty words long.

A WORD LISTS

1
Hard Words
1. courteous
2. merely
3. Argos

2
Word Practice
1. Melanthius
2. breakfast
3. Eumayus
4. Phacians
5. quarrel
6. Antinous
7. ivy

3
New Vocabulary
1. revenge
2. unearthly
3. neglect
4. custom

B VOCABULARY DEFINITIONS

1. **revenge**—When you take *revenge* on someone, you get even with that person. Here's another way of saying *He got even with the robber: He took revenge on the robber.*
   - What's another way of saying *She got even with her sister*?
2. **unearthly**—When something is *unearthly,* it is unlike things you normally find on earth.
   - What would you call a rock that is unlike rocks you normally find on earth?
3. **neglect**—When you *neglect* something, you fail to take care of it.
   - What's another way of saying *She failed to take care of her dog*?
4. **custom**—A *custom* is a way of behaving that everybody follows.
   - What do we call a way of behaving that everybody follows?

Chapter 7
Telemachus

That night, Athena went to Odysseus's palace, where Telemachus was lying awake. She disguised herself as a servant and told Telemachus that Eumayus wanted to see him the next day but could not leave his farm. Telemachus was happy for a chance to leave the palace, and he promised to go.

In the morning, just as Telemachus was leaving the palace, an eagle swept down from the sky and flew away with a large white goose that was feeding on the grass. The servants rushed out shouting, but they could do nothing.

Athena, who was still disguised, came up behind Telemachus and explained the meaning of this event. She said, "Just as the strong eagle came down from his distant hill and carried away the goose, Odysseus shall return home and take revenge on the suitors. Yes, even now he is at home and sowing the seeds of doom for them."

Telemachus turned to ask Athena how she knew all this, but she had disappeared. Then he knew the gods had come to help his family.

Eumayus and Odysseus had just lit a fire to cook breakfast when they saw Telemachus walking toward the house. The dogs welcomed him, for he was no stranger. Eumayus leaped up in delight, and the bowl in which he was making breakfast fell from his hands. Eumayus had been afraid the suitors might kill Telemachus. He ran and embraced the young man as gladly as a father welcomes a son who has long been in a far country. ◆

When Telemachus stepped into Eumayus's house, Odysseus rose from his seat, but Telemachus told him to sit down. They breakfasted on what was ready—cold pork, bread, and milk in cups of ivy wood.

As they ate, Eumayus explained that the beggar was a merchant from Phacia. Telemachus answered that he could not take strangers into his mother's house, for he was unable to protect them from the violence of the suitors. But he said he would give the beggar clothes and shoes and a sword and let him stay at Eumayus's farm.

Telemachus then asked Eumayus to get the beggar's supplies from Penelope. When they finished breakfast, Eumayus left for the palace, but Telemachus stayed behind.

After Eumayus left, the farm dogs began to whine, and they crept with their tails between their legs to a corner of the room. Telemachus could not imagine why they were afraid. But Odysseus saw the goddess Athena, who appeared to him alone. The dogs knew that something strange and unearthly was coming to the door.

Odysseus left the house, and Athena ordered him to tell Telemachus who he really was. Then she touched Odysseus with her gold wand and made him appear like himself.

Telemachus, who neither saw nor heard Athena, was stunned when Odysseus came back into the house. He thought the beggar must be a god, wandering in disguise. But Odysseus said, "No god am I, but your own father." Then they embraced and wept for joy.

At last, Odysseus told Telemachus that he had come home in a Phacian ship and that his treasure was hidden in the cave. He asked his son how many suitors there were and how they could be driven from the house.

Telemachus replied that there were one hundred eight suitors. They stayed at the palace from sunrise to sunset. There was also a minstrel, whom they forced to sing at their feasts. They were all strong young men, and they always left their swords and armor near the door.

Odysseus said he hoped to get the better of them, even though there were so many. He told Telemachus to return to the palace. Then he said, "I will come tomorrow, disguised as the old beggar. Don't quarrel with the suitors. Above all, let no one know I am your father, not even Penelope." ★

Then Odysseus went outside, and Athena changed him back into a beggar. After Eumayus returned with the supplies, Telemachus went back to the palace and comforted his mother. He told her he had been with Eumayus and looked after the farm. This story did not seem to interest Penelope, who thought she would soon be forced to marry one of the suitors.

The next morning, Odysseus and Eumayus began walking to the palace. They met Melanthius, a farmer who herded goats. He was a friend of the suitors and a rude man.

Melanthius insulted Odysseus and told him to stay away from the palace. Then he kicked Odysseus off the road. The king was tempted to hit the goat farmer, but he controlled himself. After Melanthius left, Odysseus and Eumayus resumed their journey.

When the two men reached the palace walls, a hound raised his head and pricked his ears. This hound was Argos. Odysseus had known him since he was a puppy. In the old days, the king used to hunt wild goats, deer, and rabbits with the hound. Argos had been with him when a wild boar had given Odysseus a long scar on his right leg.

Now Argos lay in the deep mud, full of lice and fleas. Yet the hound, when he was aware of Odysseus standing by, wagged his tail and dropped both his ears; but he did not have the strength to walk toward his master.

Odysseus looked aside and wiped away a tear. Then he said, "Eumayus, this hound in the mud seems to have been handsome and strong once."

Eumayus answered, "He is the hound of Odysseus. If he were as strong as he was when Odysseus left for Troy, you would marvel at the sight of his swiftness and strength. No beast could flee from this hound in the deep places of the woods, for he was the keenest hunter of them all. Now he is neglected, and his master is gone. The careless suitors do not take care of him."

While Eumayus was talking, Argos made one last effort to stand, and then he died.

Thus, the good dog knew his master. Tears came into Odysseus's eyes as he stood above the body of the hound that had loved him so well.

Eumayus went into the palace, but Odysseus sat where it was the custom for beggars to sit—on the wooden step outside the door. Telemachus saw him from his seat in the middle of the room, and he asked Eumayus to carry a loaf of bread and a piece of pork to the beggar. Odysseus laid the food on his lap and began to eat.

D VOCABULARY REVIEW

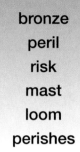

bronze

peril

risk

mast

loom

perishes

For each item, write the correct word.
1. When something dies, it ▮▮▮▮ .
2. When you take a chance, you take a ▮▮▮▮ .
3. Another word for *danger* is ▮▮▮▮ .

E COMPREHENSION

Write the answers.
1. When Athena approached Eumayus's hut, each character or animal reacted differently. Explain why.
2. How do you think Telemachus and Odysseus could defeat the suitors? Explain why your plan would work.
3. Why do you think Odysseus decided not to hit Melanthius?
4. What could the dogs in this chapter figure out that the people couldn't? Give two examples.
5. How could Odysseus's wound prove important to the story?

F WRITING

The event with the eagle and the goose had a special meaning because it showed what Odysseus might do to the suitors.

Think of another event with two animals that might have the same special meaning. Then write a paragraph that explains the event. Try to answer the following questions:
- How are the animals like Odysseus and the suitors?
- How could the meeting of these animals be like the meeting of Odysseus and the suitors?

Make your paragraph at least fifty words long.

Ⓐ WORD LISTS

1
Word Practice
1. grind
2. Antinous
3. footstool
4. grinding
5. Argos
6. none
7. nonetheless

2
New Vocabulary
1. dusky
2. courteous
3. fawn
4. feeble
5. vow
6. supple
7. uproar

Ⓑ VOCABULARY DEFINITIONS

1. **dusky**—*Dusk* is twilight. So something *dusky* is like twilight. If the shadows were like twilight, the shadows were *dusky.*
   - What's another way of saying *The shadows were like twilight*?
2. **courteous**—*Courteous* is another word for *polite.*
   - What's another way of saying *She was very polite*?
3. **fawn**—A *fawn* is a young deer.
   - What's another way of saying *The young deer jumped the fence*?
4. **feeble**—When something is *feeble,* it is very weak.
   - What's another way of saying *a very weak laugh*?

5. **vow**—A *vow* is a promise. When you *vow* to do something, you promise to do it.
   - What's another way of saying *She promised to work all day long*?
6. **supple**—When something is *supple,* it is flexible and easy to bend.
   - What's another way of saying *The leather was easy to bend*?
7. **uproar**—An *uproar* is a loud commotion.
   - What's another way of saying *There was a loud commotion in the hall*?

Chapter 8
The Suitors

When Odysseus had finished his meal on the wooden step, he decided to find out if there was one courteous man among the suitors. So he entered the hall and began to beg food from them. Some gave him crusts and bones, but the loudest one, Antinous, took up a footstool and struck Odysseus on the shoulder. Odysseus said nothing, but some of the suitors were angry with Antinous for striking a beggar.

Penelope, who stayed in an upstairs room, heard about the beggar. She told Eumayus to bring the man to her, for she thought he might have news of her husband. Odysseus said he could not see her until after sunset, when the suitors had left the palace. After giving this message to Penelope, Eumayus went to his own farmhouse. He said he would come back the next day with pigs for the suitors to eat.

After sunset, the suitors went to their houses in the town. Odysseus remained in the dusky hall, where the wood in the fireplace had burned low, and waited to see the face of his wife. The servants cleared away the food and the cups and put wood on the fire.

Then Penelope came in and ordered a chair to be brought for the beggar. When he was seated, she asked him who he was. He praised her beauty, for she was very fair, but he did not answer her question. She insisted that he tell her who he was, so he said he was a Phacian merchant. He added that he had met Odysseus on his way home from Troy and had entertained him for a week.

Penelope wept when she heard that the stranger had seen her husband. But she had heard many false stories about Odysseus from strangers who came to Ithaca. She asked how Odysseus was dressed and what kind of men were with him.

The beggar said that Odysseus wore a purple cloak and a gold medal. On the front of the medal was a picture of a hound holding a fawn in his paws.

On hearing this, Penelope wept again and said that she herself had given Odysseus the medal and the cloak. She now knew that the beggar had really met Odysseus. He went on to tell her he had heard Odysseus was still alive. The king had lost all his men, he said, and had gone to the west of Greece to seek help from Zeus. Certainly, he said, Odysseus would return that year. ◆

Penelope was unable to believe such good news, and she fell silent. At last, she asked her old nurse to wash the feet of the beggar in warm water.

The nurse brought out a pail of water. Odysseus turned his face away from Penelope, for the nurse said that he looked like her master. Then, as she washed his feet, she noticed a long scar on his leg. She remembered that Odysseus had been wounded by a wild boar long ago, before he was married.

The nurse now knew who the beggar really was, and she spoke to Odysseus in a whisper, calling him by his name. He held up his hand to hush her, for the suitors would slay him if they knew who he was. The nurse called him her child and promised she would be silent. Then Penelope, who had heard nothing, sent the nurse to fetch more hot water.

When Odysseus had finished washing, Penelope told him she could no longer refuse to marry one of the suitors. She said her husband had left a great bow that only a few people could bend. He had also left twelve iron axes, each made with a round opening in its blade. He used to set the twelve axes in a straight line and shoot an arrow through the twelve holes in the blades. Penelope had decided to bring the bow and the axes to the suitors the next day. She would marry the suitor who could string the bow and shoot an arrow through the twelve axes.

"I think," said the beggar, "that Odysseus will be here before any of the suitors can bend his bow."

Penelope made no answer. Instead, she returned to her room, and Odysseus went to find Telemachus. When the king had found his son, they went into the great hall alone. Odysseus told Telemachus he had come up with a plan.

Odysseus explained that Penelope would choose among the suitors the next day by giving them the test of the bow and arrow. He asked Telemachus to hide the suitors' swords and armor after they had come in for their feast. If the suitors asked about their weapons, Telemachus should say he had placed them out of reach in case the suitors quarreled over Penelope.

After discussing the plan, Telemachus and Odysseus also hid the shields, helmets, and spears that hung on the walls of the hall. When this was done, Telemachus went to sleep in his own room, and Odysseus lay down outside the palace. ★

There Odysseus lay, worrying if his plan would work. In the morning, he prayed to Zeus, asking for signs of his power. Suddenly, he heard a roll of thunder and then the voice of a weak old woman who was grinding corn to make bread for the suitors. All the other women of the mill had done their work, but the old woman was feeble, and the grindstone was too heavy for her.

The woman said, "Father Zeus, king of gods and men, you have thundered loudly. Help us, for we must labor all day to prepare food for the suitors. Grant me my wish, unhappy as I am. May this be the last day of the suitors' feasting in the hall of Odysseus. They have bent my back with cruel labor. May they no longer eat here!"

When he heard the woman's wish, Odysseus was glad, for he thought it would bring good luck to him.

Soon the servants were at work, and the farmers arrived at the palace with animals for the suitors. Eumayus came with pigs, and Melanthius with goats. Eumayus was as courteous to the beggar as Melanthius was rude. The goat farmer insulted Odysseus loudly as he herded his animals into a yard next to the palace. A farmer who herded cows also arrived. He hated the suitors, and he spoke to the beggar in a friendly way.

The suitors appeared last and went in to eat their meal. Telemachus asked the beggar to sit within the hall, and he ordered the servants to give the beggar as good a share of the food as the suitors received.

Then Antinous, the loud suitor, said, "This beggar has had his fair share, and I will give him a present over and above it." He picked up a cup and threw it with all his might at Odysseus, who merely moved aside. The cup struck the wall behind him.

Telemachus scolded Antinous, but the suitors only laughed wildly and began to throw food at each other. The young prince took advantage of the riot by quietly slipping away to hide the suitors' weapons. The suitors did not miss him. They called for more food and ordered the minstrel to sing.

D VOCABULARY REVIEW

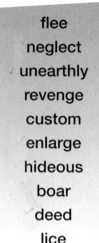

flee
neglect
unearthly
revenge
custom
enlarge
hideous
boar
deed
lice

For each item, write the correct word.
1. When you get even with a person, you take ▅▅▅ on that person.
2. When you fail to take care of something, you ▅▅▅ it.
3. A way of behaving that everybody follows is a ▅▅▅.
4. When something is unlike things normally found on earth, it is ▅▅▅.
5. When you make something bigger, you ▅▅▅ that thing.
6. When something is horrible or disgusting, it is ▅▅▅.
7. An action is a ▅▅▅.

E COMPREHENSION

Write the answers.
1. Why do you think the beggar didn't tell Penelope who he really was?
2. What do you think was better proof of Odysseus's identity—the clothes he wore or the scar on his leg? Explain your answer.
3. Describe the test that Penelope wanted to give to the suitors.
4. Why was Odysseus glad when he heard the old woman's prayer?
5. Why was Telemachus able to hide the suitors' weapons?

F WRITING

Do you think Odysseus should have told Penelope who he was?

Write a paragraph that explains your answer. Try to answer the following questions:
- What reasons does Odysseus have for keeping his secret?
- What might happen if Penelope learns his secret?

Make your paragraph at least fifty words long.

A WORD LISTS

1

Hard Words

1. victorious
2. reckoning
3. quiver
4. bewildered
5. burro
6. orchard
7. rodeo

2

Word Practice

1. caution
2. pillars
3. bedpost
4. lass
5. lasso

3

New Vocabulary

1. in vain
2. day of reckoning
3. victorious
4. quiver
5. bewildered
6. nonetheless
7. rodeo
8. lasso

B VOCABULARY DEFINITIONS

1. **in vain**—When you do something *in vain,* you do it without any success. If somebody is calling without success, that person is calling *in vain*.
   - If a person is struggling without success, that person is ___.
2. **day of reckoning**—The *day of reckoning* is a time when people are repaid for their good deeds or their bad deeds.
   - What happens on a day of reckoning?
3. **victorious**—A *victorious* person is one who wins.
   - What do we call a person who wins?
4. **quiver**—A *quiver* is a container that holds arrows.
   - What do we call a container that holds arrows?
5. **bewildered**—Someone who is *bewildered* is confused.
   - What's another way of saying *The boxer was confused*?
6. **nonetheless**—*Nonetheless* is another way of saying *in spite of that.*
   - What's another way of saying *in spite of that*?
7. **rodeo**—A *rodeo* is a show that includes bull riding and calf roping.
   - What is a rodeo?
8. **lasso**—A *lasso* is a rope that is used to catch horses and cattle.
   - What is a lasso?

Chapter 9
Penelope

The minstrel told the suitors it was bad luck to be rude to a beggar, but they paid no attention. Then the minstrel began to sing.

After a time, Penelope came through the crowd of suitors. She had the great bow and a quiver full of arrows in her hands. One of her servants followed, carrying the chest that contained the twelve iron axes. Penelope stood among the suitors and told them she would marry the man who could string the bow and shoot the arrow through the holes in the axes.

Telemachus said he would be the first to try. If he succeeded, he would not allow any of the suitors to take his mother away from her own house. Then he tried to string the bow three times, and the fourth time, he would have strung it, but Odysseus made a sign to him, and he put it down.

"I am too weak," Telemachus said. "Let a stronger man string the bow."

So the suitors tried, each in turn, beginning with the suitor who sat next to Telemachus. That suitor's hands were too weak, and he said the bow would bring bad luck to all of them. Antinous then asked Melanthius to light a fire and to bring grease for the bow to make it more supple.

The suitors warmed and greased the bow, and one after another, they tried to bend it. Meanwhile, Eumayus and the cow farmer went out into the court, and Odysseus followed them. He asked them, "Whose side would you two take if Odysseus came home? Would you fight for him or for the suitors?"

"For Odysseus!" they both cried. "If only he would come!"

"He has come, and I am he!" said their master.

Odysseus promised to give the two men land of their own if he was victorious, and he showed them the scar on his leg to prove who he was. The farmers hugged him and shed tears of joy. Then Odysseus told them to follow him back into the hall, where he would ask for the bow. He told Eumayus to place the bow in his hands no matter what the suitors said.

When the three men returned to the hall, Antinous was trying in vain to bend the bow. Finally, he begged to put off the test until the next day. On hearing that, Odysseus asked for a chance to string the bow. The suitors told him he could not, and they threatened him. ◆

But Penelope said the beggar could try his strength. She agreed that he was not a suitor and she could not marry him if he succeeded. But she would give him new clothes, a sword, and a spear and would send him wherever he wanted to go.

Suddenly, Telemachus cried out that the bow was his to give, and he would make a present of it to the beggar if he chose.

Then he ordered his mother and her servants to go to another part of the palace. Penelope was amazed to hear her son speak like the master of the house, but she went upstairs with her servants to her own room.

When Eumayus began carrying the bow to Odysseus, the suitors made such an uproar that the old man laid the weapon down, in fear for his life. But Telemachus threatened to punish him if he did not obey his master. So Eumayus placed the bow in the beggar's hands.

Odysseus turned the bow this way and that to see if it was still good. As the suitors mocked him, he suddenly bent the weapon and strung it. He plucked the string, and it made a sound like the note of a lyre. Then he took an arrow from the quiver, fitted it to the string, stood up, and shot the arrow through all twelve axe-heads.

An instant later, Telemachus drew his sword, took a spear in his left hand, and rushed to his father's side. Odysseus let his rags fall and leaped onto the table.

"Dogs!" he said. "You said I would never come home from Troy. You wasted my goods and insulted my wife and had no fear of the gods. Now the day of reckoning has come upon you! Fight or flee!"

"Get your weapons!" cried Antinous to the others. "Get your weapons!" The suitors ran to the door, but their weapons were not there. Then Odysseus shot an arrow over their heads, and the suitors were filled with fear. They fled for their lives, and they never returned to haunt the palace.

Odysseus sent the nurse to tell Penelope the good news. The good old woman ran up the stairs, laughing for joy. She came into the bedroom saying, "Come and see what you have so long desired—Odysseus in his own house and the wicked suitors gone."

"Surely you are mad, dear nurse," said Penelope, "to tell such a wild story."

The good nurse answered, "I tell you no wild tale. Odysseus is in the hall. He is that poor beggar whom the suitors struck and insulted." ★

Penelope leaped up gladly and kissed the nurse, but yet she was not sure her husband had come home. She feared he might be a god disguised as a man or an evil person pretending to be Odysseus.

"Surely Odysseus has met his death far away," she said. Even though the nurse explained that she had seen the scar on his leg, Penelope would not be convinced. "Nonetheless," she said, "let us go and see my son and the man who drove the suitors away."

So they went down the stairs. Penelope walked to the fire and sat opposite Odysseus, who was leaning against one of the four tall pillars that supported the roof. There she sat and gazed at him. This handsome man looked like Odysseus, and Telemachus told her that he was Odysseus. But she was not convinced.

"My child," she said, "I am bewildered and can hardly speak. If this man is really Odysseus, he knows things unknown to any except him and me."

Before answering his wife, Odysseus told Telemachus to put on fresh clothes, and he ordered the servants to bring the minstrel. Then he sat down on his own seat beside the fire and said, "Lady, you are the fairest and cruelest queen alive. No other woman would harden her heart against her husband when he has come home after so many years."

Penelope made no answer. Instead, she decided to give Odysseus a test. Turning to her nurse, she said, "This man may sleep outside the bedroom that Odysseus built. You can bring the bed out of that room for him."

"How can any man bring out that bed?" said Odysseus. "Did I not make it with my own hands, with a standing tree for the bedpost? No man could move that bed unless he first cut down the tree."

Then, at last, Penelope ran to Odysseus and threw her arms round his neck. "Do not be angry," she said, "for I have always feared that some strange man or god would come and deceive me, pretending to be Odysseus. But now you have told me the secret of the bed, which no person has ever seen or knows but the two of us."

Then they embraced, and it seemed as if Penelope's arms would never let go of her husband's neck.

Odysseus told her the story of his wanderings. At last, he remembered what Circe had said. He explained that he must wander again, carrying an oar on his shoulder, until he came to people who had never heard of the sea. He would start the next month and return home soon.

Then Odysseus and Penelope walked slowly away, together at last.

VOCABULARY REVIEW

supple
feeble
hideous
risk
enlarge
courteous

For each item, write the correct word.
1. Another word for *polite* is ▬▬.
2. Something that is very weak is ▬▬.
3. Something that is flexible and easy to bend is ▬▬.

COMPREHENSION

Write the answers.
1. How did the suitors try to make the bow more supple?
2. Why do you think Telemachus ordered Penelope to leave before the beggar tried to string the bow?
3. Do you think the suitors could have defeated Odysseus? Explain your answer.
4. Why was Penelope reluctant to believe Odysseus at first?
5. How did Odysseus prove to Penelope who he really was?

WRITING

People who would not recognize an oar would not know about the sea. When Odysseus meets people who have never seen an oar, what do you think he might tell them about the sea and what the sea means?

Write a paragraph that tells what Odysseus might say. Try to answer the following questions:
• How is the sea dangerous?
• How is the sea rewarding?
• How does Odysseus feel about the sea?

Make your paragraph at least fifty words long.

Ⓐ WORD LISTS

1

Hard Words
1. Eleanor
2. Clymer
3. yucca
4. mesa
5. gourd
6. corral

2

Word Practice
1. designs
2. tourist
3. sage
4. Louisa

3

New Vocabulary
1. gourd
2. squash
3. pottery
4. mesa
5. orchard
6. burro
7. corral
8. yucca

Ⓑ VOCABULARY DEFINITIONS

1. **gourd**—A *gourd* is a fruit with a hard shell. People sometimes use gourd shells as tools or containers.
   - What do people sometimes do with gourd shells?
2. **squash**—*Squash* is a vegetable that is like a pumpkin.
   - What is squash?
3. **pottery**—Dishes and pots made of clay are called *pottery.*
   - What do we call dishes and pots made of clay?

4. **mesa**—A *mesa* is a large landform with steep sides and a flat top.
   - What do we call a large landform with steep sides and a flat top?
5. **orchard**—An *orchard* is a farm where fruit trees or nut trees are grown.
   - What is an orchard?
6. **burro**—A *burro* is a small donkey.
   - What is a burro?
7. **corral**—A *corral* is a fenced area for farm animals.
   - What is a corral?
8. **yucca**—*Yucca* is a plant that grows in the desert.
   - What is yucca?

The Spider, the Cave, and the Pottery Bowl

by Eleanor Clymer
Part 1

In a certain place in the desert there is a cave, and sometimes outside the cave you can see a spider in its web. And on the shelf in my grandmother's house there is a pottery bowl. All these things are connected, and this is what I am going to tell about. But first I must tell about myself.

I am Indian. My name is an Indian word meaning One Who Dips Water. But in school they call me Kate. In winter I live with my father and mother and brother in a town near the edge of the desert. My father works in a store. There is a garage next to the store and he helps there, too. We have a garden and peach trees. We have a wooden house. We have running water and electricity. We aren't rich, but we have those things.

But in summer I go back to the mesa where my grandmother lives. We used to live there too, but we moved away. Grandmother's house is part of a village built of stone, with many small rooms, all connected, like a wall of houses around an open place. It's a small village. Some of the houses have other houses that were built on top of them when more rooms were needed. The village is very old, many hundreds of years old. When you drive across the desert you can see the mesa, like a high wall of rock ahead of you. And on top is the village. ◆

I love it on the mesa. It is windy, hot in the sun but cool in the shade of the houses, and you can see far out over the desert—the Painted Desert they call it, because it looks as if it were painted. It is beautiful on the mesa, but it is hard to live there. There is no water. The people must carry water up from springs down below. They must carry up everything they need, and they must go down to tend their gardens, and walk a long way through the desert to find grass or plants for their sheep to eat. It is hard work.

That is why some people moved away. My father doesn't mind hard work, but he needed to earn money for us. So we had to go away to the town.

But every summer we come back, my mother and my brother and I. We stay in my grandmother's house. My mother helps Grandmother with the summer work. And I help, too. We go down below and work in the garden, and we dry the corn and squash for the winter. We gather peaches from the orchard at the foot of the mesa, and we dry them. My brother plays with his friends, and rides the burros that live in the corral.

We gather firewood for the stove and

for the fireplace, and pile it up for the winter. We plaster the walls to make the house look clean. And we go a few miles away and bring home clay for the pottery.

The pottery is what I love most of all. I love to work the cool wet clay between my hands. When I was little, my grandmother gave me pieces of clay to play with, and I made things out of them. I made little animals: sheep and donkeys and birds.

Then when I got bigger, I watched my grandmother make bowls and jars. She made a flat piece for the bottom. Then she rolled pieces of clay into long rolls between her hands and coiled them on top of the flat piece till she had built up a jar. She

smoothed it with stone or a piece of shell, and shaped it in beautiful curves. When it was dry, she painted it with lovely designs. I watched her hand holding the brush of yucca leaves, slowly painting birds and leaves around the curving sides of the bowl. When she had enough bowls and jars, she built a fire and baked them hard.

People came to buy them, and my father took some to sell in the store where he works. But one bowl was never for sale. It stood on the shelf in the corner. It had been there for as long as I could remember.

The other women in the village made pottery, but I liked the things my grandmother made. There's nothing I wanted more than to make pottery like her. So I was always happy when summer came and we could go to the mesa.

But this summer was different. My mother did not come. She had to get a job.

For many days I heard my parents talking. There had been no snow during the winter, and all spring it had not rained. The springs did not give much water. The gardens were not growing well.

Where we live, everything depends on water. We are careful not to waste it. The people plant their gardens with little walls around them to save every drop that might run off. We have dances and prayers and music that help to bring rain. Even our names are like prayers for rain. That is why my name is One Who Dips Water. My brother's name is a word that means Clear Water, but his school name is Johnny. ★

Anyway, Mother and Father knew they would need money to buy food next winter. There are jobs in summer when the tourists come to stay in the hotels, and my parents decided that my mother should get such a job to earn extra money.

I said, "But what will we do? Won't we go to the mesa? What will Grandmother do?"

Mother said, "Kate, you are big, you will help Grandmother. Johnny will do his share. He is big enough to bring wood and water. Perhaps the neighbors will help with Grandmother's garden. But if the mesa springs are as dry as ours, perhaps there will not be much of a garden. When the summer is over and we come to get you, perhaps Grandmother will come with us and live here."

I did not think she would, but I did not say so.

So my father drove us to the mesa in the truck. It is about forty miles. We rode across the desert, between red and black and yellow rocks, and sand dunes covered with sage and yellow-flowered rabbit-brush. I was thinking about the work I would do. I don't mind the work, because it's important. Someday Grandmother's house will be Mother's, and then it will be mine. So I ought to know how to do everything.

A boy doesn't care so much, because the house won't belong to him when he grows up. He has to know about other things. That's why Johnny wasn't so interested in helping. Anyhow, getting wood and water isn't much fun. He wanted to play rodeo. He had a new cowboy hat and a rope for a lasso. And he wanted to go with the big boys and men to herd sheep and work in the cornfields. The little boys like it when the men are willing to take them along. Last year Johnny was too small.

"I hope they take me," he said. "I'm big enough now."

At last we saw the houses and the store and the school at the foot of the mesa. We took the narrow rocky road up the side of the mesa, and at last we came out in the open space on top.

It was good to be there. We jumped out of the truck and ran to see our friends. My best friend Louisa was there with her mother. She lives on the mesa all the time. I was so glad to see Louisa that we hugged each other. Summer is the only time we can really be together.

My grandmother was waiting for us in the doorway of her house. When I saw her I was surprised. She looked much older than the last time I had seen her. I had always thought of Grandmother as a strong, plump woman with black hair. This year she looked smaller, thinner, and her hair was gray.

Father noticed, too. He said to her, "Are you all right?"

Grandmother said, "Yes, I am well."

Father carried in the basket of food we had brought, and the boxes with our clothes. He explained why Mother had not come. Grandmother turned quickly in surprise. But she only said, "Well, if that is the way it is, it will have to be."

I said, "I will help you, Grandmother."

She nodded and said, "Yes, you are a big girl now."

And the neighbors who had come in said, "We will all help."

Father asked about Grandmother's garden. But she said she had not planted a garden this year. Then he asked if she had any pottery for him to take back, and she said, "No, I have not made any."

"Do you need clay?" he asked.

She said, "No, I don't need any clay."

Father said good-bye then. As he was leaving, he said to me, "Remember, if you need Mother or me, go down to the store and telephone, and we will come."

Then he went away, and there we were.

VOCABULARY REVIEW

> courteous
>
> hideous
>
> nonetheless
>
> bewildered
>
> in vain

For each item, write the correct word.
1. When you do something without any success, you do it ▨▨▨.
2. Someone who is confused is ▨▨▨.
3. Another word for *in spite of that* is ▨▨▨.

E COMPREHENSION

Write the answers.
1. Why is it hard to live on the mesa? Give at least three reasons.
2. Why did Kate like making pottery?
3. How were Kate's and Johnny's Indian names alike?
4. Why did Kate want to know how to do everything around Grandmother's house?
5. How do you think Kate felt at the end of this part?

F WRITING

Pretend you live on the mesa.
Write a paragraph that describes how you could save water. Try to answer the following questions:
- How could you use less water?
- How could you save the water you have?

Make your paragraph at least fifty words long.

A WORD LISTS

1
Hard Words
1. Kuka-Am
2. metate
3. juniper
4. idle

2
Word Practice
1. sight
2. sightseer
3. grey
4. greyish
5. charcoal

3
New Vocabulary
1. idle
2. plaza
3. juniper

B VOCABULARY DEFINITIONS

1. **idle**—When something is *idle*, it is still and not working.
   - What's another way of saying *Her hands were still and not working*?
2. **plaza**—A *plaza* is an open area surrounded by walls or buildings.
   - What's an open area surrounded by walls or buildings?
3. **juniper**—A *juniper* is a bush with strong-smelling berries.
   - What is a juniper?

The Spider, the Cave, and the Pottery Bowl
Part 2

I did not know what to do at first. I thought Grandmother would tell me, but she did not. So I made a fire in the stove and made coffee. We drank some. Johnny went to find his friends.

I said, "Is there something you want me to do?"

Grandmother said, "Later. Now I think I will sleep a little." And she lay down on her bed.

I went outside. It was strange for my Grandmother to be sleeping in the morning. I thought, "Well, after she has a rest, we will do things."

I went to Louisa's house. She was taking care of her baby brother. We played with him and made him laugh. Then Louisa put him to sleep in his cradle, and we went outside.

We talked about school and other things, and then Louisa's mother called out that she needed water. So we got some pails and went to the spring.

There is a big spring and a pool at the bottom of the mesa, and the men bring water up in their trucks, or on the backs of burros. But we went to another spring, a little one, on a path that goes part way down the side of the mesa. The water drips out between the layers of rock, and we hold our pails underneath and fill them.

Later, I went back to our house. It was nearly dinner time. Mother had sent some stew, so I warmed it up and cut the bread. Then I called Johnny and we ate.

Grandmother did not eat much. After dinner, she went out and sat in the sun. ◆

So the first days passed. I did everything I could think of. I tried to grind corn on the metate (the grinding stone), thinking it would please Grandmother. But I did not really know how to do it, and it was easier to cook the ready-made corn meal. I washed the cups and bowls and shook out the bedding. I swept the house.

It did not take long. There are only two rooms. In the main room there is a fireplace in one corner, a table and some chairs, the stove, and Grandmother's bed of rugs and blankets. There are the metates and the pails and jars for water, the shelves for dishes, the yucca brushes for sweeping. (Mother uses a broom but Grandmother likes the old-fashioned things.) And in another corner is the small shelf with the pottery bowl.

The other room has two beds, where Johnny and I slept, and the boxes with our clothes.

I would have liked to plaster the walls, but I did not think I could do it myself. Besides I did not want to disturb Grand-

mother. Sometimes she lay on her bed and seemed to be sleeping. Other times she sat outdoors. But her hands, which used to be so busy, were idle.

Nearly every day some tourists came. In other years, Louisa and I liked to see the tourists. They were so funny. They usually had big cars, and they were afraid of the rough road up the mesa. They went very slowly, hoping they would not meet anybody coming down. When they got to the top, they would get out of their cars and look around. And then they would buy pottery.

But this year I did not like them. I did not like the way they walked around and stared at us and our houses, as if we were something for sightseers to look at. I did not like the way some of the little boys ran after them. Once I saw Johnny and his friends go over to a car and touch it, and Johnny said, "How much did this car cost?" His friends said, "Give us money." I did not like that a bit, and I told the boys to go away.

Then, when the tourists asked for pottery, I had to say that we had none.

My grandmother used to sign her pottery. She would paint the name Anna on the bottom. Her name was Kuka-Am, which means Older Sister, but Anna was easier for white people to say, and they would often come to ask for Anna's pottery. I wondered when we were going to make some, but I did not like to ask.

Then one day I did. There had been lots of tourists, all looking for pottery. When they went away I said, "Grandmother, when will we make some?"

She said, "There is no more clay."

I knew there was none in the storeroom. Always before, there had been chunks of the greyish clay there, waiting to be ground up and soaked in water and shaped into bowls.

Grandmother used to carry it herself from a place she knew, a mile or so from the mesa. Later on, Father had brought it in the truck. But this year she had not asked him to get any.

"The bed of clay is used up," she said.

I said, "But there are other beds. Louisa's mother and the other women know where to get clay. I can go with them and get some."

She said, "The clay that I used was very fine. It needed nothing mixed with it to keep it from cracking." ★

I knew what she meant. Some kinds of clay will crack in the firing unless they are mixed with sand or ground-up bits of old pottery. But the kind she liked was good enough to be used alone. And there was no more of it.

I said, "Well, I will get some other kind, and you can show me what to do."

She nodded and said, "Perhaps. Perhaps later."

I wished my mother were there. I didn't know what to do. Grandmother did not seem to be sick. She just seemed far away.

I said, "Grandmother, shall I send a message to Mother to come? Would you like to see her?"

But she said, "No, let her do her job. That is more important now."

I asked, "When we go home, will you come with us?"

She shook her head and said, "No. My place is here. When I come to the end of my road, let it be here."

So there was nothing to be done, except to do my work and remind Johnny to do his. But most of the time he was nowhere in sight.

Johnny was disappointed, too. There were no big boys for him to go herding with, and none of the men wanted to take him to the cornfields. So all he did was play with the burros. When he wasn't doing that, he was drawing pictures in the dust of the plaza with a stick. Sometimes he found a piece of charcoal and drew on flat rocks or anything he could find. Once he drew pictures all over a house wall and got scolded for it.

Anyway, he didn't often bring firewood, so I went for it myself. One day, Louisa and I went to get some on the mesa top, beyond the village. We took cloths along, and piled juniper twigs in them. It was hot, there was no shade to protect us from the sun. The wind blew, but that only made it hotter.

I said, "I would like to have a big swimming pool here. I'd jump in and cool off."

Louisa looked at me out of the corners of her eyes. Then she said, "Maybe you wish you were back in the town, so you could go swimming."

I said, "No, I don't. I like it here. Only this summer everything is strange. Grandmother is different."

Louisa said, "My mother says she is getting very old. She thinks your mother should be here."

I said, "My mother would come if I called her. But Grandmother would not like it."

Louisa was silent for a while. She kept picking up wood and putting it in the cloth. Then she said, "I think it is because Kuka-Am fell. Something happened when she fell."

I said, "She fell? I didn't know that. How did it happen?"

Louisa said, "She went to get water, and when she was bending over, she got dizzy and fell. My mother helped her get home."

I said, "But why didn't she tell us?"

Louisa said, "She said she was well again. Perhaps I should not have told you."

I said, "I am glad you did. Now I understand better."

I did not want to understand, but I did anyway, and I felt afraid. Long ago, there would have been many aunts and cousins to help out. Now there were the neighbors, and me. If I did not send for my mother and anything happened, she would be angry with me. But Grandmother said no.

D MAIN IDEA

Write the main idea of the following paragraph. Then write four supporting details for the main idea.

Uncle Ulysses is a man with advanced ideas. He has a weakness for laborsaving devices. He equipped the lunchroom with automatic toasters, automatic coffee maker, automatic dish washer, and an automatic doughnut maker. All just the latest thing in laborsaving devices.

Use complete sentences to write the main idea and the supporting details. Indent the supporting details under the main idea, as shown below.

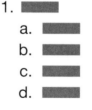

E VOCABULARY REVIEW

reckoning
minstrel
bewildered
supple
nonetheless
custom
in vain
mesa

For each item, write the correct word.
1. A way of behaving that everybody follows is called a ▆▆▆.
2. Something that is flexible is ▆▆▆.
3. The time when people are repaid for their good deeds or their bad deeds is called the day of ▆▆▆.
4. When you do something without any success, you do it ▆▆▆.
5. A person who lived at the time of Odysseus and sang songs and played the lyre was called a ▆▆▆.

F COMPREHENSION

Write the answers.
1. Why didn't Kate like the tourists this year? Give at least two reasons.
2. Why do you think Grandmother is acting strangely?
3. Why was Grandmother's clay better than regular clay?
4. Why might Kate's mother get mad at her?
5. How is Kate's life different from yours? Give at least three examples.

G WRITING

Kate is worried about her grandmother. What would you do if you were in Kate's position?

Write a paragraph that explains what you would do. Try to answer the following questions:
• How would you help Grandmother?
• What actions would you take if Grandmother became ill?
Make your paragraph at least fifty words long.

16

Ⓐ WORD LISTS

1
Hard Words
1. kachinas
2. ancestors
3. sympathize
4. cactus

2
Word Practice
1. outspread
2. polishing
3. guests
4. clattering

3
New Vocabulary
1. cross
2. affair
3. ancestors
4. ruins

Ⓑ VOCABULARY DEFINITIONS

1. **cross**—*Cross* is another word for *irritated.*
   - What's another way of saying *They were irritated in the morning*?
2. **affair**—Something that is your *affair* is your business.
   - What's another way of saying *That's his business*?
3. **ancestors**—Your *ancestors* are your relatives who lived many generations ago.
   - What do we call your relatives who lived many generations ago?
4. **ruins**—*Ruins* are the remains of old buildings.
   - What do we call the remains of old buildings?

The Spider, the Cave, and the Pottery Bowl
Part 3

We walked back with our firewood. I felt hot and dusty, and I would have liked to have a bath. Louisa was right in a way. At home, though we had to be careful with water, there was a shower, and there was a swimming pool at the school. But on the mesa there was no water for bathing.

As we came toward the village, there was a loud noise: boys' voices shouting, and burros' hoofs clattering on the stone. Johnny and three other boys had come running into the plaza. They had let the burros out of the corral and were trying to lasso them. It made a terrible dust, and people began running out of the houses shouting at them.

In the middle of all this there were some tourists in a big white car. The people inside the car looked scared.

Louisa's mother came out with a broom and chased the donkeys away. She told Johnny to go home, and she shouted at the other boys to drive the burros back to the corral.

When things had calmed down, a woman and a girl got out of the car. There was a man, but he just sat in the car.

The woman and girl stared all around. I suppose I stared at them. The girl was wearing a yellow skirt and white blouse and white sandals. She had long, yellow hair.

She looked cool, as if she had just had a shower. I guess the car was air-conditioned. She looked at me as if she was sorry for me. Then I remembered my face was dirty and my hair tangled, and it made me angry. I thought: Maybe she thinks I look like this all the time. I suppose she thinks she's better than me, because she has a big car and nice clothes.

Then I was ashamed of myself for thinking such thoughts.

The woman came over to me and said, "Where does Anna live?"

I said, "Right here." I should have asked what she wanted, but I did not think. The woman started to come in, but Louisa's mother called to her, "Anna is sleeping." ◆

The woman said she wanted pottery. Then I remembered my manners and I said, "Anna is my grandmother. She has no pottery. She has not been feeling well and hasn't made any."

Louisa's mother said, "There are other women who make pottery." But the woman said, "No, I don't want any other." She peered into the house and saw the bowl on the shelf.

"That's a nice bowl," she said. "Can I buy it?"

At this, Grandmother came to the door and said, "No, I can't sell that."

The woman asked, "Why not?"

Then the girl pulled at her mother's arm and said, "Come on, let's go."

Her mother was cross at that and said angrily, "Stop that, Elizabeth." I could see the girl's face get red.

At last, they went away. I went in with my firewood and put it down beside the stove. Johnny was sitting at the table.

Then there was a knock at the door. It was one of the old men of the village.

"Please come in," Grandmother said.

He entered and looked at Johnny. He said, "You and your friends must be more polite. Those strangers are our guests."

Johnny muttered, "They are stupid."

The old man said, "That is not your affair. If you are not careful, the kachinas will whip you."

Kachinas are the spirits that take care of people. They bring rain for the cornfields, and they bring gifts for good children and punishment for bad ones.

Johnny looked frightened.

Grandmother said, "He needs an older brother. In the old days, his father or his uncles or brothers would have been here to keep him busy, but now the men are all away." ★

The old man said, "His father expects him to keep himself busy."

After he went away, I wanted to talk about something else to make Johnny feel better, so I went over to the shelf and lifted the bowl down and held it in my hands.

"Be careful!" said Grandmother.

I said, "That lady wanted to buy Anna's pottery. She didn't know that this isn't Anna's."

Johnny said, "Isn't it? Where did it come from?"

Grandmother said, "It belonged to the Old Ones, our ancestors. Long ago, your grandfather was working with some white men in the ruins on the other side of the mesa. He brought it home to me. It was in a cave. There were other bowls, but only this one was perfect. I learned from studying it how to make my own pottery."

Johnny got up and looked into the bowl. There were some smooth stones in it. We both knew what they were. They were Grandmother's polishing stones, the ones she used for rubbing her pottery to make it smooth and shiny. Johnny reached in and took them out and felt them with his fingers.

Grandmother said, "Your grandfather found them in the bowl. A woman used them long ago, and I have used them all these years."

With his finger Johnny traced the design on the bowl. It was a bird with pointed beak and outspread wings.

"It's pretty," he said.

Then he went to put the stones back into the bowl. In doing so, he pushed my arm. The bowl fell to the floor and smashed.

D MAIN IDEA

Write the main idea of the following paragraph. Then write four supporting details for the main idea. Use complete sentences to write the main idea and the supporting details.

The machine started. Rings of batter started dropping into the hot fat. After a ring of batter was cooked on one side, an automatic gadget turned it over and the other side would cook. Then another automatic gadget gave the doughnut a little push and it rolled neatly down a little chute, all ready to eat.

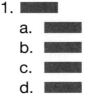

E COMPREHENSION

Write the answers.

1. How was Kate different from the tourist girl? Give at least three examples.
2. Why might the tourist girl feel she's better than Kate?
3. Why was Johnny afraid of the kachinas?
4. Why was the bowl so special to Grandmother?
5. What do you think Johnny and Kate will do about the broken bowl?

F WRITING

Do you think Kate would like to trade places with the tourist girl?

Write a paragraph that explains what you think. Try to answer the following questions:

- Why might Kate envy the tourist girl's life?
- What does Kate like about her own life?
- Which life would Kate prefer?

Make your paragraph at least fifty words long.

Ⓐ WORD LISTS

1

Word Practice
1. waist
2. carrier
3. whipping
4. kachinas

2

New Vocabulary
1. hoe
2. sympathize

Ⓑ VOCABULARY DEFINITIONS

1. **hoe**—A *hoe* is a tool that is used to break up dirt.
   - What is the purpose of a hoe?

2. **sympathize**—When you *sympathize* with someone, you understand that person's feelings.
   - What's another way of saying *He understood the crying children's feelings*?

C VOCABULARY PICTURES

hawk

jay

mockingbird

bluebird

The Spider, the Cave, and the Pottery Bowl
Part 4

We both stood there staring at the pieces on the floor. Then we looked at Grandmother. What would she say? I was sure she would be very angry. Maybe the kachinas would whip both of us. After all, I had taken the bowl down, so it was my fault just as much as Johnny's.

But Grandmother did not scold us. She only looked very sad for a moment. Then she said, "Pick up the pieces and put them in a basket. Perhaps we can mend it."

I didn't think we could, but I picked them up and put them with the polishing stones into a basket.

When I looked up, Johnny was gone. I thought, "I guess he feels pretty bad. I'll leave him alone for a while."

And I began to get supper ready. When it was done, I went out to call Johnny, but he didn't answer. I asked some of the boys if they had seen him, and they said, "Yes, up by the corral." So I went up there, and he was standing patting his favorite burro. She had her nose on his shoulder as if she was sympathizing with him.

I told him to come home and eat, and he said he wasn't hungry; but I said it was time to come anyhow, so he came with me.

I had cooked bacon and corn bread, and we had peaches and cake that I had bought at the store. I noticed Johnny ate quite a lot though he had said he wasn't hungry. ◆

After supper Grandmother lay down on her bed, but instead of going to sleep, she began to tell stories.

She told some we had heard before, ones we liked to hear again. There was the story about how our people came here. You see, for a long time they had lived in a land underground. But they did not have enough to eat, so they were looking for a way to get out. And finally they saw a hole in the roof overhead and wondered what was up there. They sent the hawk to look, but he could not fly high enough. Then they sent a mockingbird, but he too couldn't fly high enough to see what was beyond the hole. They sent a jay, but he soon came back. In the end, they sent the bluebird. He flew away and was gone so long that they thought he must be lost. But at last they heard him singing, and he had come back. He said there was a fine country beyond the hole. So the wise men used their magic to make a ladder high enough to reach the hole, and they all climbed up. And that was how they reached the earth.

She told us why the ants have thin waists. While the people were underground, they stayed in the village of the ants. There was very little food, and the ants were good to the people and gave them most of the food. So as not to feel hungry themselves, they tightened their belts till they were almost cut in half, and this is the way they are to this day.

Then she told about some things that happened while the people were looking for their proper place on this earth. For even after they came through the hole, they could not settle down. They had to wander over the earth for many years to find the right place to live. And often there was no water. So their guardian spirit gave them a little clay water jar and said, "One person will be the water carrier. If there is no water, let the water carrier plant this jar in the earth, and as long as you stay there, water will flow from the jar. When you move, you must take it along."

So they did that. "And it has happened," Grandmother said, "that people digging in the ruins, in a desert or on a mountain, have wondered how anyone could have lived there. That's because they didn't know about the magic water jar."

"And then what happened?" Johnny asked.

"They kept on wandering," Grandmother said, "until they came to their proper place, which is here. And so you see, even if things seem hard sometimes, we know it will be all right, because we are in our proper place, the place to which our people were sent."

"Who sent them?" Johnny asked.

Grandmother opened her eyes and looked at him as if she was surprised that he should ask that.

She said, "Maybe it was our Father the Sun, who made the world. Maybe it was the guardian spirit who gave them the magic water jar. But I think it may have been the Spider Woman. She is the Grandmother of us all. She helped the Sun to make animals and plants and people, and she and her twin grandsons keep things in order. If you ask her for help, she will give it to you."

I had heard of the Spider Woman. I knew you must never kill a spider, because it could be our Grandmother Spider herself.

I said, "Can we ask for anything we like?"

Grandmother said, "Yes, but not too much. You must be careful. She is very wise and will know if you are greedy." ★

Then she told us a story I had never heard before. She said, "On the far side of the mesa, there is a path that leads to the fields below. And beside the path there is a spring. It is not the spring we all use. It is a very small secret spring. There is a hollow place nearby, under the rocks. That is where Grandmother Spider lives. It is her secret house. If you see her there, spinning her web, you must not stop. You must lay a stick of firewood beside the path for the Spider Woman, and hurry on. If you stop to talk to her, she may invite you into her house. You may see her twin grandsons, and they may try to get you to come in. Once you go in, you may have to stay there. So be careful, and do not go that way."

Then she closed her eyes and I could tell from her breathing that she was asleep. Johnny was almost asleep. I pulled him up and led him over to his bed and he fell on it, and was sound asleep in a minute.

Then I went to bed myself. I thought about the stories. Why did Grandmother tell us those stories? Especially the one about the spring. Which spring was it? Could it be the one where Louisa and I sometimes went for water? No, it couldn't be. It must be one somewhere else.

I had a strange dream. I dreamed that out of the fireplace came something small and gray. It was a spider. It looked all around and waved its little feet in the air as if it was looking for something. It ran up the wall to the shelf. I looked, and there was the brown pottery bowl where it had always been. I thought: Oh, I'm so glad it wasn't broken after all. The spider ran inside the bowl and disappeared, and then I woke up and it was daylight.

Sometimes dreams fade away as soon as you wake up, but this dream was as clear as if it had been real life. The first thing I did was to jump out of bed to look at the shelf, to see if the bowl was there, but of course it wasn't.

Then I saw something else. Johnny wasn't there. I thought it was strange that he should be out so early. Most days, it was hard to get him out of bed. I looked outside the door, but he was not in sight. I wondered if he had gone for water, but the pails were empty. So I put my clothes on and went myself.

It is lovely on the mesa early in the morning. The air is cool and fresh. The sun was coming up and it made the houses look as if they were painted with light red paint. Far below, the desert was painted too, pink and red and gray. The moon was still in the sky. I was glad to be

alone out there. I got the water and started back.

At the top of the path, I met a couple of men who were going to work in their fields. I could tell because they had their hoes.

One of them was angry. He was saying, "I don't see how she could have gotten out."

I said, "Good morning, did you lose something?"

He said, "Yes, my burro. She got out of the corral somehow. I don't know how because the others aren't out. Did you see her?"

I said, "No, but I'll look for her." I hurried home. Grandmother was awake. I said, "Did you see Johnny?"

She hadn't seen him. I was sure he had something to do with the burro. It was the one he liked so much.

I thought: He must be afraid he will get a bad whipping. I knew the old man had talked about the kachinas the day before just to frighten him a little. I did not think he would really be punished much. But since he had not only taken the burros out but broken a piece of pottery, maybe he thought he had been very bad, and so he had run away.

E VOCABULARY REVIEW

ancestors

idle

custom

minstrel

cross

supple

in vain

For each item, write the correct word.
1. Another word for *irritated* is ▬▬.
2. Your relatives who lived many generations ago are your ▬▬.
3. When something is still and not working, that thing is ▬▬.
4. Something that is flexible and easy to bend is ▬▬.

 MAIN IDEA

Write the main idea of the following paragraph. Then write three supporting details for the main idea. Use complete sentences to write the main idea and the supporting details. Write **1** in front of the main idea and **a, b,** and **c** in front of the supporting details. Indent the supporting details under the main idea.

Poseidon could make storms and earthquakes. He was the god of the sea. He carried a three-pointed staff, and he had a terrible temper. He once tried to overthrow Zeus, but he did not succeed. Many Greeks were afraid of Poseidon because they believed he caused shipwrecks and other disasters.

G COMPREHENSION

Write the answers.
1. Why do you think the bluebird reached the hole and the other birds did not?
2. According to the story, why do ants have thin waists?
3. Where do you think is a "proper place" for people to live? Explain your answer.
4. According to the story, why must you never kill a spider?
5. What do you think Kate's dream means? Explain your answer.

H WRITING

Kate's grandmother told a story that explained why ants have thin waists.

Write another story that explains why ants have thin waists. Try to answer the following questions in your story:
• Where were the ants living?
• How did the ants survive in that place?
• What caused their thin waists?
Make your story at least fifty words long.

A WORD LIST

> **1**
> *Word Practice*
> 1. hoofmarks
> 2. Spaniards
> 3. cloudburst
> 4. arch

B VOCABULARY PICTURES

juniper

yucca

cactus

sagebrush

The Spider, the Cave, and the Pottery Bowl
Part 5

I said to Grandmother, "One of the neighbors' burros is missing. Maybe Johnny has taken it, not knowing the man wanted it for work this morning. I will go and see if I can find him."

Grandmother nodded and said, "He is troubled about the bowl. Tell him it does not matter. I am not angry. Last night, I was sad, but now I think that perhaps it had to be. The Old Ones may have wanted it back."

I was just going out when she said, "Wait. Eat first. And take some food with you."

So I ate some bread and cold bacon and drank some coffee, and then I wrapped some food in a cloth and put it in a basket. Then Grandmother said, "Wait," again. "Take a bottle of water."

I said, "But I'm coming right back."

She said, "You do not know. If he took the burro, you may have to go a long way. It is good to be prepared."

So I started. First, I went to the corral. It was true that the little female burro was gone. But which way did she go? I looked around on the ground and found some little hoofmarks. Then I looked to see which way they went.

Back of the village, the mesa top stretches out like a huge table. That is why it is called a mesa. It means table in Spanish, and when the Spaniards came, they made the Indians use Spanish names for things. Only we use our own names too, for things that are important. ◆

Well, this mesa stretches for miles. Desert plants grow on it, juniper and sagebrush, and some cactus. I started to walk away from the village, and I could see where twigs and leaves had been broken, and I thought that must be the way Johnny went.

I found a path where sheep had run. There were no sheep then, but sometimes the men take the sheep there when it has rained and there is fresh green stuff for them to eat. And in the path there were some little hoofprints. I followed them as fast as I could. I wondered why Johnny had gone that way. If he was going to run away, why hadn't he gone down the road and tried to get home to Mother and Father?

Then I remembered Grandmother's stories, especially the one about the Spider Woman and the spring, and I wondered if Johnny wanted to find the Spider Woman's house and go inside and escape. Perhaps he thought she would be kinder to him than the people in the village.

I wondered if the story could be true. When you go to school in town, you learn different things from what you learn on the mesa, and you wonder if the old stories can be true. But when you get back to the mesa, they have meaning for you, and you feel they are true.

The mesa has valleys in it, like big cracks in the table top. Some of those valleys are wide and have good soil for planting corn. We call them washes, because when there is a thunderstorm the water washes down them like a flood. The men put little fences of branches and twigs around their plants to protect them, so they won't be all washed away. If there is a big storm, though, some of the crops do get washed away.

I looked up at the sky and thought: I'm glad it's not going to rain today—though we had all been praying for rain for many days because it was so dry. But there were only white clouds in the blue sky, the fluffy kind that never do anything.

I was coming to one of those washes. The path led down the slope to the cornfields at the bottom. I was getting very hot and thirsty. The sun beat down on my head and I wished I had a hat. I took the cloth that was around the food and tied it over my head. Then I took a drink of water. I was glad I had it.

Then I was ready to start down into the valley. It wasn't steep, like the edge of the mesa where the village is, still it was pretty far down. I thought: How do I know Johnny is down there? I wished for one of those glasses that the tourists carry around their necks. I squinted my eyes, and yes, down in the valley I saw a boy on a burro. They looked very tiny. I yelled, "Johnny!" But of course he couldn't hear. So I started down. The ground had a lot of loose sand and stones, and I slid part way down, holding on to bushes as I went. At last, I got to the bottom and then I had to walk around a cornfield. I noticed that the corn looked thin. There hadn't been enough water. Farther down the wash were some more fields. I saw men working in them, bent over and digging. ★

I was getting tired and I thought: Why am I hurrying? Johnny knows the way back, and besides he has the burro.

But then I looked up at the sky and I saw that there was good reason to hurry. Instead of the fluffy white clouds, all of a sudden there were thunderclouds, tall gray clouds standing like mountains in the west. The sun was still bright, and as long as the clouds did not cover the sun I did not feel frightened. But they were moving. In the desert, a storm can come up in a few minutes. I began to run and to shout, "Johnny!"

He heard me and stopped, and then turned the burro and came toward me. I ran as hard as I could and pointed to the sky, and he understood. At last, I came up with him. I was out of breath and couldn't talk, but I climbed on the burro and beat her with my heels to make her run. We were in the middle of the valley and it was maybe half a mile to the opposite side, to a higher spot where we would be safe. Just in time we got there.

In a few minutes, we heard thunder. Then the cloudburst came. The rain poured down and in no time the wash was running like a river. We would never have been able to get out if the water had caught us.

Mud and rocks and tree branches came tumbling down in the roaring water. The rain poured on us. I thought: Yesterday I wanted a shower. Now I'm getting it, and my clothes are getting washed, too.

I looked down at the cornfields. The men were running up the bank to get away from the flood. I hoped the corn was not all washed away. I looked to see what Johnny was doing, but he was not beside me, only the burro with ears hanging down and the rain dripping off her.

Then I heard Johnny yell, "Come up here!"

He had found a cave, really an overhanging arch in the rock, and was standing there out of the rain. I pulled the burro and went up there too, and we sat down and watched the rain fall. We sat for a long time. I squeezed the water out of my hair and skirt, and we ate the food I had brought. Johnny was very hungry. He hadn't thought about taking food with him.

I asked, "Where were you going?"

But he wouldn't tell. I said, "Maybe you were going to look for Grandmother Spider."

Then he laughed and said, "No."

I said, "Well, then what? Did you think you'd find a magic water jar?"

He said, "If I tell you, you'll laugh at me."

I promised not to laugh. Then he said, "Grandfather found that bowl in the ruins where the Old Ones used to live. I broke it, so I was going to find another."

I said, "But Johnny, there aren't any left. The white people took them all away long ago."

He said, "White people are stupid. They couldn't find them all. I would find one that they didn't see."

I said, "But where are you going to look? I don't see any ruins around here."

He said, "Grandmother said they were on the other side of the mesa."

I said, "I think she meant a place far from here."

D MAIN IDEA

Write the main idea of the following paragraph. Then write three supporting details for the main idea. Use complete sentences to write the main idea and the supporting details. Write **1** in front of the main idea and **a, b,** and **c** in front of the supporting details. Indent the supporting details.

Odysseus told each man to select a large sheep, get under the sheep, and hold on to its fleece with his hands and feet. Then all the sheep went out through the cave doorway. Polyphemus felt the sheep, but he did not know that they were carrying out the men.

E COMPREHENSION

Write the answers.
1. How was Kate able to figure out where Johnny had gone?
2. Why do you think the Indians built their houses on the mesa instead of in the washes?
3. How did the sky change during this part?
4. Why did Kate and Johnny run to high ground?
5. Why did Johnny think he could find a bowl in the ruins?

F WRITING

As Kate walked along, she wondered if the old stories could be true. Do you think the old stories could be true?

Write a paragraph that explains your answer. Try to answer the following questions:
- What parts of the old stories are hard to believe?
- What parts of the old stories might be true?
- How do you feel about the old stories?

Make your paragraph at least fifty words long.

A WORD LISTS

1
Word Practice
1. dampness
2. buried
3. crumbled

2
New Vocabulary
1. rot
2. smudge

B VOCABULARY DEFINITIONS

1. **rot**—When something *rots,* it becomes soft and falls apart.
   - What happens when something rots?

2. **smudge**—When you *smudge* something, you smear it.
   - What's another way of saying *He smeared the window with his dirty hands*?

C VOCABULARY REVIEW

cross
hoe
bewildered
ancestors
juniper
supple

For each item, say the correct word.
1. Someone who is confused is ▬▬▬.
2. Another word for *irritated* is ▬▬▬.
3. Your relatives who lived many generations ago are called your ▬▬▬.

The Spider, the Cave, and the Pottery Bowl
Part 6

We stood up and looked around at the rock shelter we were in. It might have been a good place for the Old Ones to live, though if their houses had ever been there, they had crumbled away. But at the back, under one end of the arch, there was a crack, really a hole in the rock, partly filled with stones and sand, and we noticed that a trickle of water ran out of it and down the slope.

"There must be a spring in there," I said.

"Let's go in," Johnny said. "It looks like a deep hole. Maybe there are some ruins inside."

I said, "There could not be ruins in there."

"Well, I'm going," he said, and he got down on his hands and knees and started to crawl in.

Just then I noticed something. Near the entrance, a spider web was stretched across the branches of a little bush. I would not have seen it if the sun hadn't come out, and drops of water on the threads sparkled in the light.

In the middle of the web was the spider with her legs spread out. Some little flies were buzzing about. One of them hit the web and was trapped. At once the spider pulled in all her legs and jumped on the fly. I thought how clever she was to make her web by the spring where the flies would come.

Then I thought, "Maybe it's the Spider Woman!" And I shouted to Johnny, "Don't go in!" But it was too late. He was inside the hole. Now, I thought, the Spider Woman will get him and he will have to stay in her house forever.

I felt frightened. But I could not let him go in there alone. I tied the burro to a bush and crawled in after Johnny.

It was pretty dark inside. At first, I couldn't see anything. Then my eyes got used to the darkness, and I saw Johnny at the back of the cave. The cave was larger inside than I had thought it would be. Its floor was damp with the water that trickled down from the wall. I guess the water flowing for many years had hollowed out the cave.

"Did you find anything?" I asked.

"Yes," said Johnny. "An old basket, and a stick." ◆

I went over to look. Somebody had been digging there, and had gone away and left the things behind. I tried to lift the basket, but it was heavy. I dragged it to the entrance and looked inside.

Johnny said, "It's just a lot of dirt. I wanted to find pottery."

I said, "Johnny, you did!"

He thought I was joking. He said, "It's only sand."

I said, "It's not sand. It's clay. There's clay in this cave. We can make pottery with it."

So I got my basket, and Johnny took off his shirt. The clay was between two layers of rock in the wall at the back of the cave. We took the old digging stick and dug it out. We put it in Johnny's shirt to carry it. We wanted to take the clay we had found in the old basket, but it was heavy, and besides the basket was rotted with dampness, and I was afraid it would break, so we left it there. I wondered who the woman was who had been digging and why she had gone away and left her things behind.

We took as much clay as we could carry and went outside. The sky was blue.

The water was still running down the wash, but we could cross it. We loaded our clay on the burro and started home.

Johnny led the burro down the slope, but I stayed behind. I went back to the place where the spider web hung. The spider had sucked the juice out of the fly and was waiting for another.

I bent down and said, "Thank you, Grandmother Spider. I saw you last night in my dream. I thought you were telling me something. Now I think I understand." Then I looked around for a piece of firewood to lay beside the spring. I couldn't find one so I laid down the digging stick that I had in my hand.

Maybe this wasn't really Grandmother Spider's house. But it seemed like a good place for it. It was so quiet! The land was so big and so empty. There was no one

there but me, and farther down the slope, Johnny and the little burro. I almost expected to see the Spider Woman's twin grandsons standing in the path in front of me. But there was no one. I ran to catch up with Johnny, and we led the burro down the slope, then past the cornfields. Some of the fences had held, but others had been washed away by the storm, and some of the corn plants were torn up and drowned.

We climbed the other side of the wash and walked across the mesa to the village. It was getting toward evening. We had been gone a long time. I began to think that Grandmother must be wondering where we were. But I didn't expect what happened.

When we got to the village, the neighbors ran out to meet us looking very upset. Louisa came and hugged me, and her mother took hold of Johnny and said, "Are you all right? Nothing happened to you?"

I couldn't understand her. I said, "Why should anything happen?" ★

She said, "One of the big boys just came home and said there was a terrible flood. Then Louisa said she had not seen you all day, and your grandmother said you had gone somewhere. We thought you must be drowned. We were just going to look for you."

I said that we were not drowned, that we had climbed up away from the flood and waited till it was over. She scolded us and said, "Never go away without telling me. What if something had happened to you! What would I tell your parents?"

She wanted to know why Johnny wasn't wearing his shirt, and I said we had a present for Grandmother wrapped in it. Then we went into our house.

Grandmother was sitting inside the door waiting for us. She looked sad and small and very old.

I said, "Here we are."

She said, "So you found him. Where did you go?"

I wanted to say, "To Grandmother Spider's house." But I was afraid she would think I was joking. You must not joke about such things. So I just said, "Across the wash, and we have brought you a present from there."

I laid Johnny's shirt on the floor and untied it. She bent down and took a handful and felt it with her fingers.

"Clay!" she said. "The best kind of clay!" She smiled at me. "Where did you get it?"

I told her, "Across the wash there is a kind of cave, really just a hole in the rocks with water trickling from it. We found a basket of clay and a digging stick."

Grandmother said, "I know that place. A woman was digging there. She had her child with her, and the child was playing outside. There was a storm, and she ran out to save the child and never went back."

I asked, "Did she save the child?"

She said, "Yes, the child is grown up now. But we never went back there. We thought it was bad luck. But you see after many years it is time for good things to happen. It doesn't hurt to wait." Then she looked at Johnny and asked, "Why did you run away? And why did you take the burro?"

He looked a little scared, because he knew he shouldn't have taken the burro without permission. But he was brave.

He said, "I was sorry I broke the bowl. I wanted to find another bowl in the place where the Old Ones lived. But I didn't know how far it would be so I took the burro. It's a good thing Kate came too because I forgot to take food."

Grandmother said, "You'll remember next time. Never go out into the desert without food and water. You might have had to stay all night."

Johnny said, "But I didn't find a bowl. Kate says there are no more left. She says the white people took them all away."

Grandmother said, "They could not take them all. There are still many left, but they are buried in the earth. You would have to dig deep to find them. But what you did find is better. We will make our own bowls now."

Then she said to me, "Now we will eat, and then we will take care of the clay."

E OUTLINING

An outline helps you remember a story by showing the main ideas and the supporting details. You're going to complete part of an outline for *The Odyssey* by writing the supporting details.

The first main idea is *Odysseus blinded Polyphemus.* Tell what substance Odysseus found. Tell how Odysseus prepared that substance. Tell where Odysseus threw that substance.

The second main idea is *Circe gave Odysseus many warnings.* Tell what the men were not supposed to eat. Tell how Odysseus might finally go home. Tell what Odysseus would have to do with an oar.

The third main idea is *The men passed the Sirens safely.* Tell what the men had in their ears. Tell where

Odysseus was tied. Tell who could not hear Odysseus.

Copy each main idea on your own paper. Then use complete sentences to write the supporting details.

1. Odysseus blinded Polyphemus.
   a.
   b. ▤
   c. ▤
2. Circe gave Odysseus many warnings.
   a. ▤
   b. ▤
   c. ▤
3. The men passed the Sirens safely.
   a. ▤
   b. ▤
   c. ▤

F COMPREHENSION

Write the answers.
1. Why was Kate frightened when Johnny went into the cave?
2. What do you think Grandmother Spider was telling Kate in the dream?
3. Why were the neighbors upset with Kate and Johnny?
4. In what ways were the Indians on the mesa like the spider?
5. How were the discovery of the clay and the rainstorm alike?

G WRITING

Do you think Kate believed in the old stories now?

Write a paragraph that explains what you think. Try to answer the following questions:
- What experiences did Kate have during the day?
- How could those experiences be explained?
- What effect might those experiences have on Kate?

Make your paragraph at least fifty words long.

The Spider, the Cave, and the Pottery Bowl
Part 7

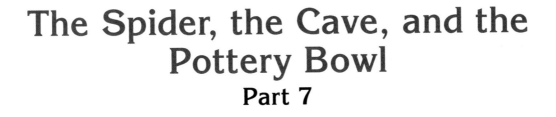

So I put the food on the table and we ate, but we were so tired that we did not do anything more till the next morning. Then Grandmother told me what to do, and watched while I did it.

I broke up the clay into lumps and ground up the lumps on the metate till it was as fine as cornmeal. I sifted out all the pebbles that were mixed in it. I wet the clay in a pail and put wet cloths over it to keep it soft.

Then I started to make a bowl. I took some clay and made a flat pancake for the bottom, using an old plate to hold it steady. I took more clay and rolled it between my hands into a long roll. I laid it along the edge of the pancake and pinched it in place.

Then I added more and more rolls till the sides of the bowl were built up. I kept wetting my hands in a pail of water and smoothing the clay. Now and then, Grandmother took the bowl and fixed it where I had made it too thick or too thin. Her hands had made so many pots that they knew just what to do.

Johnny sat watching us, and drawing lines in the dust with a stick to amuse himself. ◆

When the sides of the bowl were high enough, Grandmother took some dried pieces of gourd shell out of a basket. They were what she used for shaping the bowl. She took a piece that was curved just right and held it against the side of the bowl and pushed from inside, till it was shaped like the curve of the gourd. Then she let me do it.

When the bowl was finished, we set it in the shade to dry, not in the sun, for then it would dry too fast and crack.

I was tired. It had taken me a long time. I began to think about cooking dinner. I went into the house. The water pails were full, and there was a pile of juniper twigs for the fire. Johnny had done it while I wasn't looking.

We only made one bowl. We did not have enough clay for any more. When it was dry, it was time to put on the slip. Slip is a coating of very fine white clay. Grandmother had some in her storeroom. We made a thin paste and rubbed it on with a rag. When that was dry, the next thing was the polishing. Grandmother gave me her polishing stones and said, "They will be yours." And I polished the bowl till it was as shiny as glass.

Then we had to paint it. Grandmother sent me to the storeroom for her pot of black paint. She had made it the year before. She had gathered tansy mustard and boiled it with water till the water was all boiled away and just a black paste was left. Now it was hard and dry. We pounded it into powder and mixed it with water. Then Grandmother took the bowl, and her brush of yucca leaves, and began to paint. She painted a line all around the top with one gap in it, to keep off bad luck.

Then she gave the brush to me, to paint the design. But I had never painted, and I was afraid to spoil the bowl. I sat with the brush in my hand, wondering how to start.

Then Johnny came up behind me. He said, "Let me do it."

I said, "Do you know how?"

He took a piece of charcoal from the stove and drew a design on the wall. It was what he had been drawing in the dust, and it was the design that had been on the broken bowl, a bird with a sharp beak and strong curving wings. I gave him the brush, and he painted it around the bowl.

Grandmother watched him and said, "It is very good."

Then it was time to bake the bowl. But we didn't want to make a fire for just one bowl. We asked the neighbors if anybody wanted to bake pottery. Soon we had about a dozen pieces. Louisa's mother helped us make the fire.

It had to be made just right, with stones to set the pots on, and wood underneath and sheep dung on top. It had to be sheltered from the wind, or the pots would

be smudged. When all was ready, Grandmother sprinkled cornmeal and said a prayer. Then she lit the fire. ★

It was a long time before the fire died down and the bowls were cool enough to touch. When we took them out, our bowl was perfect, with not a single crack. Grandmother looked at it a long time.

Then she said, "Children, it is good. Now we will ask your mother to come."

I said, "Grandmother, but you are all right again!"

She said, "You are right. I was sick before, but I did not want your mother to know. She had to do her job, and it would have made her too sad. But now I think we will tell her. And maybe she will want to come home and help us make pottery. Maybe we can earn money that way, so she will not have to work in the hotel."

So Mother came and stayed the rest of the summer. She went with us to get clay. She taught me the right words to say when I was digging, because when you take something from the earth you should ask permission and give thanks.

We made pottery the rest of that summer. Johnny helped us with the designs. My mother is a good potter, almost as good as Kuka-Am. Grandmother didn't make much of the pottery, mostly she did the polishing. It was easier for her. But she signed some of the pieces, because it pleased the tourists. Father took some to sell in the store where he works, and when people heard that they could get Anna's pottery, they started coming to buy it.

One day a car came up the road to the village. It was a big white car, and it stopped and a woman and a girl got out. I went out to meet them and the girl remembered me. I remembered her, too.

I said, "Hi, you came back."

She said, "Yes. We went all the way to California, and now we're going home, but I wanted to come here on the way. My mother and father didn't want to come, but I made them."

I asked her, "Where do you live?"

She said, "We used to live in Chicago, but now we're going to live in New York. We have to move a lot on account of my father's job. I wish I could stay here."

I said, "Maybe you wouldn't like it here."

She said, "Yes, I would. It's so old. It's as if this place has been here forever. You'd always know where you belonged."

Her mother called to her to hurry up, and she went. I remembered that I envied her once. I didn't envy her any more.

I remember that she looked at the bowl on the shelf, the one Johnny painted, as if she would have liked to have it. We still keep it there, and Grandmother keeps her polishing stones in it.

Grandmother is still living in her house. It was her mother's mother's, and some day it will be mine. I'll go away, but I'll always come back, I think. And whatever happens, I'll always keep that bowl.

B OUTLINING

An outline helps you remember a story by showing the main ideas and the supporting details. You're going to complete part of an outline for *The Odyssey* by writing the supporting details.

The first main idea is *The men rowed between two dangerous places.* Tell which monster was on one side. Tell which place was on the other side. Tell what the monster did to the men.

The second main idea is *The gods freed Odysseus from Calypso.* Tell which god wanted to help Odysseus. Tell which god gave an order. Tell which god carried the order.

The third main idea is *The situation in Ithaca was very bad.* Tell what the people thought about Odysseus. Tell what some men wanted to do with Penelope. Tell what those men did at Odysseus's palace.

Copy each main idea on your own paper. Then use complete sentences to write the supporting details.
1. The men rowed between two dangerous places.
   a. ▆▆▆
   b. ▆▆▆
   c. ▆▆▆
2. The gods freed Odysseus from Calypso.
   a. ▆▆▆
   b. ▆▆▆
   c. ▆▆▆
3. The situation in Ithaca was very bad.
   a. ▆▆▆
   b. ▆▆▆
   c. ▆▆▆

C COMPREHENSION

Write the answers.
1. Why did Grandmother get well again?
2. Why was Kate's mother able to come to the mesa instead of working at the hotel?
3. Why did the tourist girl want to live on the mesa?
4. Why didn't Kate envy the tourist girl anymore?
5. Would you like to live on the mesa? Explain your answer.

D WRITING

Kate learned how to make pottery during the summer.

Write a short article that tells how to make a pottery bowl. Try to answer the following questions:
- What materials do you need?
- What steps do you follow?
- What parts are the most difficult?

Make your article at least fifty words long.

A WORD LISTS

1
Hard Words
1. apprentice
2. apprenticeship
3. average
4. guild
5. guildhall
6. lathe

2
Word Practice
1. particular
2. master
3. masterpiece
4. journeyman
5. carpentry
6. plumbing

3
Continents
1. North America
2. South America
3. Antarctica
4. Africa
5. Australia
6. Europe
7. Asia
8. Eurasia

B WORLD MAP

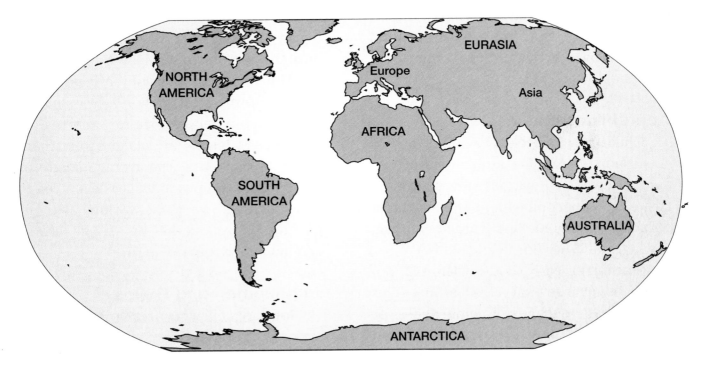

Children at Work

If you're like most kids, you spend about six hours a day in school, five days a week. After school, you might spend an hour or two on homework, but you have lots of time to play sports, read books, or just sit around visiting with your family and friends.

Seven hundred years ago, children in Western Europe weren't so lucky. By the age of twelve, almost all of them were already working ten or more hours a day, six days a week. If they lived on farms, they were in the fields, helping their parents till the soil and plant the crops. If they lived in towns, they were working without pay in small shops, learning to weave cloth, build furniture, bake bread, or make other products people needed.

Apprentices and Masters

Children who worked without pay in small shops were called **apprentices.** Most apprentices were boys, but a few were girls. (Instead of becoming apprentices, most girls stayed at home and learned cooking, sewing, and other household skills.)

Starting as early as ten years old, apprentices spent several years learning a particular craft, such as making shoes or weaving cloth. They worked for a **master**— an older person who had mastered the craft and owned a shop. Apprentices lived in the master's house and ate meals with the master's family.

In those days, people made products with hand tools. Learning to use the tools properly took a long time. Apprentices might spend months or even years just watching the master use the tools to build furniture or weave cloth. They would also run errands for the master and clean up the shop at the end of the day.

Slowly, the apprentice would begin to perform more complicated jobs for the master, such as sawing wood or measuring lengths of cloth. When the time was right, the apprentice might make a plain table or a small pair of shoes while the master looked on and asked questions. This kind of learning and testing would go on for several years until the apprentice had learned the craft.

The length of the apprenticeship depended on the craft. Bakers, for example, might keep an apprentice for only two or three years, but saddle makers kept them for up to ten years. The average length of an apprenticeship was five to seven years. After all those years of working without pay, the apprentice left his or her master and became a **journeyman.** ◆

Journeymen and Guilds

Journeymen were free to work wherever they wanted. They also got paid for working. Some stayed with the same master they had apprenticed for, but most went to work for other masters. A typical shop had one master, one journeyman, and one or two apprentices.

Being a journeyman was not an easy life. Masters hired journeymen for only a short time and paid them as little as possible. Journeymen often gathered in a central part of town and waited for masters to hire them for a day's work. If there was no work, the journeymen might wander to another town, trying to improve their luck.

The best hope for journeymen was to become masters themselves. But this was not easy. All the masters of a particular craft belonged to an organization called a **guild.** A large town might have almost a hundred guilds—one for the bakers, one for the carpenters, one for the weavers, and so on.

The guilds controlled who became masters and who did not. To become masters, journeymen first had to join the guild for their particular craft, such as the weaver's guild. Joining the guild often cost a lot of money. In return, the guild helped journeymen find jobs and places to live. The guild also invited the journeymen to its meetings, which were held in the **guildhall,** one of the biggest buildings in town.

Some of these meetings were just big parties where everybody had a good time. But at other meetings, the masters would decide which journeymen were ready to become masters. Each journeyman had to produce a "masterpiece" that the masters judged. A weaver, for example, might produce a certain amount of cloth. If the masters thought the cloth was of high quality, they made the journeyman a master. If not, the journeyman would have to try again later. ★

Changing Times

In the next lesson, you will begin reading a European folktale called "The Table, the Donkey, and the Stick." The story tells about three brothers who leave home, become apprentices, and return as journeymen. Like many folktales, the story features talking animals and other types of magic.

The first brother is a **joiner**—a type of carpenter who joins pieces of wood together to make furniture. The second brother is a **miller,** a person who grinds grain into flour. The last brother is another type of carpenter called a **turner.** He carves table legs and other round pieces of wood by turning them around and around on a lathe.

Because "The Table, the Donkey, and the Stick" is a folktale, no one knows exactly where or when it takes place. It could have happened in many parts of Western Europe between the years 1100 and 1500. During that time, guilds had a lot of power, and the apprentice system was in full swing.

That system lasted for hundreds of years, but by 1500, it was beginning to fall apart. One big reason for this change was that machines were starting to replace hand tools. Instead of training an apprentice for several years in the use of certain tools, a master could just hire somebody to run a machine.

The apprentice system didn't disappear, however. Many trades, such as carpentry and plumbing, still use the terms *apprentice, journeyman,* and *master.* And young people still spend several years learning these trades. But they start when they're much older, and they get paid for what they do.

Although "The Table, the Donkey, and the Stick" takes place hundreds of years ago, its themes are just as important as ever. As you read the story, try to figure out what it tells us about learning, working, and succeeding in life.

D RELEVANT INFORMATION

Write the answers for items 1–8.

Here are two rules about relevant information.

- Information that helps explain a fact is **relevant** to the fact.
- Information that does **not** help explain a fact is **not relevant** to the fact.

Here's a fact: *The woman sharpened her pencil.* The following items give more information about what happened before she sharpened her pencil:

The woman had been writing a letter.

1. Does that information help explain why the woman sharpened her pencil?
2. So what do you know about that information?

The woman had red hair.

3. Does that information help explain why the woman sharpened her pencil?
4. So what do you know about that information?

The pencil had an eraser.

5. Does that information help explain why the woman sharpened her pencil?
6. So what do you know about that information?

The point of the pencil was broken.

7. Does that information help explain why the woman sharpened her pencil?
8. So what do you know about that information?

E OUTLINING

Complete the following outline for "The Spider, the Cave, and the Pottery Bowl" by writing the supporting details.

Copy each main idea; then write three supporting details for each main idea. Use complete sentences to write the supporting details.

1. *At the beginning of the story, Kate's grandmother was not normal.*
   a. Tell what she did most of the time.
   b. Tell what she no longer made.
   c. Tell how she seemed to feel.
2. *Kate and Johnny found some clay.*
   a. Tell where the clay was.
   b. Tell what kind of clay it was.
   c. Tell which animal was near the clay.
3. *Kate made a pot.*
   a. Tell how she made the bottom.
   b. Tell how she made the sides.
   c. Tell how she smoothed it out.

F COMPREHENSION

Write the answers.
1. Why did apprentices need such a long time to learn a craft in the 1300s?
2. How did masters test apprentices?
3. How were journeymen different from apprentices?
4. Explain how a journeyman could become a master.
5. What was one reason the apprentice system began to fall apart?

G WRITING

What job would you like to have when you grow up?

Write an essay (a short article) that explains what job you would like to have. Try to answer the following questions:
- What job would you like to have?
- Why do you like that particular job?
- Why do you think that job is better than other jobs?
- What will you have to do to prepare yourself for that job?

Make your essay at least fifty words long.

 A WORD LISTS

1

Word Practice
1. tailor
2. churchyard
3. yardstick
4. hedge

2

New Vocabulary
1. sprouts
2. tether
3. fasting
4. devour
5. wretch
6. wrath

B VOCABULARY DEFINITIONS

1. **sprouts**—Young plants that are just starting to grow are called *sprouts.*
   - What's another way of saying *The sheep ate all the young plants*?
2. **tether**—When you *tether* an animal, you tie it with a rope or a chain to an object.
   - Why might a cowgirl tether her horse outside a house?
3. **fasting**—When you are *fasting,* you don't eat any food.
   - What's another way of saying *They are not eating any food today*?
4. **devour**—When you *devour* something, you eat it quickly.
   - What's another way of saying *The dog ate its dinner quickly*?
5. **wretch**—A *wretch* is a miserable person.
   - What's another way of saying *Those miserable people spoiled the party*?
6. **wrath**—*Wrath* is another word for anger.
   - What's another way of saying *She was filled with anger*?

The Table, the Donkey, and the Stick
Part 1

There was once a tailor who had three sons and one goat. The goat, because she fed them all with her milk, needed to eat good food. So every day the sons took turns leading her out to graze.

One day, the oldest son took the goat to the churchyard, where the best sprouts were. She ate her fill as she wandered about.

In the evening, when it was time to go home, he asked, "Well, goat, have you had enough?"

The goat answered, "I am so full that I cannot pull another blade of grass—baa! baa!"

"Then come home," said the youth, and he fastened a string to her, led her to her stall, and tethered her.

When the oldest son entered the house, the tailor asked, "Has the goat had her proper food?"

"Oh," answered the son, "she is so full that she cannot pull."

But the father, wishing to see for himself, went out to the stall, stroked his dear goat, and asked, "My dear goat, are you full?"

The goat answered, "How can I be full? There was nothing to pull, even though I looked all around—baa! baa!"

"What is this I hear?" cried the tailor. So he called out to his oldest son, "You liar, you said the goat was full when she has been hungry all the time!" And in his wrath, the tailor took up his yardstick and drove the youth out of the house. ◆

The next day was the second son's turn to feed the goat. He found a fine place in the garden hedge, where there were good green sprouts, and the goat ate them all.

In the evening, when it was time for the son to lead the goat home, he asked, "Well, goat, have you had enough?"

The goat answered, "I am so full that I cannot pull another blade of grass—baa! baa!"

"Then come home," said the youth, and he led her home and tethered her.

When the second son entered the house, the tailor asked, "Has the goat had her proper food?"

"Oh," answered the son, "she is so full that she cannot pull."

The tailor, not feeling satisfied, went out to the stall and asked, "My dear goat, are you really full?"

The goat answered, "How can I be full? There was nothing to pull, even though I looked all around—baa! baa!"

"The good-for-nothing rascal," cried the tailor, "to let the dear creature go fasting!" Running back, he chased the youth out of the house with his yardstick.

The next day was the third son's turn. To make sure the goat ate well, he found

some shrubs with the finest sprouts possible and left the goat to devour them.

In the evening, when he came to lead her home, he asked, "Well, goat, are you full?"

The goat answered, "I am so full that I cannot pull another blade of grass—baa! baa!"

"Then come home," said the youth, and he took her to her stall and tethered her.

When the third son entered the house, the tailor asked, "Has the goat had her proper food?"

"Oh," answered the son, "she is so full that she cannot pull." ★

But the tailor, not trusting his son, went out to the goat and asked, "My dear goat, are you really full?"

The goat answered, "How can I be full? There was nothing to pull, even though I looked all around—baa! baa!"

"Oh, the wretches!" cried the tailor. "The one as good for nothing and careless as the other. I will no longer have such fools around me." He grabbed his yardstick and threatened his son so mightily that the youth ran away. And so the tailor was left alone with the goat at last.

The next day, the tailor went out to the stall and let out the goat himself, saying, "Come, my dear creature, I myself will take you to graze."

So he led her by the string and brought her to the green hedges and pastures where there was plenty of food to her taste. Then he said to her, "Now, for once, you can eat to your heart's content," and he left her there till the evening.

When the tailor returned, he asked, "Well, goat, are you full?"

She answered, "I am so full that I cannot pull another blade of grass—baa! baa!"

"Then come home," said the tailor, and he led her to the stall and fastened her up. Before leaving the goat, he turned to her and said, "Now then, for once you are full."

But the goat actually cried, "How can I be full? There was nothing to pull, even though I looked all around—baa! baa!"

When the tailor heard this, he saw at once that his three sons had been sent away without reason.

"You ungrateful creature!" he cried, and he reached for his yardstick. But the goat was too quick for him, and she ran away with a jump and a spring.

The tailor felt very sad as he sat alone in his house. He would have given anything to get his sons back again, but no one knew where they had gone.

D OUTLINING

Complete the following outline for *The Odyssey* by writing the supporting details.

Copy each main idea; then write three supporting details for each main idea. Use complete sentences to write the supporting details.

1. *Odysseus visited Circe.*
   a. Tell what she did to some of the men.
   b. Tell what kind of meal she gave the men.
   c. Tell a warning she gave Odysseus.
2. *Odysseus visited the Phacians.*
   a. Tell whom he met first.
   b. Tell how he showed his strength.
   c. Tell what they gave him.
3. *Odysseus proved who he was.*
   a. Tell what he did with an arrow.
   b. Tell what he had on his leg.
   c. Tell what secret he knew.

E COMPREHENSION

Write the answers.
1. Why do you think the goat lied when the tailor asked her if she was full?
2. Why do you think the tailor trusted the goat more than he trusted his sons?
3. How did the tailor discover the goat was lying?
4. Do you think it was wise of the tailor to drive his sons away? Explain your answer.
5. What do you think the sons will do now? Explain your answer.

F WRITING

What do you think will happen next in the story?

Continue the story without looking ahead in your book. Try to answer the following questions:
- What happens to the oldest son?
- What happens to the second son?
- What happens to the youngest son?
- What happens to the tailor?
- What happens to the goat?

Make your story at least one hundred words long.

A WORD LISTS

1
Word Practice
1. apprentice
2. apprenticed
3. sparkling
4. innkeeper
5. masterpiece

2
New Vocabulary
1. subside
2. deprive
3. agreeable
4. assemble

B VOCABULARY DEFINITIONS

1. **subside**—When something *subsides,* it settles down.
   - What's another way of saying *The excitement settled down*?
2. **deprive**—When you are *deprived* of something, that thing is taken away from you. Here's another way of saying *The food was taken away from them: They were deprived of food.*
   - What's another way of saying *Sleep was taken away from him*?

3. **agreeable**—When something is *agreeable,* it is pleasing.
   - What's another way of saying *The flowers had a pleasing odor*?
4. **assemble**—When people *assemble,* they get together in a group.
   - What's another way of saying *The students got together in the gym*?

The Table, the Donkey, and the Stick
Part 2

After he was driven from home, the oldest son apprenticed himself to a joiner, and he learned his trade well. When the time came for the son to leave, his master gave him a little table. It was nothing much to look at, and it was made of common wood. But it had one great quality. When anyone set it down and said, "Table, be covered!" all at once the good little table had a clean cloth on it—and a plate, a knife, a fork, dishes with roasted and boiled meat, and a large glass of sparkling drink to cheer the heart.

The young journeyman thought he was set for life, and he went merrily out into the world. He never cared whether an inn was good or bad or whether he could get anything to eat. Whenever he was hungry—whether in the fields, the woods, or the meadows—he set down his gift and said, "Table, be covered!" In that instant, he was provided with everything his heart could wish for.

At last the youth decided to go back to his father, whose anger had probably subsided by now. Perhaps because of the wonderful table, his father might receive him again gladly.◆

On the last evening of his journey home, the young joiner came to an inn that was full of guests. They invited him to eat with them, explaining that the innkeeper had run out of food.

"No," answered the youth, "I could not think of depriving you. Instead, you had much better be my guests."

The people laughed and thought he must be joking. But the young joiner brought out his little wooden table, put it in the middle of the room, and said, "Table, be covered!" Immediately it was set with food much better than the innkeeper had been able to provide. The good smell of the food was quite agreeable to the guests' noses.

"Fall to, good friends," said the joiner. When they saw how it was, the guests didn't need to be asked twice. They took up their knives and forks and fell to work. And whenever a dish was empty, a full one immediately stood in its place.

All the while, the innkeeper stood in a corner and watched everything. He said to himself, "Such cooking as that would make my inn prosper."

The joiner and his companions ate and drank until late at night, but at last, they went to sleep. Before going to bed, the young man left his self-covering table standing against the wall. ★

The innkeeper, however, could not sleep because he kept thinking about the table. He remembered that he had an old table very much like it in his storeroom. So he fetched the old table, took away the joiner's table, and left the other one in its place.

The next morning, the joiner paid his bill and picked up the table, not dreaming that he was carrying off the wrong one. Then he went on his way. About noon, he reached home, and his father received him with great joy.

"Now, my dear son, what have you learned?" asked the old tailor.

"I have learned to be a joiner, Father," answered the son.

"That is a good trade," said the father, "but what have you brought back with you from your travels?"

"The best thing I've got, Father, is this little table," said the son.

The tailor looked at the table from all sides. Then he said, "You have certainly produced no masterpiece. It is a wretched old table.

"But it is a wonderful one," answered the son. "When I set it down and tell it to be covered, at once the finest meats are standing on it, and drink so good that it cheers the heart. Let us invite all our friends and neighbors so they can feast and enjoy themselves. The table will provide enough for all."

The guests were soon assembled at the tailor's house. Then the young joiner put his table in the middle of the room and said, "Table, be covered!" But the table never stirred, and it remained just as empty as any other table that does not understand talking.

When the poor joiner saw that the table was bare, he felt ashamed to stand there like a fool. The guests laughed at him freely, and then they returned unfilled and unhappy to their houses. The father returned to his tailoring, and the joiner went to work under another master.

D RELEVANT INFORMATION

Write the answers for items 1–8.
- What do we call information that helps explain a fact?
- What do we call information that does **not** help explain a fact?

Here's a fact: *The girl played a song on her trumpet.* The following items give more information about the fact.

She was in a brass band.
1. What kind of information is that?
2. How do you know?

She was giving a concert.
3. What kind of information is that?
4. How do you know?

The trumpet was made of metal.
5. What kind of information is that?
6. How do you know?

The trumpet had a case with a handle.
7. What kind of information is that?
8. How do you know?

E MAIN IDEA

Write the main idea of the following paragraph. Then write three supporting details for the main idea. Use complete sentences. Write **1** in front of the main idea and **a, b,** and **c** in front of the supporting details. Indent the supporting details.

The steamship came rushing down upon our left side. Our captain roared at the steamer, and all at once I could see people moving wildly on her deck. The steamer veered again, and our fishing boat also changed its course. Both ships were trying to get away from each other, but it was too late. There was a tremendous crash, and the steamer plowed right into us.

F COMPREHENSION

Write the answers.
1. What did the magic table do when the young joiner spoke to it?
2. Why did the young joiner think he was set for life?
3. Do you think it was wise of the young joiner to use his magic table at the inn? Explain your answer.
4. Explain how the innkeeper fooled the joiner.
5. Why do you think the joiner didn't go back to the inn?

G WRITING

What would you have done with the magic table if you had been the young joiner?

Write a story that tells what you would have done. Begin the story when you receive the table and end it after you return home. Try to answer the following questions:
- Where would you have used the table?
- What would you have done with the table at the inn?
- Why would your plan work?
- What would happen to you at the end?

Make your story at least fifty words long.

A WORD LISTS

1

Word Practice
1. gold-spitting
2. knothole
3. clothful

2

New Vocabulary
1. remarkable
2. exchange
3. rejoice
4. bricklebrit

B VOCABULARY DEFINTIONS

1. **remarkable**—When something is *remarkable,* it is uncommon or unusual.
   • What's another way of saying *She had an unusual voice*?
2. **exchange**—When you *exchange* something, you trade it for something else. If you trade bikes with a friend, the two of you *exchange* bikes.
   • What's another way of saying *The two friends traded gifts*?
3. **rejoice**—When you *rejoice,* you feel great joy or delight.
   • What's another way of saying *The mother felt great joy to see her children again*?
4. **bricklebrit**—*Bricklebrit* is a nonsense word, like *abracadabra,* that people use to cast a spell.
   • What might somebody say if he or she wanted to cast a spell?

The Table, the Donkey, and the Stick
Part 3

The second son apprenticed himself to a miller. When the young man's time was up, his master said to him, "As you have behaved so well, I will give you a remarkable donkey. He will not pull a cart or carry a sack."

"What is the good of him then?" asked the new journeyman.

"He spits out gold," answered the miller. "If you put a cloth before him and say 'Bricklebrit,' out come gold pieces."

"That is a wonderful thing," said the journeyman. Thanking the master, he went out into the world. Whenever he wanted gold, he had only to say "Bricklebrit" to his donkey, and there was a shower of gold pieces. Wherever the young miller visited, he lived like a king. Cost was no matter because his purse was always full.

After the young miller had looked around the world a long time, he thought he would return to his father. Perhaps the tailor would forget his anger and receive him kindly because of the gold-spitting donkey. ◆

Now, it happened that the young miller stopped at the same inn where his brother's table had been exchanged. When the young miller stood outside the inn with his donkey, the innkeeper offered to lead the donkey to the stable. But the young miller said, "Don't trouble yourself, old fellow. I will take him into the stable myself and tie him up, and then I shall know where to find him."

The innkeeper thought this was very strange. He didn't believe that a man who looked after his own donkey would have much to spend. But when the miller reached into his pocket and took out two gold pieces to pay for dinner, the innkeeper ran inside and laid the table.

After dinner, the young miller asked for his bill. Wanting to get all the profit he could, the innkeeper said it would amount to two gold pieces more. The miller felt in his pocket, but his gold had come to an end.

"Wait a moment, innkeeper," said he, "I will go and fetch some money." Then he left the room, carrying the tablecloth with him. Curious to know where the miller was going, the innkeeper slipped after him.

The young man went to the stable and shut the door, but the innkeeper peeped in through a knothole. Then he saw how the miller spread the cloth before the donkey and said "Bricklebrit." All at once, the donkey spat out gold pieces that rained onto the cloth.

"Dear me," said the innkeeper, "that is an easy way of getting gold. A purse of money like that is no bad thing." ★

After the miller had paid his bill and gone to bed, the innkeeper slipped down to the stable in the middle of the night. He led the gold-spitting donkey away and tied up another donkey in his place.

The next morning, the miller set forth with his donkey, never doubting that it was the right one. By noon, he came to the house of his father, who rejoiced to see him again and received him gladly.

"What trade have you taken up, my son?" asked the father.

"I am a miller, dear father," answered the son.

"And what have you brought home from your travels?" continued the father.

"Nothing but a donkey," answered the son.

"We have plenty of donkeys here," said the father. "You had much better have brought me a nice goat!"

"Yes," answered the son, "but this is no common donkey. When I say 'Bricklebrit,' the good creature spits out a whole clothful of gold pieces. Let us call all the neighbors together. I will make rich people of them all."

"That will be fine!" said the tailor. "Then I need labor no more with my needle." So he rushed out and called all the neighbors together. As soon as they were all assembled, the miller brought in the donkey and spread a cloth before him.

"Now, pay attention," said he. Then he cried "Bricklebrit!" But no gold pieces came, and the donkey just stared back at him.

The poor miller made a long face when he saw that he had been fooled. Then he begged pardon of the neighbors, who went home as poor as they had come. The tailor took up his needle again, and the young miller went off to find a new master.

D MAIN IDEA

Write the main idea of the following paragraph. Then write three supporting details for the main idea. Use complete sentences. Write **1** in front of the main idea and **a, b,** and **c** in front of the supporting details.

The man built large, deep boxes in his yard. Then he filled the boxes with soil and planted seeds in the soil. He watered the soil every day. Soon, the boxes were blooming with the green shoots of tomato plants, string beans, potatoes, onions, and parsley.

E COMPREHENSION

Write the answers.
1. The story says that "cost was no matter" to the miller when he had the magic donkey. Explain what that phrase means.
2. Why do you think the miller wanted to tie up the donkey by himself at the inn?
3. Tell how the innkeeper discovered the miller's secret.
4. Why did the miller want to show the donkey to all the neighbors?
5. How do you think the tailor feels about his sons now? Explain your answer.

F WRITING

What do you think will happen to the youngest son?
   Without looking ahead, write your own ending to the story. Try to answer the following questions:
   • What trade does the youngest son learn?
   • What present does the youngest son get from his master?
   • Where does the youngest son go?
   • What happens in the end?
Make your story at least fifty words long.

Ⓐ WORD LISTS

1

Hard Words
1. conduct
2. content

2

Hard Words
1. creature
2. treasure
3. mercy
4. generous
5. valuable
6. comparison
7. splendor

3

New Vocabulary
1. precious
2. exhausted
3. collapse
4. goblin
5. abroad
6. grisly

Ⓑ VOCABULARY DEFINITIONS

1. **precious**—When something is *precious,* it has great value or costs a lot of money. Gems that cost a lot are *precious* gems.
   - What's another way of saying *His house was full of art that cost a lot*?

2. **exhausted**—When you are *exhausted,* you are very tired.
   - What's another way of saying *The runner was very tired after the long race*?

3. **collapse**—When you *collapse,* you fall down suddenly.
   - What's another way of saying *The actor fell down suddenly on the stage*?

4. **goblin**—A *goblin* is an ugly and wicked fairy.
   - What's another way of saying *The ugly and wicked fairy tormented the queen*?

5. **abroad**—When you go *abroad,* you travel outside your country.
   - What's another way of saying *We will travel outside the country in the spring*?

6. **grisly**—When something is *grisly,* it is horrible and disgusting.
   - What's another way of saying *The goblin was a horrible and disgusting creature*?

The Table, the Donkey, and the Stick
Part 4

The third son apprenticed himself to a turner. Because turning is a difficult trade, it took him a long time to learn it. One day, he received a letter from his brothers with all their bad news. They explained how the innkeeper had stolen their treasures on the last night of their travels.

Finally, the young turner had learned his trade and was ready to travel around the world. To reward the apprentice for his good conduct, the master gave him a sack and told him there was a stick inside it.

"The sack may be useful to me," said the new journeyman. "But what is the good of the stick?"

"I will tell you," answered the master. "If anyone does you any harm, just say, 'Stick, out of the sack!' Then the stick will jump out upon them and beat them so soundly that they will not be able to move for a week. It will not stop until you say, 'Stick, into the sack!'"

The journeyman thanked the master, took up the sack, and started on his travels. When anyone attacked him, he would say, "Stick, out of the sack!" Then the stick would immediately jump out and deal a shower of blows on the attacker, quickly ending the affair.

One evening, the young turner reached the inn where his two brothers had been fooled. He laid his sack on the table and began to describe all the wonderful things he had seen in the world.

"Yes," he said loudly, "you may talk of self-covering tables, gold-spitting donkeys, and so forth. These are good things, but they are nothing in comparison with the treasure I carry with me in my sack!"

Then the innkeeper opened his ears.

"What in the world can it be?" he thought. "Very likely the sack is full of precious stones. I have a perfect right to it, for all good things come in threes." ◆

When bedtime came, the young turner stretched himself on a bench and put his sack under his head for a pillow. Thinking the turner was sound asleep, the innkeeper crept up to the bench. He stooped down and pulled gently at the sack, which he planned to replace with another.

But the turner had only been waiting for this to happen. Just as the innkeeper was giving a last gentle pull, the turner cried, "Stick, out of the sack!" The stick flew out directly and worked its magic on the innkeeper's back. In vain, the innkeeper begged for mercy. But the louder he cried, the harder the stick beat time on his back.

At last, the innkeeper fell exhausted to the ground. Then the turner said, "If you do not give me the table and the donkey right away, this game shall begin all over again."

"Oh, dear, no!" cried the innkeeper, quite collapsed. "I will gladly give them back again if you will only make this terrible goblin go back into the sack."

So the young turner said, "I will be generous—but beware!" Then he cried, "Stick, into the sack!" and left the innkeeper in peace.

The next morning, the turner set out with the table and the donkey on his way home to his father. The tailor was very glad to see him again and asked what he had learned abroad.

"My dear father," answered he, "I have become a turner."

"A very difficult trade," said the father. "And what have you brought with you?"

"A most valuable thing, dear father," answered the son. "A stick in a sack!"

"What!" cried the father. "A stick! You can cut one from any tree!"

"But it is not a common stick, dear father," said the young man. "When I say, 'Stick, out of the sack!' out jumps the stick upon anyone who means harm to me and makes him dance. It does not quit until the person is beaten to the earth and asks pardon."

Then the turner showed his father the table and the donkey and said, "With this stick, I have recovered the table and the donkey that the thieving innkeeper took from my two brothers. Now send for both of them and invite all the neighbors, too. They shall all eat and drink to their hearts' content, and we will fill their pockets with gold." ★

The old tailor could not quite believe in such a thing, but he called his other sons and all the neighbors together. Then the turner brought in the donkey, opened a cloth before him, and said to his brother, "Now, my dear brother, speak to him."

So the miller said, "Bricklebrit!" The cloth was immediately covered with gold pieces until all the people had more than they could carry away.

After that, the turner set down the table and said, "Now, my dear brother, speak to it."

So the joiner said, "Table, be covered!" and it was immediately covered with the richest dishes. All the people sat down to eat, and the whole company remained through the night, merry and content.

The next day, the tailor locked up his needle and thread and lived ever after with his three sons in great joy and splendor.

But what became of the goat, the unlucky cause of the tailor's sons being driven out? I will tell you. She felt so ashamed of what she had done that she ran into a fox's hole and hid herself.

When the fox came home, he caught sight of two great eyes staring at him out of the darkness. He was so frightened that he ran away.

A bear met him and asked, "What is the matter, brother fox, that you look so frightened?"

"Oh, dear," answered the fox. "A grisly beast is sitting in my hole, and he stared at me with fiery eyes!"

"We will soon drive him out," said the bear, so he went to the hole and looked in. But when he caught sight of the fiery eyes, he was likewise seized with terror. Not wishing to have anything to do with so grisly a beast, he ran off.

The bear was soon met by a bee, who said, "Bear, you look depressed. What has become of your high spirits?"

"You may well ask," answered the bear. "In the fox's hole, there sits a grisly beast with fiery eyes, and we cannot drive him out."

The bee answered, "I am just a poor feeble little creature, but I think I can help you."

So she flew into the fox's hole and stung the goat so severely that the goat jumped up, crying, "Baa! Baa!" Then she ran out like mad into the world, and to this day, no one knows where she went.

D RELEVANT INFORMATION

Write the answers for items 1–4.

Information that is not relevant is called **irrelevant.**

- What is the word for information that is not relevant?

So information that does not help explain a fact is **irrelevant** to the fact.

Here's a fact: *The boy fell off his bike.* The following items give more information about the fact.

His bicycle had ten gears.
1. Is that information relevant or irrelevant?

He had ridden into a pothole.
2. Relevant or irrelevant?

He hadn't been looking at the road.
3. Relevant or irrelevant?

He was riding to the swimming pool.
4. Relevant or irrelevant?

E OUTLINING

Complete the following outline for "The Table, the Donkey, and the Stick." Copy each main idea; then write three supporting details for each main idea. Use complete sentences to write the supporting details.

1. The tailor's three sons went out into the world.
2. The oldest son got a magic table.
3. The second son got a magic donkey.
4. The youngest son got a magic stick.

F COMPREHENSION

Write the answers.
1. Explain how the turner fooled the innkeeper.
2. What do you think the joiner learned in this story?
3. Which son do you think was the smartest? Explain your answer.
4. How was the goat like the innkeeper?
5. What lesson or lessons do you think this story teaches? Explain your answer.

G WRITING

The story about the goat and the bee has the same theme as the story about the innkeeper and the three sons. In both stories, small and weak creatures defeat a big and powerful one.

Write another story with that same basic theme. Try to answer the following questions in your story:
- Who are the small and weak creatures or people?
- Who is the big and powerful creature or person?
- What bad things does the big creature or person do to the small ones?
- How do the small creatures or people win in the end?

Make your story at least one hundred words long.

Ⓐ WORD LISTS

1
Hard Words
1. DeMarco
2. Adeline
3. Amelia
4. Reinhardt
5. Agatha
6. Callahan
7. Grotowski
8. pumpernickel

2
Word Practice
1. starvation
2. busybody
3. parsley
4. drenched
5. thyme
6. matzo

3
New Vocabulary
1. dependable
2. coop
3. preen
4. tenant
5. twining
6. mirage
7. outrage

Ⓑ VOCABULARY DEFINITIONS

1. **dependable**—Something that always works without failing is *dependable.* Here's another way of saying *The washer always worked: The washer was dependable*.
   - What's another way of saying *The washer always worked*?
2. **coop**—A *coop* is a cage for small animals.
   - What is a coop?
3. **preen**—When a bird *preens* itself, it uses its beak to fluff its feathers.
   - What is a bird doing when it uses its beak to fluff its feathers?
4. **tenant**—A person who rents space in a building is a *tenant.*
   - What do we call a person who rents space in a building?

5. **twine**—When something *twines,* it wraps around something else. When plants wrap around a post, they twine around the post.
   - What's another way of saying *The ivy wrapped around the fence*?
6. **mirage**—A *mirage* is something that seems to be there, but is really not there at all.
   - What do we call something that only seems to be there?
7. **outrage**—An *outrage* is a great insult.
   - What's another way of saying *His statement was a great insult*?

Ireland

The next story you will read is titled "Mrs. Dunn's Lovely, Lovely Farm." The story tells about the Dunns, a family that moves from Dublin, Ireland, to New York City around the year 1900. Dublin is the capital of Ireland, and New York is the biggest city in the United States.

The Dunns were among the millions of people who started moving away from Ireland in 1845, when the Irish Potato Famine began. Potatoes were the main crop that Irish farmers raised, and many Irish people ate almost nothing but potatoes. In 1845, a disease called "potato blight" began destroying Irish potatoes, leaving many people with nothing to eat. The blight continued until 1849. During that time, more than a million Irish starved to death. Others left the country.

People continued to leave Ireland even after the potato famine ended. By 1900, only about half as many people lived in Ireland as in 1845. The families who moved away, such as the Dunns, had to start life all over in their new homes.

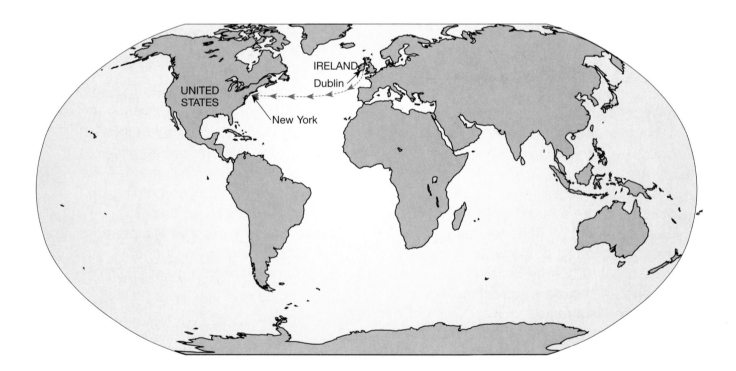

Mrs. Dunn's Lovely, Lovely Farm
by Myron Levoy
Part 1

Focus Question: What was unusual about Mrs. Dunn's farm?

Mrs. Dunn had always wanted a farm. Back in the old country, she had lived in the great city of Dublin with its crowded streets and noisy carts over the cobblestones, with its men forever looking for work, and its thin children, forever hungry.

She had made her husband promise that when they came to America they would save every penny they possibly could, so that in time they could buy a farm. A lovely farm with chickens and cows and potatoes, with the smell of sweet clover and the giggle of a brook always beyond the door. Where their children, Cathy and Neil, could have good fresh food, could grow and run and tumble. A lovely, lovely farm.

When they arrived in New York, with other thousands from Ireland and Italy and Hungary and Russia, they moved into a little apartment on the third floor of a building near Second Avenue. One of their neighbors was named DeMarco and another was named Kandel. In Dublin everyone had Irish names; this was something new and different, and a little frightening. But the neighbors said hello and smiled and warned them about Mr. Warfield, the terrible, horrible landlord. And Mr. and Mrs. Dunn felt much better, because in Dublin the land-

lords had been terrible and horrible, too. Things were becoming familiar very quickly.

The next task was for Mr. Dunn to find work. After much searching, he found a job hauling coal. He helped send the coal roaring like a river down a metal chute into the basements of buildings. Sometimes he would stand on the mound of coal in the back of the truck and coax it down through a square hole into the chute. And sometimes he would stand on the coal pile down in the cellar, clearing the coal away from the bottom of the chute so that more coal and still more coal could come roaring down into the coal bin.

Mr. Dunn would come home every night looking just like a great lump of coal, himself. But after a good washing and a hot dinner, Mr. Dunn looked almost like Mr. Dunn again.

And though they could pay the rent and buy coats for the winter, and could afford a little more lamb and butter than they could in Dublin, they couldn't seem to save much money. After a year, Mrs. Dunn counted four dollars and ninety-two cents in her secret empty cereal box, and Mr. Dunn had eight dollars and twelve cents in his shaving mug.

At that rate, they would never have enough for a farm. There were new shoes needed, and a new blanket, and a bigger stew pot, and this, and that, and the other. So Mrs. Dunn made a firm decision. They must buy their farm now, as much of it as they could, or the money would vanish like a mist over the chimneys of Dublin. And Mr. Dunn had to admit she was right. ◆

That very next day, Mrs. Dunn bought a hen. They had told her at the market that it was a good dependable laying hen, a Rhode Island Red, the best. Mrs. Dunn wrapped the hen in a scarf, tucked it under her arm, and carried it five blocks back to her kitchen. Then she put the hen on the floor and watched it strut on the yellow linoleum.

The children named it Amelia for no special reason, and fed it cereal and corn and crusts of bread. Mr. Dunn brought home scraps of wood from the coal yard and built a coop. Then with more wood and some chicken wire, he built a little barnyard filled with dirt and pebbles in which Amelia could scratch. And he took some old felt hats and shaped them into nice, soft nests.

Soon, Amelia was joined by Agatha, and then Adeline. Now there were two eggs, sometimes three, every morning in the hat-

nests, fresh and delicious. Cathy and Neil loved Agatha and Amelia and Adeline as if they were their own sisters. Each hen was different: Amelia was very, very proud and strutted as if she were a rooster; Agatha was a busybody, forever poking into everything; Adeline was shy and loved to sit in the coop and preen. Soon, the other children in the building started bringing the three hens little presents: Aaron Kandel brought pieces of a huge, flat, dry cracker called *matzo* which Adeline particularly loved; Fred Reinhardt brought scraps of thick bread; and Vincent DeMarco brought dried seeds called chick peas. And sometimes, Mrs. Dunn would give one of the children a freshly laid egg to take home. ★

Now, it was time for the vegetables, for who ever heard of a farm without vegetables? Mr. Dunn built large, deep boxes, filled them with earth, and planted seeds. Then he put them on the fire escape outside the bedroom window. When the fire escape landing was covered with boxes, he put new boxes on the iron stairs leading up to the next landing. Soon, the fire escape was blooming with the green shoots of tomato plants, string beans, potatoes, onions, and parsley. And on every windowsill were pots of spices: rosemary, thyme, mint, chives.

On weekdays, Mrs. Dunn carefully weeded and watered the fire-escape garden and fed the chickens. And on Sundays, after he had tried to wash the last of the coal from his face and hands for the third time, Mr. Dunn would repair the chicken wire, and prop up the growing vegetables with tall sticks and string, and build new boxes. Then he and Mrs. Dunn would walk from room to room, admiring the pots of spices, the vegetables, the chickens, and the mushrooms growing in flat boxes on the kitchen shelves.

But one day, Mr. Warfield, the terrible, horrible landlord, came to collect the rents. As he was about to enter the building, a sudden shower drenched his hat. He took off the hat and looked at it with disbelief, for there wasn't a cloud in the sky. Perhaps a tenant had spilled some dishwater on him, from above. He looked up and shook his fist toward the top of the building at the hidden enemy.

His mouth dropped in astonishment and he forgot to bring down his fist, for up above, three stories up, was a hanging garden twining about the metal bars of the fire escape. A lady was watering the green mirage with a watering can, and some of it had dripped down the fire escape from landing to landing until it finally splashed on Mr. Warfield's head.

"This is an outrage!" Mr. Warfield muttered to himself. "It's completely unreasonable."

Then he plunged into the building and rushed toward the stairs.

E OUTLINING

Complete the following outline for
"Children at Work." Copy each main
idea; then write three supporting details
for each main idea. Use complete
sentences to write the supporting
details.

1. In the 1300s, one type of worker was
   called an apprentice.
2. Another type of worker was called a
   journeyman.
3. A third type of worker was called a
   master.

F COMPREHENSION

Write the answers.
1. Why did people begin moving away
   from Ireland in 1845?
2. Why did the Dunns save every penny
   they could?
3. Why were the Dunns already familiar
   with people like Mr. Warfield?
4. What was unusual about Mrs. Dunn's
   farm?
5. What do you think Mr. Warfield will
   say to Mrs. Dunn?

G WRITING

Pretend you have to grow a garden to
get food.
   Write an essay that explains how you
would grow the garden and what
problems you might have. Try to answer
the following questions:
- Where would you plant your garden?
- What things would you plant?
- How would you take care of the
  plants?
- What problems might you have?
- When would you pick the plants?
- What foods would you make with the
  plants?
Make your essay at least fifty words
long.

Ⓐ WORD LISTS

1

Hard Words
1. lunatic asylum
2. Foreign Legion
3. Niagara Falls
4. geraniums
5. squat

2

Word Practice
1. chandelier
2. premises
3. Grotowski
4. Callahan
5. relevant
6. irrelevant

3

New Vocabulary
1. lunatic asylum
2. nourishment
3. roost
4. dainty
5. superb
6. tamper

Ⓑ VOCABULARY DEFINITIONS

1. **lunatic asylum**—*Lunatic asylum* is an old term for a place where mentally ill people live.
   • What's an old term for a place where mentally ill people live?
2. **nourishment**—The ingredients of food that help your body work and grow are called *nourishment.*
   • What do we call the ingredients of food that help your body work and grow?
3. **roost**—When birds *roost*, they sit on a branch or a perch.
   • Where do birds roost?

4. **dainty**—When something is *dainty,* it is fine and delicate.
   • What's another way of saying *a delicate napkin*?
5. **superb**—When something is *superb,* it is truly great.
   • What's another way of saying a *truly great cook*?
6. **tamper**—When you *tamper* with something, you meddle with that thing.
   • What's another way of saying *He meddled with the machine*?

Mrs. Dunn's Lovely, Lovely Farm
Part 2

Focus Question: How did the neighbors try to help Mrs. Dunn?

"Ah, Mr. Warfield," said Mrs. Callahan at the first landing, "and when, pray tell, are you going to fix m'stove? The divil of a thing's got only one burner working. Do you expect me to pay m'rent when I can't cook soup and stew at the same time?"

"Oh blast!" said Mr. Warfield. "I'll see you later. I've got a madhouse here. A madhouse! Let me go by, Mrs. Callahan."

"And what might be the trouble, if I may ask?" said Mrs. Callahan.

"Somebody's growing a tree on the fire escape!"

"Ah, to be sure, to be sure." And with that, Mrs. Callahan nudged her little girl, Noreen, standing next to her. Without a word, Noreen turned and raced up the two flights of stairs to warn her friend Cathy Dunn that Warfield, the monster landlord, was on his way up. "And tell me now, Mr. Warfield, but how would a tree gain the necessary nourishment on a fire escape, do you know?"

"I intend to find out, Mrs. Callahan, if you'll let me get by!"

"But m'stove, Mr. Warfield. I'm paying rent for three rooms and four burners."

"Yes, yes, yes, yes! Very reasonable request. We'll have it fixed in seventy-two hours. Now please let me get—"

"Seventy-two hours, is it? Make it

twenty-four," said Mrs. Callahan.

"But that's only *one day*. That's unreasonable. Make it . . . forty-eight hours."

"Thirty-six, Mr. Warfield, or I'll have the Board of Health, I will."

"Forty!"

"Thirty-eight!"

"All right! We'll have it fixed within thirty-eight hours! Now let me *through!*"

And Mr. Warfield raced up the flight of stairs to the second landing.

"Hello, Mr. Warfield!" Mrs. Grotowski called. "I dreamt about you last night! And what did I dream?"

"I don't care!" said Mr. Warfield. "Let me go by!"

"I'll *tell* you what. I dreamt that I took the money for your rent and tore it up into little shreds. Then I put a little pepper on it, a little salt, stirred in some nice chicken fat, and made you eat every dollar of it until you choked. And *why?*"

"Please, Mrs. Grotowski! This isn't the time for your dreams!"

"I'll tell you why. Because you promised to have my apartment painted two months ago. Two months! Where are the painters? Did they join the Foreign Legion? Or is it possible that they've gone over Niagara Falls in a barrel?"

"We'll have the painters soon."

"When?"

"Soon. Very soon."

"How soon?"

"Very, very soon. Let me go by, Mrs. Grotowski, before I lose my temper."

"This week! I want them *this* week."

"Next week."

"By Friday!"

"By next Wednesday, Mrs. Grotowski."

"By next Monday, Mr. Warfield."

"Tuesday."

"All right. But it better be Tuesday," said Mrs. Grotowski.

"Tuesday. Absolutely, positively, you will have the painters on Tuesday." ◆

Meanwhile, up in the Dunns' apartment, people were flying back and forth. Cathy and Neil had each grabbed a chicken and raced out the door. One chicken went into the DeMarco apartment, the other clucked away in Mrs. Kandel's kitchen. But the chicken left behind, Amelia—or was it Adeline?—had gotten so excited from all the rushing about that she'd flown up to the ceiling and was now roosting comfortably on top of the chandelier in the living room. Mr. Dunn wasn't at home, but Mrs. Dunn took vegetable boxes off the fire-escape landing and slid them under the bed. And from the apartment above, Mrs. Cherney climbed out of her bedroom window onto the fire escape, took more boxes off the iron stairs, and hid them in her own apartment. But try though they did, there just wasn't enough time to hide everything.

For Mr. Warfield had finally reached the third floor and was pounding at the Dunns' door. Three Rhode Island Reds answered with a chorus of *berawk-bawk-bawks:* one in Mrs. Kandel's kitchen, one in Mrs. DeMarco's bathroom and one on Mrs.

Dunn's chandelier. But fortunately, Mr. Warfield knew they weren't chickens, because that would be impossible. It was the children making chicken noises at him. Why did they all hate him? He was a good man. Fair. Reasonable. Wasn't he always reasonable?. . . But what was *this?* There were feathers in the hallway. Children having a pillow fight? Very likely. Ah well, children must play. No harm. Not like trees on the fire escape!

Then Mr. Warfield pounded on the door again; not the dainty tap-tap of a salesman, nor the thump-thump of a bill collector, but the Shaboom-Shaboom of a landlord. And again, from three apartments, three children in a superb imitation of three chickens, *berawk-bawked* away at Mr. Warfield.

Why? thought Mr. Warfield. Why? He had three children of his own and they *loved* him. Didn't they? Of course they did. ★

At last the door opened a crack, and Mrs. Dunn's hand appeared with an envelope holding the rent money. She waved the envelope up and down at Mr. Warfield. Mr. Warfield took the envelope, but also pushed firmly on the door.

"Mrs. Dunn, I'd like a word or two with you," he said.

"I'm feeling a bit ill today, Mr. Warfield, sir. Would you be so kindly as to stop back next week?"

"Mrs. Dunn! There is a tree growing on your fire escape!"

"Mr. Warfield," said Mrs. Dunn rapidly. "You're blessed. There's many a man who would trade this very building for your keen eyesight. But still, a tree cannot truly grow on a fire escape. Unless, of course, it's a miracle. With which you would not want to tamper, Mr. Warfield, would you? Good day to you now."

"Good day my foot! I demand to see the condition of that fire escape. As landlord, I have the right to enter and inspect the premises at reasonable hours. I'm a reasonable man and I would never come at an unreasonable hour."

"Why it's nearly four o'clock. I've got to do m'husband's supper. 'Tis not a reasonable hour at all," said Mrs. Dunn.

"Either you let me enter, madam, or I'll call the police. *And* the fire department. A tree on the fire escape is a fire hazard. Let me in!"

"Tomorrow."

"NOW!" shouted Mr. Warfield. And with that, the chicken on the chandelier clucked again. "Did you hear that, Mrs. Dunn?"

"Sounded like a cuckoo clock. Cuckoo, cuckoo. 'Tis four o' the clock, you see."

"Nonsense. You have a *chicken* in there! My building has *chickens!*" At that, all three hens in all three apartments *be-rawk-bawked* again. "This isn't an apartment house! It's a lunatic asylum!" Then Mr. Warfield pushed his way past Mrs. Dunn and stormed into her living room.

"My chandelier!" shouted Mr. Warfield.

"'Tisn't *your* chandelier. I've paid the rent. 'Tis *my* chandelier," said Mrs. Dunn.

D RELEVANT INFORMATION

Write the answers for items 1–4.

Here are two facts:

Fact A: *Frank got on the bus.*

Fact B: *Frank took out his keys.*

Some items below are relevant to fact A; some are relevant to fact B; and some are irrelevant to both facts.

He did not own a car.
1. Is that item relevant to fact A, relevant to fact B, or irrelevant?

He was wearing a round hat.
2. Is that item relevant to fact A, relevant to fact B, or irrelevant?

He wanted to get into his house.
3. Is that item relevant to fact A, relevant to fact B, or irrelevant?

His last name was Mitchell.
4. Is that item relevant to fact A, relevant to fact B, or irrelevant?

E COMPREHENSION

Write the answers.
1. How did the neighbors try to help Mrs. Dunn?
2. How do the tenants feel about Mr. Warfield? Why?
3. How does Mr. Warfield feel about the tenants? Explain your answer.
4. What do you think of Mr. Warfield? Explain your answer.
5. What do you think will happen to Mrs. Dunn's farm? Why?

F WRITING

Pretend Mrs. Dunn doesn't have money for the rent, but she does have a lot of vegetables.

Make up a conversation between Mrs. Dunn and Mr. Warfield. In the conversation, Mrs. Dunn is trying to talk Mr. Warfield into taking vegetables instead of money for the rent. Try to answer the following questions:
- How does Mrs. Dunn try to convince Mr. Warfield to take the vegetables instead of money for the rent?
- How does Mr. Warfield feel about the vegetables?
- What happens at the end of the conversation?

Make your conversation at least fifty words long.

28

A WORD LISTS

1

Hard Words
1. Greenwich Village
2. Mr. Behrman
3. studio
4. pneumonia
5. gnarled

2

Word Practice
1. affectionately
2. geraniums
3. greenery

3

New Vocabulary
1. health hazard
2. stalk
3. squat
4. studio
6. pneumonia

B VOCABULARY DEFINITIONS

1. **health hazard**—Something that is dangerous to your health is a *health hazard.*
   • Smoking is dangerous to your health. So what do we call smoking?
2. **stalk**—When a hunter *stalks* an animal, the hunter follows the animal quietly.
   • What's another way of saying *The lion followed the zebra quietly*?
3. **squat**—When something is *squat,* it is short and thick.
   • What's another way of saying *They lived in a short and thick building*?
4. **studio**—A *studio* is a room where an artist works.
   • What do we call a room where an artist works?
5. **pneumonia**—*Pneumonia* is a disease that attacks the lungs.
   • What is pneumonia?

Mrs. Dunn's Lovely, Lovely Farm
Part 3

Focus Question: What agreement did
Mrs. Dunn and Mr. Warfield make?

Mr. Warfield rushed through to the bedroom and stared at the remains of the farm on the fire escape. "My fire escape!" His face was flushed, his eyes were bulging. "Unbelievable! Mrs. Dunn, what are these weeds supposed to *be?*"

"That? Why that's onions, Mr. Warfield."

"*This* is an *onion?*"

"Oh, you can't see it. The onion's beneath the dirt. Least I hope 'tis."

"And *this?*" he said, pointing.

"That's supposed to be potatoes. But I fear for them. The soil's not deep enough."

"Incredible!" he said. "Don't you like geraniums, Mrs. Dunn? I thought people liked to grow geraniums. Look out the window, across the street. See the windowsills? There and there. And over there. Everyone *else* is growing geraniums.

"That's a good *idea*, Mr. Warfield," said Mrs. Dunn. "'Twould brighten up the house. I'll fetch some seed tomorrow."

"No, no. I didn't mean . . . Mrs. Dunn, look here. This is a firetrap! And that chicken—"

"I have two more, visiting with the neighbors."

"Well, that, Mrs. Dunn, is a relief. I thought *all* the tenants had gone insane."

"No, 'tis only m'self. But I do think I'm as sane as you, if not a bit saner. Because you see, I shall have the freshest vegetables in the city of New York. I already have the freshest eggs."

"Those chickens, in an apartment, are a health hazard. You'll have to remove them! Sell them to a farmer or a butcher."

"I shan't. They stay right here."

"That's unreasonable. I'm a reasonable man, Mrs. Dunn. Say something reasonable, *ask* something reasonable, and I'll say: *that's* reasonable."

"Very well. Why don't you pretend that you hadn't come at all today. Then you wouldn't have seen anything, would you, and your mind would rest easy," said Mrs. Dunn.

"Completely unreasonable! And *that's* why you tenants don't like me. Because *I'm* reasonable, and you're all *un*reasonable. Simple as that."

"Oh, I like you, Mr. Warfield."

"Nonsense.

"Any landlord who would offer me the use of his roof for a fine little garden must be a very likable *and* reasonable man."

"I didn't offer you any roof, Mrs. Dunn."

"You were going to. I saw it on the tip of your lips.

"My *lips?*"

"And you were going to say how much better 'twould be if the chickens had a much bigger coop up there on the roof."

"I was never going to say—"

"Tut tut, Mr. Warfield," said Mrs. Dunn. "You've as good as said it. And I was going to answer that for such generosity you should surely receive some fresh string beans and onions and potatoes in season. And you were going to say, 'Ah, and how lovely the roof would look with greenery all about.' And I was about to answer, 'Yes, Mr. Warfield, and the tenants would surely look at you most affectionately.' Would they not, now?"

"*Hmm,*" said Mr. Warfield, thinking.

"Reasonable or unreasonable?" asked Mrs. Dunn.

"*Hmm* . . . well . . . I'd have to give this some thought."

"But you're a man of *action,* Mr. Warfield. You pound on the door like a very tiger."

"Yes. Well . . . it's not *unreasonable,*" said Mr. Warfield. "If you didn't already *have* any chickens or trees or onions, I would say no. But since you *do* have all this *jungle* of creatures and vines . . . I would, after careful consideration, being after all a human being, I would . . . *ahem, ahem . . .* say . . . *ahem . . .* yes."

"Oh, you are a darling man, Mr. Warfield. A darling, *darling* man."

"Here, Mrs. Dunn! Watch your language! I mean to say! *Darling* man?"

"Oh, back in the old country, it only means you're nice, that's all."

"Oh. Now remember, Mrs. Dunn, a bargain's a bargain. I expect one-tenth of everything you grow as my roof rent. Is that a deal?"

"'Tis a deal."

"Except the onions. You can keep them all. I hate onions. My whole family hates onions." ◆

And with that, Mr. Warfield slammed his hat on his head, only to find it was still wet from Mrs. Dunn's watering can. Without a word, he turned and marched out to the living room. At that moment, Amelia—or was it Adeline?—up on the chandelier decided it was time to come down. For there, on top of Mr. Warfield's head, was her nest-shaped-like-a-hat, moving by. And down she came, wings beating, feathers flying, on top of Mr. Warfield's head. "Oh blast!" shouted Mr. Warfield as he raced to the hallway with the chicken flapping on top of him.

"She likes you!" called Mrs. Dunn. "She knows you have a good heart! Chickens can tell right off!" ★

But Mr. Warfield didn't hear this very clearly, for as he raced out to the hallway and down the stairs, all three chickens started their *berawk-bawking* again, and the loudest of all was the one on top of Mr. Warfield. He finally escaped by leaving his nest-shaped-like-a-hat, behind.

And so Mrs. Dunn moved everything to the roof, and Mr. Dunn added still more boxes for vegetables. Cathy and Neil and their friends went up to the roof every afternoon to feed the chickens and water the plants. And Mrs. Dunn had her lovely, lovely farm—or at least she thought she did, which comes to the same thing in the end.

VOCABULARY REVIEW

dainty

tamper

nourishment

tenant

superb

mirage

outrage

For each item, write the correct word.
1. When something is truly great, it is ▆▆▆▆.
2. Something that is very fine and delicate is ▆▆▆▆.
3. The ingredients of food that help your body to work and grow are called ▆▆▆▆.
4. When you meddle with something, you ▆▆▆▆ with that thing.

E MAIN IDEA

Write the main idea of the following paragraph. Then write three supporting details for the main idea. Use complete sentences.

Being a journeyman was not an easy life. Masters hired journeymen for only a short time and paid them as little as possible. Journeymen often gathered in a central part of town and waited for masters to hire them for a day's work. If there was no work, the journeymen might wander to another town, trying to improve their luck.

F COMPREHENSION

Write the answers.
1. What agreement did Mrs. Dunn and Mr. Warfield make?
2. Why do you think Mrs. Dunn kept praising Mr. Warfield?
3. For Mrs. Dunn, what were the advantages of having the garden on the roof instead of the fire escape?
4. What advantage did Mr. Warfield get from the roof garden?
5. What lessons do you think this story teaches about solving problems and making agreements?

G WRITING

Mrs. Dunn was able to make a deal with Mr. Warfield by being kind and clever.

Write a new ending for the story to show what would have happened if Mrs. Dunn had not been so kind or so clever. Try to answer the following questions:
- How does Mrs. Dunn treat Mr. Warfield?
- What happens to Mrs. Dunn?
- Why does that happen?

Make your ending at least fifty words long.

A WORD LISTS

1
Hard Words
1. Persephone
2. Demeter
3. easel
4. idiotic
5. palette

2
Word Practice
1. Greenwich Village
2. Mr. Behrman
3. thermometer
4. mercury
5. skeleton

3
New Vocabulary
1. one chance in ten
2. swagger
3. accomplish
4. gnarled
5. decayed
6. broth

B VOCABULARY DEFINITIONS

1. **one chance in ten**—Let's say there's a group of ten people. If there's *one chance in ten* that somebody in the group will get sick, one of those people will probably get sick.
   - What does it mean if there's one chance in ten that somebody in the group will win a prize?
2. **swagger**—When you *swagger,* you walk around with great confidence.
   - What are you doing when you walk around with great confidence?
3. **accomplish**—When you *accomplish* something, you succeed in doing that thing.
   - What's another way of saying *They succeeded in doing the job*?
4. **gnarled**—When something is *gnarled,* it is twisted and full of knots.
   - What do we call something that is twisted and full of knots?
5. **decay**—When something *decays,* it rots.
   - What's another way of saying *The wood had rotted*?
6. **broth**—Clear soup is called *broth.*
   - What do we call clear soup?

STORY BACKGROUND

O. HENRY AND NEW YORK

The next story is titled "The Last Leaf." The author is O. Henry, but the real name of the man who wrote the story is William Sydney Porter. He changed his name to O. Henry when he was in prison in Ohio for stealing money from a bank. While in prison, O. Henry started writing stories and selling them to magazines.

O. Henry moved to New York City in 1902, shortly after he was released from prison. He soon got a job writing one story a week for a newspaper. Before his death in 1910, O. Henry wrote hundreds of stories, and he became one of the most famous writers of his time. Many of his stories are set in New York City, and they often end with a surprise.

"The Last Leaf" takes place in a section of New York City called Greenwich Village. The map below shows where Greenwich Village is located.

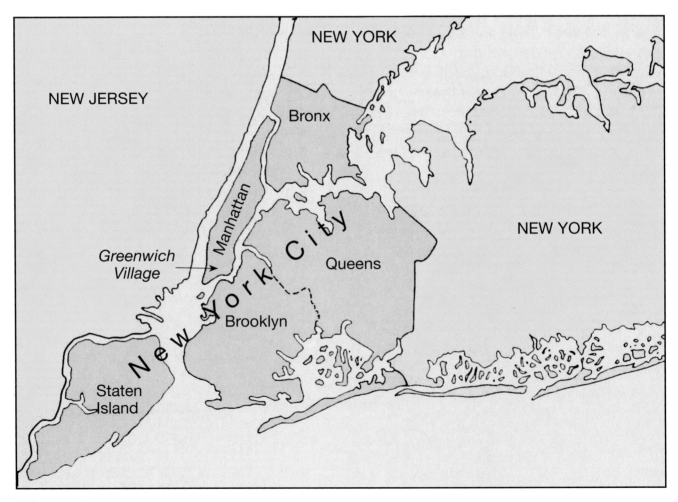

The Last Leaf
*by O. Henry**
Part 1

Focus Question: Why did Joan think she was like the ivy leaves?

In Greenwich Village, the streets run crazy. They are broken into strange angles and curves. One street even crosses itself a time or two. Artists love this neighborhood, and so many live here that it is often called an artists' colony.

At the top of a squat three-story building in Greenwich Village, Sue and Joan had their painting studio. Sue was from Maine; Joan was from California. They had met at a restaurant, and they had found their tastes in art so similar that they had decided to share this studio.

That was in May. In November, a cold unseen stranger, called pneumonia by the doctors, stalked around the colony, touching people here and there with his icy fingers. Pneumonia was not a well-mannered stranger, and Joan, who was very thin, was no match for him. But pneumonia touched her nonetheless. For more than a week, she lay on her bed, scarcely moving, and looking through the small windowpanes at the blank side of the next brick house.

One morning, the busy doctor invited Sue into the hallway to discuss her sick friend. "Joan has one chance in ten of surviving," he said as he shook down the mercury in his thermometer. "But she won't even have one chance in ten unless she wants to live. Your friend has made up her mind she's not going to get well. Is there anything she really wants to do?"

"She...she wanted to paint a picture of the bay someday," said Sue.

"Paint? Bosh! Has she anything on her mind worth thinking about?"

Sue said nothing.

"Well, it seems she has very little to live for," said the doctor. "I will do all that science can accomplish. But whenever my patient begins to think of death, I subtract fifty percent of my power." ◆

After the doctor had gone, Sue went into the workroom and cried into a napkin until it became a pulp. Then, with great effort, she swaggered into Joan's room with her drawing board, whistling gaily.

Joan lay with her face toward the window, scarcely making a ripple under the blankets. Sue stopped whistling, thinking Joan was asleep.

Sue arranged her board and began a pen-and-ink drawing for a magazine story.

* Adapted for young readers

As she was sketching the figure of the hero, an Idaho cowboy, she heard a low sound, several times repeated. She went quickly to Joan's bedside.

Joan's eyes were open wide. She was looking out the window and counting—counting backward.

"Twelve," she said, and, a little later, "eleven" and then "ten" and "nine" and then "eight" and then "seven."

Sue looked out the window. What was there to count? There was only a bare, dreary yard to be seen and the blank side of the brick house twenty feet away. An old, old ivy vine, gnarled and decayed at the roots, climbed halfway up the brick wall. The cold breath of autumn had blown the leaves from the vine until its skeleton branches clung, almost bare, to the crumbling bricks.

"What is it, dear?" asked Sue.

"Six," said Joan, in almost a whisper. "They're falling faster now. Three days ago there were almost a hundred. It made my head ache to count them. But now it's easy. There goes another one. There are only five left now."

"Five what, dear?"

"Leaves. On the ivy vine. When the last one falls, I must go, too. I've known that for three days. Didn't the doctor tell you?" ★

"Oh, I never heard such nonsense," Sue objected. "What do the old ivy leaves have to do with your getting well? Why, the doctor told me this morning that your chances for getting well soon were—let's see exactly what he said—he said the chances were ten to one! Why, that's almost as good a chance as we have in New York when we ride on the streetcars or walk past a new building. Try to drink some broth now, and let me go back to my drawing. If I sell it, I can buy you more broth."

"You needn't get any more broth," said Joan, keeping her eyes fixed out the window. "There goes another. No, I don't want any broth. That leaves just four. I want to see the last one fall before it gets dark. Then I'll go, too."

"Joan, dear," said Sue, bending over her, "will you promise me to keep your eyes closed and not look out the window until I am finished working? I must hand in these drawings by tomorrow. I need the light, or I would pull the shade down."

"Couldn't you draw in the other room?" asked Joan coldly.

"I'd rather be here by you," said Sue. "Besides, I don't want you to keep looking at those silly ivy leaves."

"Tell me as soon as you've finished," said Joan, closing her eyes and lying as still as a fallen statue. "I want to see the last one fall. I'm tired of waiting. I'm tired of thinking. I want to turn loose my hold on everything and go sailing down, down, just like one of those poor, tired leaves."

"Try to sleep," said Sue. "I want to see Mr. Behrman. I'll not be gone a minute. Don't try to move 'til I come back."

E COMPREHENSION

Write the answers.
1. The author made pneumonia seem like a person. Why do you think the author did that?
2. Why do you think the doctor disliked painting?
3. Why did the doctor think Joan's chance of surviving was particularly low?
4. Why did Joan think she was like the ivy leaves?
5. How do you think Sue could help Joan?

F WRITING

Joan thought she was like a leaf. What plant or animal do you think you are like?

Write an essay that explains what plant or animal you are like. Try to answer the following questions:
- Which plant or animal are you like?
- In what ways do you resemble that plant or animal?
- How do you feel about that plant or animal?
- What would you do if you actually were that plant or animal?

Make your essay at least fifty words long.

Ⓐ WORD LISTS

1
Hard Words
1. Hades
2. Cerberus
3. Demeter
4. prudent
5. Persephone

2
New Vocabulary
1. scoff at
2. canvas
3. palette
4. easel
5. contempt
6. idiotic
7. persistent

Ⓑ VOCABULARY DEFINITIONS

1. **scoff at**—When you *scoff at* something, you make fun of that thing.
   • What's another way of saying *She made fun of the boy's behavior*?
2. **canvas**—*Canvas* is a tough cloth that artists paint on.
   • What is canvas?
3. **palette**—A *palette* is a thin board that artists use for mixing paint.
   • What is a palette?
4. **easel**—An *easel* is a frame that artists use to hold a picture.
   • What is an easel?
5. **contempt**—When you show *contempt,* you show hatred or disrespect.
   • What's another way of saying *The queen showed disrespect for the minstrel*?
6. **idiotic**—When something is *idiotic,* it is stupid.
   • What's another way of saying *Their plan was stupid*?
7. **persistent**—When something is *persistent,* it won't give up.
   • What do we call a person who won't give up?

The Last Leaf
Part 2

Focus Question: What was Mr. Behrman's masterpiece?

Old Mr. Behrman was a painter who lived on the ground floor beneath Joan and Sue. He was past sixty and had a huge beard that curled down his chest. Mr. Behrman was a failure as an artist. He had been painting for forty years. He had always been about to paint a masterpiece but had never yet begun it.

For several years, he had painted nothing except advertising posters. But he still talked of his coming masterpiece. He was a fierce little old man who scoffed terribly at softness in anyone. He regarded himself as the protector of the two young artists in the studio above.

Sue found Mr. Behrman in his dimly

lighted apartment. In one corner was a blank canvas on an easel that had been waiting there for twenty-five years to receive the first line of the masterpiece.

Sue told Mr. Behrman how Joan felt about the leaves. She said that Joan was as light and fragile as a leaf and that she would float away when her slight hold on life grew weaker.

Mr. Behrman shouted his contempt for such idiotic imaginings.

"Vot!" he cried. "Iss dere people in de world wid de foolishness to die because leafs dey drop off from a stupid vine? I haf not heard of such a thing. Vy do you allow dot silly business to come into her brain? Ach, dot poor leetle Miss Joan."

"She is very ill and weak," said Sue, "and the fever has left her mind full of strange thoughts."

"Go on," Behrman answered. "I come wit you. Dis iss not any place in which one so goot as Miss Joan shall lie sick. Someday, ve shall all go away."

Joan was sleeping when they went upstairs. Sue pulled the shade down to the windowsill and motioned Behrman into the other room. In there, they peered out the window fearfully at the ivy vine. Then they looked at each other for a moment without speaking. A persistent, cold rain was falling, mingled with snow.

A moment later, Behrman turned and went back downstairs. ◆

When Sue awoke the next morning, she found Joan with dull wide-open eyes, staring at the pulled-down window shade.

"Open the shade. I want to see," Joan ordered in a whisper.

Wearily, Sue obeyed.

Even after the beating rain and the fierce gusts of wind that had lasted the whole night, one ivy leaf still stood out against the brick wall. It was the last on the vine. It was dark green near its stem, but its edges were tinted yellow with decay. It hung bravely from a branch some twenty feet above the ground.

"It is the last one," said Joan. "I thought it would surely fall during the night. I heard the wind. It will fall today, and I shall die at the same time."

"Dear, dear!" said Sue, leaning over and embracing Joan. "Think of me if you won't think of yourself. What would I do if you died?"

But Joan did not answer.

The day wore away, and even through the twilight, they could see the lone ivy leaf clinging to its stem against the wall. And then, with the coming of the night, the north wind blew again while the rain still beat against the windows and pattered down from the roof.

When it was light enough the next morning, Joan commanded that the shade be raised again.

The ivy leaf was still there.

Joan lay for a long time looking at it. And then she called to Sue, who was stirring her chicken broth over the gas stove.

"I've been a bad girl, Sue," said Joan. "Something has made that last leaf stay there to show me how wicked I was. I no longer want to die. You may bring me a little broth now and some milk. No; bring me a hand mirror first and then pack some pillows around me, and I will sit up and watch you cook." ★

An hour later, Joan said, "Someday I hope to paint a picture of the bay."

The doctor came in the afternoon, and Sue went with him into the hallway.

"Now her chances are fifty-fifty," said the doctor, taking Sue's thin, shaking hand in his. "With good nursing, you'll win. And now I must see another case downstairs. Behrman, his name is—some kind of an artist, I believe. Pneumonia, too. He is an old, weak man, and the attack is severe. There is no hope for him."

The next day the doctor said to Sue: "Joan is out of danger. You've won. Good food and care now—that's all she needs."

That afternoon Sue came to the bed where Joan lay, contentedly knitting a blue woolen scarf. Sue put her arm around Joan.

"I have something to tell you," Sue said. "Mr. Behrman died of pneumonia today in the hospital. He was ill only two days. The janitor found him on the morn-ing of the first day in his room downstairs, helpless with pain. His shoes and clothing were wet through and icy cold. The janitor couldn't imagine where Behrman had been on such a dreadful night. Then the janitor found a lantern, still lit, and a ladder that had been dragged from its place, and some scattered brushes, and a palette with green and yellow colors mixed on it. Look out the window, Joan, at the last ivy leaf on the wall. Didn't you wonder why it never fluttered or moved when the wind blew? Ah, Joan, that leaf is Behrman's masterpiece—he painted it there two nights ago—the night that the last real leaf fell."

D VOCABULARY REVIEW

stalks
broth
gnarled
decayed
accomplish
swagger
squat

For each item, write the correct word.
1. When you succeed in doing something, you ▇▇▇ that thing.
2. When a hunter follows an animal quietly, the hunter ▇▇▇ the animal.
3. Something that is twisted and full of knots is ▇▇▇.
4. Another word for *rotted* is ▇▇▇.

E OUTLINING

Complete the following outline for "The Last Leaf." Copy each main idea; then write three supporting details for each main idea. Use complete sentences to write the supporting details.

1. Joan thought she was going to die.
2. Mr. Behrman lived downstairs.
3. Joan did not die.

F COMPREHENSION

Write the answers.
1. Why do you think Mr. Behrman had never painted a masterpiece?
2. Compare the doctor and Mr. Behrman. How were they different? How were they alike?
3. What did Joan mean when she said, "I've been a bad girl"?
4. Why did Mr. Behrman get wet and cold?
5. Why do you think Mr. Behrman painted the leaf?

G WRITING

The story doesn't tell exactly what Mr. Behrman did on the night he painted the leaf.

Write a short story that tells what he did. Try to answer the following questions:
- How did Mr. Behrman feel?
- What was he thinking?
- What was the weather like?
- What difficulties did he have?

Make your story at least one hundred words long.

Finding Yourself

People lose things all the time—hats, coats, wallets, purses, and keys. But what happens if you lose yourself? Where do you go to find out who you really are?

The characters in the following stories answer those questions in different ways. Some travel to the ends of the earth; others stay put; still others wait for time to set their path. But they all find answers. In doing so, they find themselves.

A WORD LISTS

1
Hard Words
1. Hades
2. Hecate
3. Cerberus
4. dominions
5. triumphant
6. sea nymphs

2
Word Practice
1. Persephone
2. necklace
3. demon
4. Demeter
5. nostrils

3
New Vocabulary
1. prudent
2. wilt
3. cavern
4. triumphant
5. sullen
6. excessive
7. massive
8. splendor

B VOCABULARY DEFINITIONS

1. **prudent**—When you are *prudent,* you are wise and careful.
   - What's another way of saying *Mrs. Dunn always tried to be wise and careful*?
2. **wilt**—When plants *wilt,* they dry up and droop.
   - What's another way of saying *The leaves drooped and dried up*?
3. **cavern**—A large cave is a *cavern.*
   - What do we call a large cave?
4. **triumphant**—*Triumphant* is another word for *victorious.*
   - What's another way of saying *The Greek army was victorious at Troy*?
5. **sullen**—When you are *sullen,* you are gloomy and silent.
   - What's another way of saying *The gloomy and silent boy had no fun at the party*?

6. **excessive**—*Excessive* means "too much."
   - What's another way of saying *too much noise*?
7. **massive**—When something is *massive* it is very large.
   - What's another way of saying *The tree was very large*?
8. **splendor**—*Splendor* is another word for *beauty.*
   - What's another way of saying *They stared at the beauty of the castle*?

Demeter and Hades

The next story you will read, "Persephone," is a Greek myth. Several Greek deities (gods and goddesses) appear in the story, including Demeter and Hades.

Demeter was the goddess of the earth. She helped plants grow and kept the fields green. Although Demeter could have stayed on Mount Olympus with the chief god, Zeus, she spent almost all her time on earth.

Hades was the god of the underworld. He was one of Zeus's brothers. Zeus's other brother was Poseidon, god of the sea. Hades lived in the underworld, a magic cave below the ground where people went after they died.

Demeter

Hades

Persephone
Part 1

Focus Question: What happened when Persephone picked the most magnificent flowers in the world?

Demeter was the goddess of the earth. She was quite fond of her daughter, Persephone, who was a beautiful young woman of sixteen.

One day, Demeter was very busy because she had to take care of the wheat, the corn, the rye, and all the crops of every kind all over the earth. The growing season had begun late, and it was necessary to make the harvest ripen more rapidly than usual. So Demeter got into her chariot and was just ready to set off for the fields.

"Mother," said Persephone, "I shall be lonely while you are away. Do you mind if I run down to the shore and ask some of the sea nymphs to come up out of the waves and talk to me?"

"No, I do not mind," answered Demeter. "The sea nymphs are good creatures and will never lead you into any harm. But you must take care not to stray away from them, nor to go wandering about the fields by yourself. You never know when the other gods will play tricks on you."

Persephone promised to be as prudent as if she were a grown woman. By the time Demeter's chariot had whirled out of sight, Persephone was already on the shore, calling to the sea nymphs. They knew her voice and were not long in showing their glistening faces and sea-green hair above the water. They brought a great many beautiful shells with them. Then they sat down on the moist sand, where the waves broke over them, and made a necklace, which they soon hung around Persephone's neck. To show her gratitude, Persephone asked the sea nymphs to go with her into the fields so that they might gather flowers for more necklaces.

"Oh, no, Persephone!" cried the sea nymphs. "We dare not go with you on dry land. We grow faint unless we can sniff the salt breeze of the ocean. Don't you see how careful we are to let the waves break over us every moment or two, so as to keep ourselves comfortably moist? If it were not for the waves, we should soon look like bunches of uprooted seaweed dried in the sun."

"It is a great pity," said Persephone. "Wait for me here while I gather my apron full of flowers. I will be back again before the waves have broken ten times over you. I long to make you some necklaces that will be as lovely as the one you have given me."

"We will wait, then," answered the sea nymphs. "But while you are gone, we may as well lie down on a bank of soft sponge under the water. The air today is a little too dry for our comfort. We will pop up our heads every few minutes to see if you have returned." ◆

Persephone ran quickly to a spot where, only the day before, she had seen a great many flowers. These, however, were now a little past their bloom and showed signs of wilting. Persephone wished to give her friends the freshest and loveliest blossoms, so she strayed farther into the fields, where she soon found some flowers that delighted her. Never had she seen such dazzling flowers before—large, fragrant violets; rich and delicate roses; and many others, some of which seemed to be of new shapes and colors.

Two or three times, it seemed that a tuft of splendid flowers suddenly sprouted from the earth before her very eyes, as if to tempt her a few steps farther. Persephone's apron was soon filled and brimming over with delightful blossoms. She was ready to turn back to rejoin the sea nymphs when she saw a large shrub a little farther on. It was completely covered with the most magnificent flowers in the world.

"They're beautiful!" cried Persephone. Then she thought to herself, "I was looking at that spot only a moment ago. How strange it is that I did not see the flowers! It is really the most beautiful shrub that ever sprang out of the earth. I will pull it up by the roots and carry it home and plant it in my mother's garden."

Holding up her apron full of flowers with her left hand, Persephone seized the large shrub with the other. She pulled and pulled but was hardly able to loosen the soil about its roots. What a deep-rooted plant it was! As Persephone pulled with all her might, she observed that the earth began to stir and crack around the shrub. She gave another pull but relaxed her hold, imagining there was a rumbling sound right beneath her feet.

Did the roots extend down into an enchanted cavern? Then, laughing at herself for so childish a thought, Persephone made another effort. Up came the shrub, and she staggered back. She held the stem triumphantly in her hand and gazed at the deep hole its roots had left in the soil.

Much to her astonishment, this hole kept spreading wider and wider and growing deeper and deeper until it seemed to have no bottom. And all the while there came a rumbling noise out of its depths, louder and louder and nearer and nearer and sounding like the tramp of horses, hooves and the rattling of wheels. Too frightened to run away, she stood straining her eyes into this wonderful cavern. ★

Persephone soon saw a team of four black horses, snorting smoke out of their nostrils and tearing their way out of the earth with a splendid golden chariot whirling at their heels. They leaped out of the bottomless hole, chariot and all, and there they were, tossing their black manes and swishing their black tails. In the chariot sat a man, richly dressed, with a crown on his head, all flaming with diamonds. He looked noble and rather handsome, but he seemed sullen and discontented. He kept rubbing his eyes and shading them with his hand, as if he did not like the sunshine.

Persephone did not know it, but the stranger was Hades, king of the underworld. As soon as he saw the frightened young woman, he beckoned her to come a little nearer.

"Do not be afraid," said he with a smile as cheerful as he could put on. "Come,

would you like to ride a little way with me in my beautiful chariot?"

But Persephone was so alarmed that she wished for nothing but to get out of his reach. And no wonder! The stranger did not look very good-natured, in spite of his smile. And as for his voice, its tones were deep and stern and sounded like the rumbling of an earthquake. Persephone's first thought was to call for her mother.

"Mother!" she cried, trembling. "Come quickly and save me!"

But her voice was too faint for her mother to hear. Indeed, Demeter was then a thousand miles off, making the corn grow in a distant country. Even if she had been within hearing, Demeter could not have helped her poor daughter. As soon as Perse-phone began to cry out, Hades leaped to the ground, caught her in his arms, mounted the chariot, shook the reins, and shouted to the four black horses to set off. These demon horses immediately broke into so swift a gallop that they seemed to fly through the air.

In a moment Persephone had lost sight of the pleasant valley in which she had always lived. Another moment and even Mount Olympus had become tiny in the distance. But still Persephone screamed. She scattered her apron full of flowers along the way, leaving a long trail behind the chariot. Many mothers ran quickly to see if anything had happened to their children—but Demeter was not one of them. She was a great way off, and she could not hear her daughter's cry.

Ⓔ VOCABULARY REVIEW

gnarled
persistent
canvas
contempt
scoff at
idiotic
stalks
decayed

For each item, write the correct word.
1. When you mock or ridicule something, you ▰▰▰ that thing.
2. Another word for *hatred* is ▰▰▰.
3. Something that is very stupid is ▰▰▰.
4. Something that won't give up is ▰▰▰.
5. Something that is twisted and full of knots is ▰▰▰.

F OUTLINING

Complete the following outline for "Mrs. Dunn's Lovely, Lovely Farm." Copy each main idea; then write three supporting details for each main idea. Use complete sentences to write the supporting details.

1. Mrs. Dunn started a farm in her apartment.
2. The neighbors tried to protect Mrs. Dunn from Mr. Warfield.
3. Mrs. Dunn and Mr. Warfield made an agreement.

G COMPREHENSION

Write the answers.
1. What happened when Persephone picked the most magnificent flowers in the world?
2. How can you tell that the shrub Persephone pulled up was magic?
3. Do you think it was wise of Persephone to pull up the shrub? Explain your answer.
4. What should you do if a stranger offers you a ride?
5. Where do you think Hades will take Persephone? Explain your answer.

H WRITING

What do you think Demeter should do when she finds out what has happened to Persephone?
Write an essay that explains what she should do. Try to answer the following questions:
- Whom should Demeter talk to about Persephone?
- What evidence should Demeter use to find Persephone?
- What powers might Demeter use?
- Where should Demeter go?

Make your essay at least fifty words long.

A WORD LISTS

1
Hard Words
1. illuminated
2. delicacies
3. morsel
4. threshold

2
Word Practice
1. Cerberus
2. Hecate
3. Hades
4. spaniel
5. soothe
6. crystal

3
New Vocabulary
1. illuminated
2. lofty
3. summon
4. morsel
5. delicacies
6. motive
7. threshold

B VOCABULARY DEFINITIONS

1. **illuminated**—When something is *illuminated,* it is lit up.
   - What's another way of saying *The park was lit up*?
2. **lofty**—When something is *lofty,* it is very high.
   - What's another way of saying *The eagle's nest was on a very high cliff*?
3. **summon**—When you *summon* a person, you order that person to go somewhere.
   - What's another way of saying *They ordered Henry to court*?
4. **morsel**—A *morsel* is a bit of food.
   - What's another way of saying *She didn't have a bit of food*?
5. **delicacies**—*Delicacies* are the finest and richest foods.
   - What's another way of saying *Nancy had never seen such rich foods*?
6. **motive**—A person's *motive* for doing something is a person's reason for doing that thing.
   - What's another way of saying *Nobody could understand her reason for helping the beggar*?
7. **threshold**—The entrance of a place is the *threshold* of that place.
   - What do we call the entrance of a place?

Persephone
Part 2

Focus Question: Why did Hades capture Persephone?

As the horses galloped on, Hades did his best to soothe Persephone.

"Why should you be frightened, my dear girl?" he said in his rough voice. "I promise not to do you any harm."

"Let me go home!" cried Persephone. "Let me go home!"

"My home is better than your mother's," answered Hades. "It is a palace all made of gold, with crystal windows. And because there is little or no sunshine, the rooms are illuminated with diamond lamps. You never saw anything half so magnificent as my throne. If you like, you may sit on it and be my queen, and I will sit on the foot-stool."

"I don't care for golden palaces and thrones," sobbed Persephone. "O my mother, my mother! Carry me back to my mother!"

"Do not be foolish, Persephone," Hades said in a rather sullen tone. "I offer you my palace, my crown, and all the riches under the earth, but you treat me as if I were doing you an injury. The one thing my palace needs is a woman to cheer the rooms with her smile. This is what you must do for Hades."

"Never!" answered Persephone, looking miserable. "I shall never smile till you set me down at my mother's door."

She might just as well have talked to the wind that whistled past them, for Hades urged on his horses, and they went faster than ever. Persephone continued to cry out. She screamed so long and so loudly that her poor voice became a hoarse whisper. Then Persephone happened to cast her eyes over a great broad field of waving grain. There she saw Demeter, making the corn grow. The goddess was too busy to notice the golden chariot as it went rattling along. Persephone gathered all her strength and gave one more scream, but the chariot was out of sight before Demeter had time to turn her head. ◆

Hades had taken a road that soon became gloomy. It was bordered on each side with sharp rocks. The rumbling of the chariot wheels echoed off the rocks with a noise like rolling thunder. The trees and bushes that grew between the rocks had dismal leaves. Although it was only noon, the air was darkened by a gray twilight.

The black horses had rushed along so swiftly that they were already beyond the limits of sunshine. The darker it grew, the more satisfied Hades' face became. He soon stopped twisting his features into a smile. Persephone peeped at his wicked face through the gathering dusk. She hoped he might not be as evil as he appeared.

"Ah, this twilight is truly refreshing after the ugly glare of the sun," said Hades. "Torchlight is so much more agreeable, particularly when it is reflected from diamonds! My palace will be a magnificent sight!"

"Is it much farther?" asked Persephone. "And will you carry me back when I have seen it?"

"We will talk of that by and by," answered Hades. "We are just entering my dominions. Do you see that tall gateway before us? When we pass those gates we are at home. And there lies my faithful dog at the threshold. Cerberus! Cerberus! Come here, my good dog!"

So saying, Hades pulled at the reins and stopped the chariot right between the tall, massive pillars of the gateway. The dog got up from the threshold and stood on his hind legs, so as to put his forepaws on the chariot wheel. What a strange dog he was! He was a big, rough, ugly-looking monster with three fierce heads. Fierce as they were, Hades patted them all. He seemed as fond of his three-headed dog as if it had been a sweet little spaniel with silken ears and curly hair.

Cerberus was pleased to see his master, and he expressed his love by wagging his tail. Persephone saw that the tail was actually a live dragon with fiery eyes and poisonous fangs.

"Will the dog bite me?" asked Persephone. "What an ugly creature he is!"

"Oh, never fear," answered her companion. "He never harms people unless they try to enter my dominions without being sent for or if they try to get away when I wish to keep them here. Down, Cerberus! Now, my dear Persephone, we will drive on." ★

On went the chariot past the gates, and Hades seemed greatly pleased to find himself once more in his own kingdom. He showed Persephone the rich veins of gold among the rocks, and he pointed to several places where one stroke of a pickaxe would loosen a bushel of diamonds. Sparkling gems could be seen all along the road. They would have been of immense value above ground, but they were merely common here.

When the chariot arrived at the palace, Hades got out and led Persephone up a lofty flight of steps into the great hall. The room was splendidly illuminated by large precious stones. They seemed to burn like lamps, and they glowed radiantly all through the vast palace. And yet there was a kind of gloom in the midst of this enchanted light. Not a single object in the hall was pleasing to the eyes, except for Persephone. She was a lovely young woman. She still carried one earthly flower she had not let fall from her hand.

Hades had never been happy in his palace. That is why he had kidnapped Persephone. He wanted a wife instead of cheating his heart any longer with this tiresome magnificence. Her presence was like a sunbeam that had somehow found its way into the enchanted hall.

Hades now summoned his servants and told them to lose no time in preparing a magnificent banquet. He made sure they set a golden flask of enchanted water by Persephone's plate. Those who drink this water forget everything they know.

"I will neither drink that nor anything else," said Persephone. "Nor will I taste a morsel of food, even if you keep me forever in your palace." Because her mother was a goddess, Persephone did not need food to survive, although she did enjoy eating fresh fruit and certain other foods.

"I should be sorry for that," replied Hades, for he really wished to be kind if he had only known how. "You are spoiled, Persephone. But when you see the nice things my cook will make for you, you will regain your appetite."

Then, sending for the head cook, he gave strict orders that all sorts of delicacies should be set before Persephone. He had a secret motive in this, for the law said that if anyone in Hades' palace ever tasted any food there, that person could never leave.

Now, if Hades had been cunning enough to offer Persephone some fruit or bread, she would soon have been tempted to eat it. But he left the matter entirely to his cook, who considered nothing fit to eat unless it was rich pastry or highly seasoned meat or spiced sweetcakes—foods that Persephone's mother had never given her. The smell of these foods took away her appetite instead of sharpening it.

D CONTRADICTIONS

Write the answer to item 1.

Here's a rule about contradictions: *If a statement is true, a contradiction of that statement is false.*

Here's a statement: *Jack was in Chicago at 5:00 a.m. on July 1, 2001.* If that statement is true, these statements are false:

- Jack was in New Orleans at 5:00 a.m. on July 1, 2001.
- Jack was in St. Louis at 5:00 a.m. on July 1, 2001.
- Jack was in Milwaukee at 5:00 a.m. on July 1, 2001.

These statements contradict the true statement because Jack couldn't be in Chicago and other cities at the same time.

Here's another true statement: *Yesterday Darla was fifteen years old.* These statements contradict the true statement:

- Yesterday Darla was twelve years old.
- Yesterday Darla was twenty years old.
- Yesterday Darla was eighteen years old.

These statements contradict the true statement because Darla can't be fifteen years old and any other age at the same time.

Let's say this statement is true: *Maria is shorter than everybody else in her family—her father, her mother, and her sister, Jane.*

- Make up three statements that contradict the true statement about how short Maria is.

Let's say this statement is true: *Mr. Green had red hair and brown eyes.*

- Make up three statements that contradict the true statement about Mr. Green's hair and eyes.

Let's say this statement is true: *Phillip could speak only English.*

1. Write three statements that contradict the true statement.

E COMPREHENSION

Write the answers.
1. Why did Hades capture Persephone?
2. Why do you think Cerberus stayed at the gateway of the underworld?
3. The story says that gems "would have been of immense value above ground, but they were merely common here." Explain what that statement means.
4. What happens to people who taste food in Hades' palace?
5. Why wasn't Persephone tempted by the food the cook prepared?

F WRITING

If you could live in a palace, what would it look like?

Write an essay that describes your palace. Try to answer the following questions:

- Where is your palace located?
- What is your palace made of?
- How many rooms does your palace have?
- What do the rooms look like?

Make your essay at least fifty words long.

33

A WORD LISTS

1
Hard Words
1. melancholy
2. pomegranate
3. wretched
4. recollect

2
Word Practice
1. innocent
2. enchantment
3. assure
4. Hecate

3
New Vocabulary
1. apt
2. entice
3. melancholy
4. shriveled
5. behold
6. compose

B VOCABULARY DEFINITIONS

1. **apt**—When you are *apt* to do something, you are likely to do it.
   - What's another way of saying *He is likely to take a nap in the afternoon*?
2. **entice**—When you *entice* somebody, you tempt that person.
   - What's another way of saying *The queen tempted him into the secret garden*?
3. **melancholy**—When you are *melancholy,* you are sad.
   - What's another way of saying *She was sad*?
4. **shriveled**—When something is *shriveled,* it is wrinkled and withered.
   - What's another way of saying *The apple was wrinkled and withered*?
5. **behold**—When you *behold* something, you observe it.
   - What's another way of saying *She will observe the great mountains*?
6. **compose**—When you *compose* something, you make up that thing.
   - What's another way of saying *She made up a letter to her friend*?

Persephone
Part 3

Focus Question: How did Demeter try to find Persephone?

Our story must now move out of Hades' dominions to observe what Demeter has been doing since her daughter was kidnapped. You will remember that we had a glimpse of her, half-hidden among the waving grain, while Persephone went swiftly whirling by in Hades' chariot. You will remember, too, the loud scream Persephone gave just when the chariot was out of sight.

Of all Persephone's outcries, this last shriek was the only one that reached Demeter's ears. She had mistaken the rumbling of the chariot wheels for a peal of thunder. She imagined a rain shower was coming and that it would help her make the corn grow.

At the sound of Persephone's shriek, Demeter looked about in every direction. She did not know where the shriek had come from, but she felt almost certain it was her daughter's voice.

It seemed unlikely that Persephone should have strayed over so many lands and seas. Nevertheless, Demeter decided to go home and assure herself that her daughter was safe. She quickly left the field in which she had been working. Because her work was only half done, the grain looked as if it needed both sun and rain and as if something was wrong with its roots.

Demeter's chariot was also swift. In less than an hour, she arrived at her home and found it empty. Knowing that Persephone might be at the seashore, she hastened there as fast as she could. She soon beheld the wet faces of the poor sea nymphs peeping over a wave. These good creatures had been waiting on the sponge bank. Every minute or so, they popped their heads above water to see if Persephone had come back. When they saw Demeter, they sat down on the crest of a wave and let it toss them ashore at her feet.

"Where is Persephone?" cried Demeter. "Where is my daughter? Tell me, you naughty sea nymphs, have you enticed her under the sea?"

"Oh, no, Demeter," said the innocent sea nymphs, tossing back their green hair and looking her in the face. "We never should dream of such a thing. Persephone had been making necklaces with us. But she left us a long while ago, meaning only to run a little way on the dry land to gather some flowers for a necklace. This was early in the day, and we have seen nothing of her since." ♦

Demeter scarcely waited to hear what the nymphs had to say. She made inquiries all through the neighborhood, but nobody

told her anything that could help her guess what had become of Persephone. A fisherman had noticed Persephone's footprints in the sand as he went homeward along the beach with a basket of fish. A shepherd had seen her stooping to gather flowers. Several people had heard either the rattling of chariot wheels or the rumbling of distant thunder. And one old woman had heard a scream but did not take the trouble to look up.

The people were no help at all, and they took such a long time to tell the nothing that they knew. Day turned to night before Demeter discovered she must seek her daughter elsewhere. So she lit a torch and set forth, resolving never to come back until she found Persephone.

Demeter thought she could search more thoroughly on foot. So she began her sorrowful journey, holding her torch before her and looking carefully at every object along the path. She had not gone far before she found one of the magnificent flowers that grew on the shrub Persephone had pulled up.

"Ah," thought Demeter, examining it by torchlight, "there is mischief in this flower! The earth did not produce it by any help of mine, nor did it develop by itself. It is the work of enchantment and is therefore poisonous. Perhaps it has poisoned my poor daughter."

Demeter put the poisonous flower in her cloak, not knowing whether she might ever find any other sign of Persephone.

All night long, Demeter knocked at the door of every cottage and farmhouse and asked the weary farmers if they had seen her daughter. They stood, gaping and half asleep, and answered her with sympathy. They begged her to come in and rest.

At the gates of every palace, Demeter made so loud a summons that the servants thought she must be some great queen.

When they saw only a sad and anxious woman with a torch in her hand, they spoke rudely and sometimes threatened to set the dogs on her. ★

But nobody had seen Persephone, nor could anyone give Demeter the least hint where to seek her. The night passed, and still Demeter continued her search without sitting down to rest or stopping to take food. She even forgot to put out the torch, although the glad light of the morning sun made its red flame look thin and pale. This torch was magical, for it burned dimly throughout the day, and at night was as bright as ever. It was never darkened by the rain or wind in all the weary days and nights that followed.

Demeter went wandering about for nine long days and nights, finding no trace of Persephone except for now and then a withered flower. She picked these up and put them into her cloak because she thought they might have fallen from her poor daughter's hand. All day she traveled onward through the hot sun, and at night again the flame of the torch would redden and gleam along the pathway. Demeter con-tinued her search by its light, never sitting down to rest.

On the tenth day, Demeter chanced to see the mouth of a cavern. A torch flickered and struggled within the darkness of the gloomy space. Demeter had resolved to leave no spot without a search, so she peeped into the entrance of the cavern and lighted it up a little more by holding her own torch before her. In so doing, she caught a glimpse of what seemed to be a woman, sitting on a great heap of brown leaves.

This woman was by no means beauti-ful, for her head was shaped very much like a dog's, and she wore a necklace of snakes. Demeter knew the woman was the witch Hecate, who put all her enjoyment in being miserable. Hecate would not talk to others unless they were as melancholy and wretched as she.

"I am wretched enough now," thought poor Demeter, "to have a conversation with Hecate."

So she stepped into the cave and sat down on the shriveled leaves by the dog-headed woman's side.

D CONTRADICTIONS

Write the answers to items 1 and 2.

Assume this statement is true: *Tom could not drive a car.* Then this statement is a contradiction: *Tom was driving a station wagon down Fifth Street.* Here is why the statement is a contradiction: *If Tom could not drive a car, then he could not drive a station wagon down Fifth Street.*

Assume this statement is true: *Abby swam all morning.* Then this statement is a contradiction: *Abby rode her bike at 10:00 a.m.* Here is why the statement is a contradiction: *If Abby swam all morning, then she could not have ridden her bike at 10:00 a.m.*

Assume this statement is true: *Gina loved to eat all fruits.* Then this statement is a contradiction: *Gina hated to eat pears.*

1. Explain why the statement is a contradiction. Start by saying the true statement. Then tell what couldn't also be true. Use this format: *If* ▬▬, *then* ▬▬.

Assume this statement is true: *Jason always sleeps from noon to 6:00 p.m.* Then this statement is a contradiction: *Jason was fishing today at 3:00 p.m.*

2. Explain why the statement is a contradiction. Use this format: *If* ▬▬, *then* ▬▬.

E VOCABULARY REVIEW

morsel
stalks
lofty
delicacies
summon
motive
illuminated
triumphant
excessive
persistent

For each item, write the correct word.
1. The finest and richest foods are ▬▬.
2. A bit of food is called a ▬▬ of food.
3. When something is lit up, it is ▬▬.
4. When you order a person to go somewhere, you ▬▬ that person.
5. A person's reason for doing something is a person's ▬▬.
6. Something that is very high is ▬▬.
7. Another word for *victorious* is ▬▬.
8. A word that means "too much" is ▬▬.

F COMPREHENSION

Write the answers.

1. How did Demeter try to find Persephone?
2. What was the most important piece of evidence Demeter found? Explain your answer.
3. Demeter stopped at farmhouses and palaces. What was different about the treatment she received at each place?
4. Why do you think Demeter was able to search without ever resting?
5. Do you think Hecate will be able to help Demeter? Explain your answer.

G WRITING

How do you think Demeter's wandering compares with Odysseus's wandering?

Write an essay that compares Demeter's wandering with Odysseus's wandering. Try to answer the following questions:

- How was Demeter's wandering the same as Odysseus's wandering?
- How was her wandering different from his?
- What did each one learn on his or her wanderings?

Make your essay at least fifty words long.

Ⓐ WORD LISTS

1
Hard Words
1. frivolous
2. elegant
3. exquisite
4. pomegranate
5. contradiction
6. recollect

2
New Vocabulary
1. exquisite
2. frivolous
3. recollect
4. indignant
5. gratify

Ⓑ VOCABULARY DEFINITIONS

1. **exquisite**—When something is *exquisite,* it is beautifully made.
   - What's another way of saying *a beautifully made painting*?
2. **frivolous**—*Frivolous* is another word for *foolish.*
   - What's another way of saying *The king was foolish*?
3. **recollect**—*Recollect* is another word for *remember.*
   - What's another way of saying *He could not remember the stranger's name*?
4. **indignant**—When you are *indignant,* you are angry and insulted.
   - What's another way of saying *She was angry and insulted over his unjust claim*?
5. **gratify**—*Gratify* is another word for *satisfy.*
   - What's another way of saying *His kind manner satisfied her*?

Persephone
Part 4

Focus Question: How did Demeter change as she searched for her daughter?

"Oh, Hecate," said Demeter, "if ever you lose a daughter you will know what sorrow is. Have you seen my poor child Persephone pass by the mouth of your cavern?"

"No," answered Hecate in a cracked voice. Then, with many sighs, she continued, "No, Demeter, I have seen nothing of your daughter. But my ears hear all cries of distress all over the world. Nine days ago, I heard the voice of a young woman shrieking as if in great distress. Something terrible has happened to that young woman, you may rest assured. As well as I could judge, a dragon or some other cruel monster was carrying her away."

"You kill me by saying so," cried Demeter, almost ready to faint. "Where was the sound, and which way did it seem to go?"

"It passed very swiftly along," said Hecate, "and at the same time, there was a heavy rumbling of wheels toward the east. I can tell you nothing more. The best advice I can give you is to live in this cavern, where we will be the two most miserable women in the world."

"Not yet, miserable Hecate," replied Demeter. "When there shall be no more hope of finding Persephone, I will show you what it is to be miserable. But until I know

she has perished from the face of the earth, I will not allow myself to grieve."

Just then, a thought struck Demeter.

"There is one god," she exclaimed, "who must have seen my poor child and can doubtless tell me what has become of her. Why did I not think of him before? It is Apollo."

"What?" said Hecate. "The young god that always sits in the sunshine? Oh, do not think of going near him. He is a cheerful, light, frivolous young fellow, and he will only smile in your face. Besides, there is such a glare of the sun about him that he will blind you."

But Demeter only ignored Hecate's remarks and immediately went in search of Apollo. By and by, after a long journey, she arrived at the sunniest spot in the whole world. There she beheld a beautiful young god with long curly hair that seemed to be made of golden sunbeams. His garments were like light summer clouds, and his face was so bright that Demeter held her hands before her eyes. He had a lyre in his hands and was making sweet music. ◆

As Demeter approached, Apollo smiled at her cheerfully, but she was too filled with grief to know or care whether Apollo smiled or frowned.

"Apollo," she exclaimed, "I am in great trouble and have come to you for assistance. Can you tell me what has become of my daughter, Persephone?"

"Persephone? Persephone. Is that her name?" answered Apollo, trying to recollect. There was such a constant flow of pleasant ideas in his mind that he was apt to forget unpleasant things. "Ah, yes, I remember her now. A very lovely young woman indeed. I am happy to tell you, my dear woman, that I did see Persephone not many days ago. You may set your mind at rest. She is safe and in excellent hands."

"Oh, where is my daughter?" cried Demeter, clasping her hands.

"Why," said Apollo—and as he spoke he kept touching his lyre so as to make a thread of music run in and out among his words—"she was gathering flowers and was suddenly snatched up by Hades and carried off to his dominions. I have never been in that part of the world. The royal palace, I am told, is built of the most splendid and costly materials. Gold, diamonds, pearls, and all manner of precious stones will surround your daughter. I recommend to you, my dear lady, not to worry."

Demeter answered indignantly, "What is there to gratify her heart? What are all the splendors you speak of, without love? I must have her back again. Will you go with me, Apollo, to demand my daughter back from wicked Hades?" ★

"Please, excuse me," replied Apollo in an elegant tone. "I certainly wish you success, and I regret that I cannot have the pleasure of helping you. Besides, Hades' three-headed dog would never let me pass the gateway. I would bring sunbeams along with me, and sunbeams are forbidden in Hades' kingdom."

"Ah, Apollo," said Demeter with bitter meaning in her words, "you have a harp instead of a heart. Farewell."

"Won't you stay a moment," asked Apollo, "and hear me turn the pretty and touching story of Persephone into poetry?"

Demeter did not answer Apollo. She simply turned her back on him and began to search for the entrance to Hades' dominions. But she never found that entrance, for Hades had hidden it from her sight.

Poor Demeter! It is sad to think of her, pursuing her task alone and holding up that never-dying torch. The torch's flame seemed to contain all the grief and hope that burned in her heart. So much did she suffer that her face, which had been quite youthful when her troubles began, soon became old and wrinkled.

At last, in her despair, she decided that not a stalk of grain nor a blade of grass nor any other plant should grow until her daughter was returned to her. She even forbade the flowers to bloom because she did not want anybody's heart to be cheered by their beauty.

D CONTRADICTIONS

Write the answers to items 1 and 2.

Assume this statement is true: *Libby loved all animals.* Then this statement is a contradiction: *Libby hated rats.*

1. Explain why the statement is a contradiction. Use this format: *If* ▮▮▮, *then* ▮▮▮.

Assume this statement is true: *At 6:00 a.m. yesterday, I was in Paris, France.* Then this statement is a contradiction: *At 6:00 a.m. yesterday, I was in London, England.*

2. Explain why the statement is a contradiction. Use this format: *If* ▮▮▮, *then* ▮▮▮.

E VOCABULARY REVIEW

summon

behold

persistent

illuminated

entice

shriveled

compose

excessive

melancholy

morsel

apt

lofty

For each item, write the correct word.

1. Another word for *sad* is ▮▮▮.
2. When something is lit up, that thing is ▮▮▮.
3. When you observe something, you ▮▮▮ it.
4. Something that is very high is ▮▮▮.
5. When something is wrinkled and withered, it is ▮▮▮.
6. When you make up something, you ▮▮▮ that thing.
7. When you are likely to do something, you are ▮▮▮ to do it.
8. A word that means "too much" is ▮▮▮.
9. When you tempt somebody to do something, you ▮▮▮ that person to do it.

F OUTLINING

Complete the following partial outline for "Persephone." Copy each main idea; then write three supporting details for each main idea. Use complete sentences to write the supporting details.

1. One character was named Demeter.
2. One character was named Persephone.
3. One character was named Hades.

G COMPREHENSION

Write the answers.

1. Why had Hecate heard Persephone's cry?
2. Describe Apollo.
3. Why do you think Apollo didn't offer to help Demeter?
4. How did Demeter change as she searched for her daughter?
5. Why did Demeter forbid the plants to grow?

H WRITING

Demeter told Apollo, "You have a harp instead of a heart."

Write an essay that explains what she meant by that. Try to answer the following questions:
- How did Apollo treat Demeter?
- What was Apollo doing as he spoke to Demeter?
- How did Demeter feel about Apollo?

Make your essay at least fifty words long.

A WORD LISTS

1

Hard Words

1. juicy
2. snake
3. snaky
4. pomegranate
5. juiciest

2

New Vocabulary

1. of your own accord
2. pomegranate
3. detained

B VOCABULARY DEFINITIONS

1. **of your own accord**—When you do something *of your own accord,* you do it willingly.
   • What's another way of saying *They stayed in the cave willingly*?
2. **pomegranate**—A *pomegranate* is a red fruit that contains many seeds.
   • What is a red fruit that contains many seeds?

3. **detained**—When you are *detained,* you are held against your will.
   • What's another way of saying *They were held against their will in prison*?

Pomegranates

A fruit called a pomegranate appears in the next part of "Persephone." Pomegranates, which grow on trees, are about the size of an orange, and they have a hard red skin. Inside are many little bits of fruit, and inside each bit is a small seed.

Some people eat pomegranates by biting into them and picking out the bits of fruit with their teeth. Other people cut the pomegranates in half and pick out the fruit with a knife or spoon.

One picture below shows a whole pomegranate; the other two show a pomegranate that has been sliced in half.

Persephone
Part 5

Focus Question: How did the condition of the earth change because of Demeter's actions?

Now let us find out what Persephone has been doing since we saw her last.

Persephone had declared that she would not taste a mouthful of food as long as she remained in Hades' palace. She had maintained her resolution against all odds. It was now six months since she had left the outside of the earth, and not a morsel had yet passed between her lips. Hades had tempted her day after day with delicacies of every sort. But her good mother had often warned her not to eat these foods, and Persephone refused to taste them.

Since Persephone's arrival, the palace had lost some of its dismal quality. The inhabitants all felt this, and Hades more than any of them.

"Persephone," he once said, "I wish you could like me a little better. We gloomy people often have warm hearts. If you would only stay of your own accord, it would make me happier than to own a hundred palaces such as this one."

"Ah," said Persephone, "you should have tried to make me like you before carrying me off. The best thing you can do now is to let me go again. Then I might remember you sometimes and think you were kind. Perhaps I might even come back and pay you a visit."

"No, no," answered Hades with his gloomy smile, "I will not trust you for that. You are too fond of living in the broad daylight and gathering flowers. What an idle and foolish pleasure that is! Are not these gems prettier than a violet?"

"Not half so pretty," said Persephone, snatching the gems from Hades' hand and flinging them to the other end of the hall. "Oh, my sweet flowers!" she cried. "Shall I never see you again?" ◆

"Are you not terribly hungry?" asked Hades. "Is there nothing I can get you to eat?"

Hades had a cunning purpose in asking these questions. If Persephone tasted a morsel of food in his dominions, she would never be able to leave.

"No, indeed," said Persephone. "Your head cook is always baking and stewing and roasting and making one dish or another that he imagines may be to my liking. But he might just as well save himself the trouble. I have no appetite for anything in the world unless it were a slice of bread of my mother's own baking or a little fruit out of her garden."

When Hades heard this, he began to see the best method of tempting Persephone to eat. The cook's dishes were not

half so delicious, in the girl's opinion, as the simple food her mother gave her. Hades therefore sent one of his trusty servants with a large basket to get some of the finest and juiciest pears, peaches, and plums that could be found in the upper world. ★

But when the servant came to the upper world, he discovered that Demeter had forbidden any fruits or vegetables to grow. After seeking all over the earth, he found only a single pomegranate, and it was so shriveled that it was not worth eating. Nevertheless, he picked the fruit, put it into his basket, and began his trip back to Hades' dominions.

Now it so happened that while the servant was returning to the palace, Zeus was thinking about the condition of the earth.

Because of Demeter's actions, the earth was turning browner every day, and the people were getting hungry. Zeus knew all that had happened, and he finally decided to send the messenger god, Hermes, to Hades' dominions. Hermes carried a simple order: Release Persephone.

The messenger god made his way to the great gate, took a flying leap over the three-headed dog, and soon stood at the door of the palace. The servants recognized both his face and his clothes, for his winged cap and snaky staff were known to all. He requested to see Hades immediately.

Strangely enough, just as Hermes was going up the steps to meet Hades, the servant was bringing the pomegranate into Persephone's room.

E CONTRADICTIONS

Write the answers to items 1 and 2.

Here's one way to find a contradiction in a passage:

- Assume that what the writer says first is true.
- Read until you find a contradiction.
- Make up an if-then statement that explains the contradiction.

Here's a passage with an underlined statement: *Andrea went to a museum when she was in Egypt. The museum was quite large. It had several sculptures and many different kinds of pottery. Andrea has never left the United States.*

Assume the underlined statement is true. If that statement is true, then it can't be true that Andrea has never left the United States. Here's how to explain the contradiction: *If Andrea went to Egypt, then she must have left the United States.*

Here's another passage. Assume the underlined statement is true. Find the statement that contradicts the underlined statement.

We have only girls in our club. We have meetings twice a week. John is a member of the club, and he loves it. We are thinking of building a clubhouse.

1. Which statement is a contradiction?
2. Explain the contradiction using an if-then statement.

F MAIN IDEA

Write the main idea of the following paragraph; then write three supporting details for the main idea. Use complete sentences.

Hades began to see the best method of tempting Persephone to eat. The cook's dishes were not half so delicious, in the girl's opinion, as the simple food her mother gave her. Hades therefore sent one of his trusty servants with a large basket to get some of the finest and juiciest pears, peaches, and plums that could be found in the upper world.

G VOCABULARY REVIEW

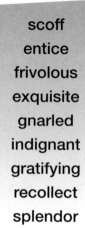

scoff

entice

frivolous

exquisite

gnarled

indignant

gratifying

recollect

splendor

For each item, write the correct word.
1. Something that is beautifully made is ▨▨▨.
2. When you are angry and insulted, you are ▨▨▨.
3. When you tempt somebody to do something, you ▨▨▨ that person to do it.
4. Another word for *beauty* is ▨▨▨.
5. Another word for *remember* is ▨▨▨.
6. Someone who is foolish is ▨▨▨.
7. Another word for *satisfying* is ▨▨▨.

H COMPREHENSION

Write the answers.
1. How did the condition of the earth change because of Demeter's actions?
2. How had Hades' palace changed since Persephone's arrival?
3. Compare Hades and Persephone. How are they alike? How are they different?
4. Why couldn't Hades' servant find any fresh fruit above ground?
5. Why did Zeus want Hades to release Persephone?

I WRITING

How do you think "Persephone" will end?

Without looking ahead, write your own ending to the story. Try to answer the following questions:
• What will Persephone do when she gets the pomegranate?
• What will Hades say to Hermes?
• What will Demeter do above ground?
• How will the story end?
Make your story at least fifty words long.

A WORD LISTS

1

Hard Words

1. liberty
2. emerge
3. wardrobe

2

Word Practice

1. fatal
2. idle
3. idly
4. oyster

3

New Vocabulary

1. emerge
2. lush
3. liberty

B VOCABULARY DEFINITIONS

1. **emerge**—When something *emerges* from a place, it comes out of that place. Here's another way of saying *The campers came out of their tents: The campers emerged from their tents.*
   - What's another way of saying *The students came out of the school*?

2. **lush**—When plants are *lush,* they are growing well and have lots of leaves.
   - What's another way of saying *The plants in the garden have lots of leaves*?

3. **liberty**—*Liberty* is another word for *freedom.*
   - What's another way of saying *The slaves wanted their freedom*?

Persephone
Part 6

Focus Question: According to this myth, why do the seasons change?

As soon as Persephone saw the pomegranate in the basket, she told the servant he had better take it away.

"I shall not touch it, I assure you," said she. "I would never think of eating such a miserable, dry pomegranate as that."

"It is the only one in the world," said the servant.

He set the wrinkled pomegranate on a table and left the room. When he was gone, Persephone could not help coming close to the table and eagerly examining this poor dried fruit. Suddenly, she felt six months of appetite. It was a very wretched-looking pomegranate, and it seemed to have no more juice in it than an oyster shell. But there was no choice of such things in Hades' palace. This was the first fruit she had seen in the underworld. She feared this fruit might be the last she would see. Unless she ate it immediately, it would become drier than it already was, and it would be unfit to eat.

"At least I may smell the pomegranate," thought Persephone.

So she took up the pomegranate and held it to her nose, and somehow or other, the fruit found its way into her mouth. Before Persephone knew what she was doing, she had bitten into the pomegranate. Just as this fatal deed was done, the door of the room opened, and in came Hades and Hermes. At the first noise of their entrance, Persephone withdrew the pomegranate from her mouth. Neither god saw what she had done. ◆

"Persephone," said Hades, sitting down, "here is Hermes, who has ordered me to release you. To confess the truth, I had already decided it was not right to take you away from your good mother. But then you must consider that this vast palace is so gloomy that I had to seek a wife. I hoped you would grow to like it here."

"I never shall," whispered Persephone.

Hades answered, "I can see plainly enough that you think my palace is a prison and that I am the iron-hearted keeper of it. And an iron heart I would surely have if I detained you here any longer when it is now six months since you have tasted food. I give you your liberty. Go with Hermes and return to your mother."

Hermes hurried the girl away. "Come along quickly," he whispered in her ear, "or Hades may change his mind."

In a very short time, they had passed the great gateway and emerged onto the surface of the earth. As they hastened along, how the path grew lush behind them! Wherever Persephone set her foot, there was at once a beautiful flower.

Demeter had returned to her deserted home and was sitting on the doorstep with her torch burning in her hand. She had been idly watching the flame for some time when all at once it flickered and went out.

"What does this mean?" she thought. "This is an enchanted torch. It should keep burning till my daughter comes back."

Lifting her eyes, she was surprised to see a sudden brilliance flashing over the brown and barren fields. ★

"Does the earth disobey me?" exclaimed Demeter indignantly. "It cannot become green until my daughter is returned to my arms!"

"Then open your arms, dear Mother," cried the familiar voice of Persephone, "and take your daughter into them."

Persephone came running and flung herself into her mother's arms. The two women shed a great many tears of joy. When their hearts had grown a little more quiet, Demeter looked anxiously at Persephone and said, "Did you taste any food while you were in Hades' palace?"

"Mother," answered Persephone, "I will tell you the whole truth. Until this very morning not a morsel of food had passed my lips. But today they brought me a pomegranate, and I was tempted just to bite it. The instant I tasted it, Hades and Hermes came into the room. I had not swallowed a morsel—but six of the pomegranate seeds remained in my mouth."

"Ah, unfortunate child and miserable me!" exclaimed Demeter. "For each seed, you must spend one month of every year in Hades' palace. Six months with me, and six in Hades' dominions!"

And the two wept in each other's arms. At last, Persephone said, "I can bear to spend six months in his palace if he will only let me spend the other six with you."

And so, for the next six months, Demeter blessed all the plants of the earth and made them grow. But when Persephone's time was up, the plants withered and died, and a new season settled on the land. This season was called winter. For six long months, the earth waited for Persephone to return. When she did, Demeter blessed the plants once again, and spring came for another joyful stay.

D CONTRADICTIONS

Write the answers to items 1 and 2.

Here's one way to find a contradiction in a passage:

- Assume that what the writer says first is true.
- Read until you find a contradiction.
- Make up an if-then statement that explains the contradiction.

Here's a passage with an underlined statement: *Cape Canaveral is in Florida. Rockets are launched from the Cape, and many people work there. Every year we go to Alabama to visit Cape Canaveral. We love to watch rocket launchings.*

Assume the underlined statement is true. If that statement is true, then it can't be true that Cape Canaveral is in Alabama. Here's how we explain the contradiction: *If Cape Canaveral is in Florida, then it can't be in Alabama.*

Here's another passage. Assume the underlined statement is true. Find the statement that contradicts the underlined statement.

The Camberra family was preparing a Fourth of July picnic. Mr. Camberra was frying chicken. Mrs. Camberra was making sandwiches. The children were packing cookies. They all thought it was a great way to celebrate Thanksgiving.

1. Which statement is a contradiction?
2. Explain the contradiction using an if-then statement.

E VOCABULARY REVIEW

apt
frivolous
indignant
gratifying
lofty
entice

For each item, write the correct word.
1. When you tempt somebody, you ▆▆▆ that person.
2. When you are likely to do something, you are ▆▆▆ to do it.
3. Another word for *satisfying* is ▆▆▆ .
4. When you are angry and insulted, you are ▆▆▆ .

F COMPREHENSION

Write the answers.
1. Why did Hades agree to release Persephone?
2. How did the earth change when Persephone returned?
3. According to the myth of Persephone, why do the seasons change?
4. Why do the seasons really change?
5. Why do you think the Greeks had a myth about the seasons?

G WRITING

The myth of Persephone explains why the seasons change.

Make up a different story that explains why the seasons change. Think about the following questions as you write your story:
- Who are the characters in your story?
- Where and when do they live?
- What happens to those characters?
- How does the story explain why the seasons change?

Make your story at least one hundred words long.

Ⓐ WORD LISTS

1

Hard Words
1. decorate
2. bedstead
3. tolerate
4. climate
5. possession

2

New Vocabulary
1. obliged
2. frail
3. plume
4. wardrobe
5. adorn
6. skylight

Ⓑ VOCABULARY DEFINITIONS

1. **obliged**—When you are *obliged* to do something, you are required to do it.
   - What's another way of saying *She was required to visit Mrs. Jones*?
2. **frail**—Somebody who is *frail* is weak and delicate.
   - What's another way of saying *The leaf was weak and delicate*?
3. **plume**—A *plume* is a large feather. People sometimes wear plumes on hats.
   - What do we call large feathers?
4. **wardrobe**—All the clothes you have are called your *wardrobe.*
   - What is your wardrobe?
5. **adorn**—When you *adorn* something, you decorate it.
   - What's another way of saying *Her hat was decorated with plumes*?
6. **skylight**—A *skylight* is a window in the roof of a house.
   - What is a skylight?

The British Empire

In this lesson, you will begin reading the novel *Sara Crewe*, by Frances Hodgson Burnett. The novel takes place in London around 1880, and the main character is a girl named Sara. She attends a boarding school—a type of school where students live. Students stay at a boarding school all the time except for holidays, when they usually go home.

Sara's father lives in India, where he is a captain in the British Army. At that time, India was a colony in the British Empire. It was one of many colonies around the world that were ruled from London by British kings and queens. The British Army stayed in India to keep control of the colony.

Sara's mother is dead. Because Sara is a frail child who cannot tolerate the hot weather in India, her father decides to send her to boarding school in London. The map below shows the location of India and London.

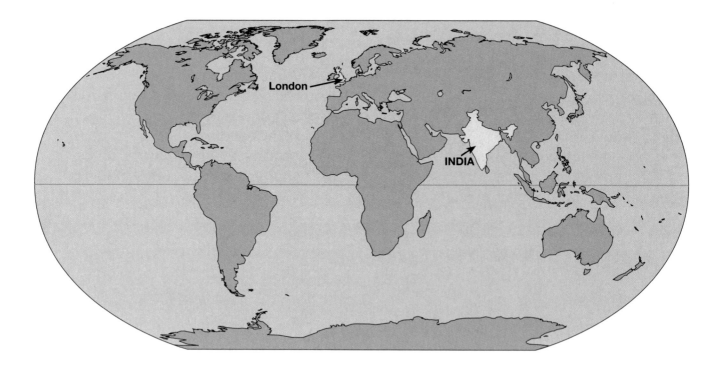

Sara Crewe
*by Frances Hodgson Burnett**

* Adapted for young readers

Chapter 1
Miss Minchin

Focus Question: How did Sara feel about going to boarding school?

Miss Minchin lived in London. Her home was a large, dull, tall one in a large, dull square where all the houses were alike and all the sparrows were alike and where all the door knockers made the same heavy sound. On still days, the door knockers seemed to echo around the square.

On Miss Minchin's door was a brass plate with the following words:

> MISS MINCHIN'S
> BOARDING SCHOOL
> FOR YOUNG LADIES

When Sara Crewe was eight years old, she was brought to Miss Minchin's Boarding School. Her father, Captain Crewe, brought her all the way from India. Her mother had died when she was a baby, and her father had kept Sara with him as long as he could. Then, because the hot Indian climate was bad for Sara's health, he brought her to England to live in Miss Minchin's boarding school. Except for Sara, Captain Crewe did not have a relative in the world, so he was obliged to place her at a boarding school.

Sara was not a pretty child. She was thin, and she had a weird, interesting little face, short black hair, and very large green-gray eyes with heavy black lashes. ◆

When Sara and her father came into the school, Miss Minchin took them into her office and said, "Sara is a beautiful and promising little girl, Captain Crewe. She will be a favorite pupil."

Miss Minchin was tall and had large, cold, fishy eyes and large, cold hands, which seemed fishy, too, because they were so damp. She touched Sara on the forehead, and chills ran down Sara's back as Miss Minchin repeated, "Yes, she will be a favorite pupil, *quite* a favorite pupil."

Captain Crewe was very sad at the thought of parting with his little girl. She was all he had left to remind him of her beautiful mother, whom he had dearly loved. He wanted his daughter to have everything the most fortunate little girl could have, so he took Sara out and bought her many beautiful clothes. ★

The saleswomen in the shops said, "Here is our very latest thing in hats. The plumes are exactly the same as those we sold to Lady Diana Sinclair yesterday." Captain Crewe immediately bought what was offered and paid whatever was asked. The result was that Sara had a most extraordinary wardrobe. Her dresses were silk and velvet. Her hats and bonnets were covered with bows and plumes. Her slips were adorned with real lace. Captain Crewe also bought her a large doll named Emily, whose dresses were as extraordinary as Sara's.

When they had finished shopping, they took a horse-drawn cab back to the school. Then Captain Crewe gave Miss Minchin some money and went away.

For several days, Sara would neither touch the doll nor her breakfast nor her dinner nor her tea and would do nothing but crouch in a small corner by the window and cry. She cried so much that she made herself ill. She was a strange child, with old-fashioned ways and strong feelings. She adored her father and could not believe that London and Miss Minchin were better for her than India. She had already begun to hate Miss Minchin and to think little of Miss Amelia, who was Miss Minchin's younger sister.

E CONTRADICTIONS

Write the answers to items 1–3.

Here's how to find a contradiction in a passage:
- Assume that what the writer says first is true.
- Read until you find a contradiction.
- Make up an if-then statement that explains the contradiction.

There are no underlined statements in the following passage. Read the passage and find a statement that contradicts an earlier statement.

Bert was getting ready for his camping trip. At six in the morning, he started filling his backpack. He put in three shirts, an extra pair of pants, and some socks. When he left a few minutes later, the sunset was turning the sky red. Bert looked forward to his trip.
1. Write the statement you assume to be true.
2. Write the contradiction.
3. Write an if-then statement that explains the contradiction.

F VOCABULARY REVIEW

detain
gratifying
lush
liberty
emerges

For each item, write the correct word.
1. Plants that are growing well are ▬▬ .
2. When something comes out of a place, it ▬▬ from that place.
3. Another word for *freedom* is ▬▬ .

G COMPREHENSION

Write the answers.
1. How did Sara feel about going to boarding school?
2. How is a boarding school different from a regular school?
3. In what ways was Miss Minchin like a fish?
4. Why did Captain Crewe buy Sara such extraordinary clothes?
5. Why did Sara have to leave India?

H WRITING

What kind of school would you rather go to, a boarding school or a regular school?

Write an essay that explains what kind of school you would prefer. Try to answer the following questions:
- In what ways are boarding schools better than regular schools?
- In what ways are regular schools better than boarding schools?
- Which type of school would you prefer? Why?

Make your essay at least fifty words long.

Ⓐ WORD LISTS

1

Hard Words
1. distinguished
2. inherit
3. bedstead

2

New Vocabulary
1. decked out
2. mount
3. distinguished
4. inherit
5. bedstead
6. twitch

Ⓑ VOCABULARY DEFINITIONS

1. **decked out**—When you are *decked out*, you are dressed up.
   - What's another way of saying *The dancers were dressed up in fancy clothes*?
2. **mount**—When you *mount* something, you climb it.
   - What's another way of saying *She climbed the stairs*?
3. **distinguished**—A *distinguished* person is an outstanding person.
   - What's another way of saying *They met an outstanding gentleman*?
4. **inherit**—When you *inherit* things, you receive them from somebody who has died.
   - What's another way of saying *When her father died, she received his fortune*?
5. **bedstead**—A *bedstead* is the frame of a bed.
   - What is the frame of a bed called?
6. **twitch**—A *twitch* is a quick nervous gesture.
   - What is a twitch?

Chapter 2
The Attic

Focus Question: Why did Miss Minchin change her opinion of Sara?

For the first year, Sara was a favorite pupil of Miss Minchin's. When the boarding school girls went walking, two by two, Sara was always decked out in her grandest clothes. Miss Minchin would lead Sara by the hand at the head of the procession. And when the parents of any of the pupils came, Sara was always called into the parlor to meet them. Sara often overheard Miss Minchin saying that Captain Crewe was a distinguished Indian officer and that Sara would someday inherit a great fortune.

Sara hoped her father would leave the army soon and come to live in London. Every time a letter came, she wanted it to say that he was coming and that they were going to live together again.

But about the middle of the third year, when Sara was eleven, a letter came bringing very different news. Because he was not a business man himself, Sara's father had given his bank books to a friend he trusted. His friend had deceived and robbed him. The friend and the money were gone; no one knew exactly where. The shock was so great to Captain Crewe that he lost his strength. He was attacked by jungle fever shortly afterward, and he died, leaving Sara with no one to take care of her.

Miss Minchin's cold and fishy eyes had never looked so cold and fishy as they did when Sara went into the parlor a few days after the letter was received.

Because she was mourning for her father, Sara was wearing a black velvet dress. When she came into the room, she looked like the saddest little figure in the world. The dress was too short and too tight, her face was pale, and her eyes had dark rings around them. She had wrapped her doll, Emily, in a piece of old black velvet, and she held the doll under her arm.

Sara fixed her eyes steadily on Miss Minchin as she slowly advanced into the parlor, clutching her doll.

"Put your doll down!" said Miss Minchin in an unfriendly tone.

"No," said the child, "I won't put her down. I want her with me. She is all I have. She has stayed with me all the time."

Sara's determination made Miss Minchin feel uncomfortable. Miss Minchin decided not to enforce her command. Instead, she looked at Sara as severely as possible.

"You will have no time for dolls in the future," she said. "You will have to work and make yourself useful."

Sara kept her big odd eyes fixed on her teacher and said nothing.

"Everything will be very different

now," Miss Minchin went on. "I sent for you to talk to you and make you understand. Your father is dead. You have no friends. You have no money. You have no home and no one to take care of you." ◆

Sara's pale little face twitched nervously, but her green-gray eyes did not move from Miss Minchin's—and still Sara said nothing.

"What are you staring at?" demanded Miss Minchin sharply. "Are you so stupid that you don't understand what I mean? I tell you that you are quite alone in the world and have no one to do anything for you unless I choose to keep you here."

Miss Minchin could not bear to find herself with a little beggar on her hands.

"Now listen to me," she went on, "and remember what I say. If you work hard and make yourself useful, I shall let you stay here. You are only a child, but you are a sharp child, and you learn things almost without being taught. You speak French very well, and in a year or so, you can begin to help with the younger pupils. By the time you are fifteen, you ought to be able to do that much at least."

"I can speak French better than you," said Sara. "I always spoke it with my father in India." Sara's statement was not at all polite, but it was painfully true because Miss Minchin could not speak French at all. But Miss Minchin was a clever business woman. She knew that this determined child could be very useful to her and save her the trouble of paying large salaries to French teachers.

"Don't be rude, or you will be punished," Miss Minchin cautioned. "You will have to improve your manners if you expect to earn your bread. You are not a favorite pupil now. If you don't please me, and I send you away, you will have no home but the street."

Sara turned away.

"Stay," commanded Miss Minchin. "Don't you intend to thank me?" ★

Sara turned toward her. The nervous twitch came back into her face, and she tried to control it.

"Why should I thank you?" Sara said.

"For my kindness to you," replied Miss Minchin. "For my kindness in giving you a home."

Sara went two or three steps nearer to Miss Minchin. Her thin little chest was heaving up and down, and she spoke in a strange, unchildish voice.

"You are not kind," she said. "You are not kind." And she turned again and went out of the room, leaving Miss Minchin staring after her strange, small figure in stony anger.

The child walked up the staircase, holding tightly to her doll. She meant to go to her bedroom, but at the door she was met by Miss Amelia.

"You are not to go in there," she said. "That is not your room now."

"Where is my room?" asked Sara.

"You are to sleep in the attic."

Sara walked on. She mounted two flights more and reached the door of the attic room. She opened the door and went in, shutting the door behind her. Then she stood against the door and looked around. The room was painted white and had a slanted roof. There was a rusty stove, an iron bedstead, and some odd pieces of worn-out furniture. Under the skylight in the roof, which showed nothing but a piece of dull gray sky, there was a battered old red footstool.

Sara went to the footstool and sat

down. She was unlike other children because she seldom cried anymore. She did not cry now. She laid her doll Emily across her knees and put her face down on the doll and her arms around her. Sara's little head rested on the doll, and she sat there, not saying one word, not making one sound.

D CONTRADICTIONS

Write the answers to items 1–3.

Here's how to find a contradiction in a passage:

- Assume that what the writer says first is true.
- Read until you find a contradiction.
- Make up an if-then statement that explains the contradiction.

There are no underlined statements in the passage below. Read the passage and find a statement that contradicts an earlier statement.

Pine trees stay green all year round. Pine trees are very common, and many forests have nothing but pine trees. Sometimes, pine trees are called evergreens. Pine trees are really beautiful in the fall, when they turn brown. Some people collect pine cones.

1. Write the statement you assume to be true.
2. Write the contradiction.
3. Write an if-then statement that explains the contradiction.

E OUTLINING

Complete the following outline for "Persephone." Copy each main idea; then write three supporting details for each main idea. Use complete sentences.

1. Hades kidnapped Persephone.
2. Demeter looked for Persephone.
3. Persephone had to visit Hades every year.

F VOCABULARY REVIEW

wardrobe
adorn
liberty
detain
frail
obliged
skylight

For each item, write the correct word.
1. When you are required to do something, you are ▮▮▮▮ to do it.
2. Somebody who is weak and delicate is ▮▮▮▮.
3. All the clothes you have are called your ▮▮▮▮.
4. When you decorate something, you ▮▮▮▮ it.

G COMPREHENSION

Write the answers.
1. Why do you think Miss Minchin was nice to Sara at first?
2. Why did Miss Minchin change her opinion of Sara?
3. What do you think of Miss Minchin?
4. How did Sara feel at the end of the chapter?
5. Why do you think Sara didn't cry?

H WRITING

When Miss Minchin found out that Sara's father had died, she might have discussed the matter with Miss Amelia.

Write a conversation between Miss Minchin and Miss Amelia in which they discuss Sara's future. Before writing the conversation, think about the following questions:
- How is Miss Amelia different from Miss Minchin?
- Which person is more powerful?
- Which one is more likely to support Sara?
- How do they reach a decision?

Make your conversation at least fifty words long.

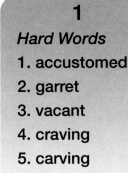 WORD LISTS

1
Hard Words
1. accustomed
2. garret
3. vacant
4. craving
5. carving
6. figurative

2
New Vocabulary
1. accustomed
2. outcast
3. garret
4. vacant
5. discard
6. craving

B VOCABULARY DEFINITIONS

1. **accustomed**—When you are *accustomed* to something, you are used to that thing.
   - What's another way of saying *They were used to fancy parties*?

2. **outcast**—An *outcast* is somebody who is thrown out of a group.
   - What would you call somebody who is thrown out of a team?

3. **garret**—*Garret* is another word for *attic*.
   - What's another way of saying *She lived in the attic*?

4. **vacant**—*Vacant* is another word for *empty*.
   - What's another way of saying *She stared at us with an empty expression*?

5. **discard**—When you *discard* something, you throw it away.
   - What's another way of saying *She wore clothes that had been thrown away*?

6. **craving**—When you have a *craving* for something, you have a great desire for that thing.
   - What's another way of saying *He had a great desire for pickles*?

Chapter 3
Emily

Focus Question: How do Sara's feelings about Emily change in this chapter?

Sara's life changed entirely after she moved into the attic. Sometimes she felt it was another life altogether, the life of some other child. She was sent on errands by Miss Minchin, Miss Amelia, and the cook. Nobody took any notice of her except when they ordered her around. She was often kept busy all day. At night, she would sit in the deserted schoolroom with a pile of books to learn her lessons.

Sara had never been close friends with the other pupils, and her once-fine clothes soon became so shabby that the other pupils began to look on her as an outcast. They were rather dull young people, accustomed to being rich and comfortable. These pupils were suspicious of Sara, her cleverness, her dreary life, and her odd habit of staring at people.

Sara never made any mischief or interfered with anyone. She talked very little, did as she was told, and thought a great deal. Nobody knew, and nobody cared, whether she was unhappy or happy. The only person who might have cared was her doll, Emily, who lived in the attic and slept on the bed at night. Sara thought Emily understood her feelings, even though she was only made of wax. Sara used to talk to her at night.

One of Sara's "pretends" was that Emily was a kind of good witch who could protect her. Poor Sara! Everything was "pretend" with her. She had a strong imagination. There was almost more imagination than there was Sara. Her whole life was made up of imaginings. She imagined and pretended things until she almost believed them. She would not have been surprised at any remarkable thing that could have happened. So she insisted to herself that Emily understood all about her troubles and was really her friend. ◆

"You are the only friend I have in the world," she would say to her. "Why don't you say something? Why don't you speak? Sometimes I am sure you could if you would try. You ought to, because you are the only thing I have. If I were you, I would try. Why don't you?"

Sara's feelings about Emily came from her loneliness. She did not like to admit that her only friend could feel and hear nothing. She wanted to believe that Emily understood and sympathized with her. She wanted to believe that Emily heard her, even though she did not answer.

Sara used to put Emily in a chair sometimes and sit opposite her on the old red footstool. She would stare at Emily and think about her until her eyes grew large with a feeling that was almost like fear. This

feeling was strongest at night when the attic was still and the only sound that could be heard was the occasional squeak of rats in the walls. There were ratholes in the attic, and Sara hated rats and was always glad Emily was with her when she heard their hateful squeak and rush and scratching.

"Emily doesn't speak," Sara used to say to herself. "But I don't speak very often myself. I never answer when I can help it. When people are insulting you, the best thing is to keep quiet. Just look at them and think. Miss Minchin turns pale with rage when I keep quiet. Miss Amelia looks frightened and so do the girls. They know I am stronger than they are because I am strong enough to hold in my rage and they are not—and they say stupid things they wish afterwards they hadn't said. There's nothing so strong as rage except what makes you hold it in—that's stronger. It's a good thing not to answer your enemies. I scarcely ever do. Perhaps Emily is more like me than I am like myself. Perhaps she would rather not answer her friends. She keeps it all in her heart." ★

Although Sara tried to satisfy herself

with these explanations for Emily's silence, she did not find it easy. It was not easy on days when she had been sent here and there, sometimes on long errands, through wind and cold and rain. It was not easy when she came in wet and hungry and was sent out again. It was not easy when she had been given only harsh words and cold looks for thanks. It was not easy when Miss Minchin was in her worst moods. And it was not easy when she had seen the girls sneering at her among themselves and making fun of her poor, outgrown clothes. At these times, Sara did not find Emily quite all that her sore heart needed, for Emily just sat in her little old chair and stared.

One night, Sara came up to the garret cold, hungry, and tired. Emily's stare seemed so vacant and inhuman that Sara lost all control over herself.

"I am suffering!" she said at last.

Emily stared.

"I can't bear this!" said the poor child, trembling. "I know I shall die. I'm cold, I'm wet, and I'm starving to death. I've walked a thousand miles today, and they have done nothing but scold me from morning until night. And because I could not find that last thing they sent me for, they would not give me any supper. Some people laughed at me because my old shoes made me slip down in the mud. I'm covered with mud now. And they laughed! Do you hear?"

She looked at the staring glass eyes and calm wax face. Suddenly, a sort of heartbroken rage seized her. She lifted her hand and knocked Emily off the chair, bursting into a passion of sobbing.

"You are nothing but a doll!" she cried. "Nothing but a doll—doll—doll! You care for nothing. You are stuffed with sawdust. You never had a heart. Nothing could ever make you feel. You are a doll!"

Emily lay on the floor with her legs doubled up over her head and a new flat place on the end of her nose. But she was still calm, even dignified.

Sara hid her face with her arms and sobbed. Some rats in the wall began to fight and bite each other and to squeak and scramble. But Sara was not in the habit of crying. After a while, she stopped, and when she stopped, she looked at Emily, who seemed to be gazing at her around the side of one ankle. Sara bent and picked her up. She was overcome with sadness.

"You can't help being a doll," Sara said with a sigh, "any more than those girls downstairs can help not having any sense. We are not all alike. You are just being yourself."

D FIGURATIVE LANGUAGE

Write the answers for items 1–7.

Sometimes people use figurative language. When people use figurative language, they make statements that are not really accurate but still give a good picture of what they mean.

Here are some examples of figurative language:

- Her eyes were like emeralds.
- He ran like a rocket.
- The voice of Zeus sounded like thunder.

Each statement tells how two things are the same. The first statement says *Her eyes were like emeralds.*

1. How could her eyes and emeralds be the same?

2. Name one way that her eyes and emeralds are not the same.

The second statement says *He ran like a rocket.*

3. How could his running and a rocket be the same?

4. Name one way that his running and a rocket are not the same.

The third statement says *The voice of Zeus sounded like thunder.*

5. What two things are the same in that statement?

6. How could those two things be the same?

7. Name two ways those two things are different.

E VOCABULARY REVIEW

gratifying

gnarled

frail

adorn

wardrobe

lush

For each item, write the correct word.

1. When you decorate something, you ▮▮▮ it.
2. All the clothes you have are called your ▮▮▮.
3. Something that is twisted and full of knots is ▮▮▮.

F COMPREHENSION

Write the answers.
1. Why did the other students look on Sara as an outcast?
2. Why do you think Sara had such a strong imagination?
3. How did Sara's feelings about Emily change in this chapter?
4. Why was it hard for Sara to admit that Emily was just a doll?
5. Why do you think Sara finally admitted that Emily was just a doll?

G WRITING

Sara had a strong imagination. What kinds of things do you imagine?

Write an essay that tells about something you have imagined or dreamed of, such as starring in a movie, being the president, or visiting other planets. Try to answer the following questions:

- What have you imagined or dreamed of doing?
- What happens to you in your dream?
- How does your dream compare to reality?

Make your essay at least fifty words long.

A WORD LISTS

1

Hard Words
1. Bastille
2. dramatic
3. awe
4. gypsies
5. fascinate
6. revolution
7. gesture

2

New Vocabulary
1. gift
2. subscribe
3. dramatic
4. forlorn
5. awe
6. crimson
7. Bastille

B VOCABULARY DEFINITIONS

1. **gift**—One meaning of *gift* is "talent."
   - What's another way of saying *She had a talent for writing poems*?
2. **subscribe**—When you *subscribe* to a magazine, you pay money to the magazine and receive each issue in the mail.
   - How do you subscribe to a magazine?
3. **dramatic**—When speech or gestures are *dramatic,* they produce emotion.
   - What's another way of saying *Her gestures produced emotion*?
4. **forlorn**—When you are *forlorn,* you are sad and lonely.
   - What would you call a child who is sad and lonely?
5. **awe**—When you are *awed* by something, you are amazed by that thing.
   - What's another way of saying *She was amazed by her father's talent*?
6. **crimson**—*Crimson* is a deep red color.
   - What is a deep red color?
7. **Bastille**—The *Bastille* was a prison in Paris, France, where French kings kept prisoners. During the French Revolution in 1789, citizens opposed to the king stormed the Bastille and released the prisoners.
   - What was the Bastille?

Chapter 4
Erma

Focus Question: Why did Sara and Erma decide to become friends?

Most of Miss Minchin's pupils did not like to read or do schoolwork. But Sara, who took her lessons at odd hours, using tattered and discarded books, had a craving for schoolwork. She often envied the other pupils. They had books they never read; she had books that had been discarded. When she had something to read, she did not feel so lonely. She liked romances and history and poetry—she would read anything.

A maid in the school bought newspapers and subscribed to a magazine. The magazine was filled with stories of counts and dukes who always fell in love with gypsies and servant-girls and married them. Sara often did chores for this maid, who would then let her read these romantic stories.

But Sara soon found a better source of books—a friendly pupil named Erma Johnson. Erma's father was a college professor, and he constantly sent Erma valuable and interesting books. But the books were only a source of grief to Erma. Sara had once found her crying over a big package of them. The sight of books always gave Sara a hungry feeling, and she could not help drawing near to them.

"What is the matter with you?" Sara asked.

"My father has sent me some more books," answered Erma woefully, "and he expects me to read them."

"Don't you like reading?" said Sara.

"I hate it!" replied Erma. "And he will ask me questions when he sees me. He will want to know how much I remember. How would you like to have to read all those books?"

"I'd like it better than anything else in the world," said Sara.

Erma wiped her eyes to look at Sara.

Sara returned the look with interest. A sudden plan formed in her sharp mind.

"Look here," she said, "if you'll lend me those books, I'll read them first, and then I can help you read them."

"Do you think you could?" said Erma.

"I know I could," answered Sara. "I like to read, and I always remember. I'll take care of the books, too. When I give them back to you, they will look just as new as they do now."

Erma put her handkerchief in her pocket.

"If you'll do that," she said, "and if you'll help me learn, I'll give you—I'll give you some money."

"I don't want your money," said Sara. "I want your books—I want them." And her eyes grew big and strange.

"Then take them," said Erma.

Sara picked up the books and marched off with them. The next day, she brought one back and helped Erma understand it. ◆

After that day, Erma always handed her books over to Sara, and Sara would carry them to her garret and study them.

After she had read each book, she would return it and help Erma. Sara had a gift for making things interesting. Her imagination helped her make everything sound like a story. Sara spoke so well that Erma gained more information about her books than if she had read them three times over. When Sara sat down by her and helped her read a story about travel or history, she made the travelers and historical people seem real. Sometimes, Erma would look at Sara's dramatic gestures, her thin cheeks, and her shining, odd eyes with amazement.

"It sounds nicer than it seems in the book," she would say. "I never cared about Henry the Eighth before, and I always hated the French Revolution. But you make it seem like a story."

"It is a story," Sara would answer. "They are all stories. Everything is a story—everything in this world. You are a story. I am a story. Miss Minchin is a story. You can make a story out of anything, even Emily."

"'Who is Emily?"

"Emily is . . . a person . . . I know," Sara replied.

"Do you like her?"

"Yes, I do," said Sara.

Erma examined Sara's strange little face and figure again. Sara did look odd. She was wearing a faded blue skirt, which barely covered her knees; a scratchy brown cloth shirt; and a pair of worn, olive-green stockings. Yet Erma was slowly beginning to admire the girl. Sara was thin and forlorn, but she could read and remember and tell you things so they did not tire you out. She could speak French and was learning German. Erma could not help staring at her and feeling interested. ★

"Do you like me?" said Erma, finally, at the end of her examination.

"Of course," answered Sara. "I like you because you are kind, and you let me read your books, and you don't make fun of me as the other girls do."

"I like you too, Sara," said Erma.

"Let's be best friends."

Sara agreed immediately, and she felt herself smiling for the first time in months.

"Sara," Erma said, "how can you stand to live in the attic?"

"If I pretend it's different, I can stand it," Sara answered. "I pretend it's a place in a story."

Sara spoke slowly. Her imagination was beginning to work for her.

"Other people have lived in worse places," she went on. "Think of the prisoners in the Tower of London. Think of the people in the Bastille!"

"The Bastille," whispered Erma, watching Sara and beginning to be fascinated. She remembered Sara's stories of the French Revolution.

A glow came into Sara's eyes.

"Yes," Sara said, "that will be a good place to pretend about. I am a prisoner in the Bastille, and Miss Minchin is the jailer."

Erma was awed.

"Maybe I will creep up there, whenever it is safe, and visit with you. Then it will seem as if we were more 'best friends' than ever."

"Yes," answered Sara, nodding. "That would be wonderful."

D FIGURATIVE LANGUAGE

Write the answers for items 1–7.

Sometimes people use figurative language. When people use figurative language, they make statements that are not really accurate but still give a good picture of what they mean.

Here are some examples of figurative language:

- Joan was like a leaf.
- Persephone was like a sunbeam.
- Miss Minchin was like a fish.

Each statement tells how two things are the same. The first statement says *Joan was like a leaf.*

1. How could Joan and a leaf be the same?

2. Name two ways that Joan and a leaf are not the same.

The second statement says *Persephone was like a sunbeam.*

3. How could Persephone and a sunbeam be the same?

4. Name two ways that Persephone and a sunbeam are not the same.

The third statement says *Miss Minchin was like a fish.*

5. What two things are the same in this statement?

6. How could those two things be the same?

7. Name two ways those two things are different.

E VOCABULARY REVIEW

craving
accustomed
liberty
wardrobe
frail
inherit
distinguished
outcast
discard
vacant

For each item, write the correct word.

1. An outstanding person is a ▮▮▮▮ person.
2. When you have a great desire for something, you have a ▮▮▮▮ for that thing.
3. Another word for *empty* is ▮▮▮▮.
4. Somebody who is thrown out of a group is an ▮▮▮▮.
5. When you are used to something, you are ▮▮▮▮ to that thing.
6. When you throw something away, you ▮▮▮▮ it.
7. When you receive things from somebody who has died, you ▮▮▮▮ those things.

F COMPREHENSION

Write the answers.
1. Why did Sara and Erma decide to become friends?
2. What was Sara's plan for helping Erma with her reading?
3. Why do you think Sara thought everything was a story?
4. How was the attic like the Bastille?
5. How was Miss Minchin like a jailer?

G WRITING

Do you agree with Sara that everything is a story?

Write an essay that explains what you think. Try to answer the following questions:
- What are stories?
- What things in real life are like stories?
- What things in real life are not like stories?
- Do you think everything is a story? Why or why not?

Make your essay at least fifty words long.

A WORD LIST

1

Word Practice

1. fleecy
2. coral
3. sooty
4. quilt
5. corral

B VOCABULARY REVIEW

subscribe
inherit
dramatic
awed
forlorn
distinguished
twitch

For each item, say the correct word.

1. Somebody who is sad and lonely is _____.
2. When you are amazed by something, you are _____ by that thing.
3. When you receive each issue of a magazine in the mail, you _____ to the magazine.
4. Speech or gestures that create emotion are _____.
5. An outstanding person is a _____ person.

Chapter 5
The Sparrow

Focus Question: Why did Sara like the attic?

There were fine sunsets, even in London, but Sara could see only parts of them between the chimneys and over the roofs. From the kitchen windows, she could not see the sunsets at all. She could only guess the sun was setting because the bricks looked warm and the clouds looked rosy or yellow for a while.

There was, however, one place from which she could see all the splendor of the sunsets—the piles of red or gold clouds in the west or the purple ones edged with dazzling brightness or the fleecy ones tinged with rose and looking like flights of pink doves. She could see all this from the garret window.

When the streets outside began to glow in an enchanted way and to look wonderful in spite of their sooty trees and fences, Sara knew something was going on in the sky. When it was possible to leave the kitchen without being missed, she always stole away and crept up to the attic. Then she would climb on an old table and get her head and body as far out of the window as possible. When she had accomplished this, she always drew a long breath and looked all around her. It seemed as if she had all the sky and the world to herself.

Generally, the windows were closed in the other attics, but even if they were propped open, no one ever seemed to look out of them or come near them. There Sara would stand, sometimes turning her face upward to the blue that seemed so friendly and near—just like a ceiling—sometimes watching the west and all the wonderful things that happened there. The clouds would melt or drift or slowly change to pink or crimson or purple. Sometimes they looked like islands or great mountains; sometimes like dark cliffs jutting into strange, lost seas; sometimes like slender strips of wonderful lands. There were places in the clouds where it seemed that one could run or climb or stand and wait to see what was coming next—until, perhaps, one could float away. At least it seemed so to Sara, and nothing had ever been quite so beautiful to her as the things she saw as she stood on the table with her body half out of the skylight. The sparrows always twittered softly on the roof when these marvels were going on. ◆

One evening, soon after Sara and Erma had become best friends, Sara was watching a particularly beautiful sunset. She was so enchanted that several moments went by before she realized someone was

knocking on her door. Sara rushed to open the door—and there was Erma.

"Quick!" Sara said. "Come see the sunset."

A moment later, both girls were standing on the table and looking out the window.

The sky seemed so much nearer than it did from the street that Erma was enchanted. From the attic window, among the chimneys, the things happening in the world below seemed almost unreal. The girls could scarcely believe in the existence of Miss Minchin and Miss Amelia and the schoolroom. The roll of wagon wheels in the street seemed like a sound from another world.

"Oh, Sara!" cried Erma. "I like this attic—I like it! It is nicer than downstairs!"

"Look at that sparrow," whispered Sara. "I wish I had some crumbs to throw to him."

"I have some," said Erma. "I have part of a bun in my pocket. I bought it yesterday, and I saved a bit."

When they threw out a few crumbs, the sparrow jumped and flew away to a nearby chimney top. He was evidently startled by the unexpected gift. But when Erma remained quite still and Sara chirped very softly—almost as if she were a sparrow herself—the bird became less alarmed. He put his head on one side and, from his perch on the chimney, looked down at the crumbs with twinkling eyes.

"Will he come?" whispered Erma.

"His eyes look as if he would," Sara whispered back. "He is thinking and thinking whether he dare. Yes, he will! Yes, he is coming!"

The sparrow flew down and hopped toward the crumbs. But he stopped a few inches away from them, putting his head on one side again as if wondering if Sara and Erma might turn out to be big cats and jump on him. At last he hopped nearer and nearer, darted at the biggest crumb with a lightning peck, seized it, and carried it away to the other side of his chimney.

"Now he knows," said Sara. "And he will come back for the others."

He did come back and even brought a friend. The friend went away and brought a relative, and between them, they made a hearty meal from the crumbs. Every now and then, a bird would put his head on one side and examine Sara and Erma. Both girls were delighted. ★

When the sunset was finally over, Sara showed Erma around the room. "It is so little and so high above everything," Sara said, "that it is almost like a nest in a tree. The slanting ceiling is so funny. See, you can scarcely stand up at this end of the room. When the morning begins, I can lie in bed and look right up into the sky through the window. It is a square patch of light. If the sun is going to shine, little pink clouds float about, and I feel as if I could touch them. If it rains, the drops patter and patter as if they were saying something. If there are stars, I can lie and try to count how many go into the patch. And just look at that tiny, rusty stove in the corner. If it were polished and had a fire in it, just think how nice it would be. You see, it's really a beautiful little room."

Sara walked around the small room, making gestures that described all the beauties she was making herself see. She made Erma see them, too. Erma could always believe in the things Sara made pictures of.

"You see," Sara went on, "there could be a thick, soft blue Indian rug on the floor. And in that corner there could be a soft little sofa, with cushions to curl up on. Just over it could be a shelf full of books so one could reach them easily. There could be a fur rug before the fire and hangings and pictures on the wall to cover up the cracks. The pictures would have to be little, but they could be beautiful. And there could be a lamp with a deep rose-colored shade, and a table in the middle. It could be beautiful. Perhaps we could coax the sparrows until we made such friends with them they would come and peck at the window and ask to be let in."

"Oh, Sara!" said Erma. "It really could be beautiful."

When Erma had gone downstairs again, Sara stood in the middle of the room and looked about her. The enchantment of her imaginings had died away. The bed was hard and covered with its dingy quilt. The wall showed its broken patches, the floor was cold and bare, the stove was broken and rusty, and the battered footstool was tilted sideways. Sara sat down on the footstool for a few minutes and let her head drop into her hands. Erma had come and gone away again, and that made things seem a little worse—just as prisoners feel a little lonelier after visitors come and go, leaving them behind.

"It's a lonely place," Sara said. "Sometimes it's the loneliest place in the world."

D FIGURATIVE LANGUAGE

Write the answers.

The advertising man was like a sandwich.

1. Name two things that are the same in that statement.
2. How could those two things be the same?
3. Name two ways those two things are different.

His feet felt like lead.

4. Name two things that are the same in that statement.
5. How could those two things be the same?
6. Name two ways those two things are different.

E MAIN IDEA

Write the main idea and three supporting details for the following paragraph.

"You see," Sara went on, "the room really could be beautiful. There could be a thick, soft blue Indian rug on the floor. And in that corner there could be a soft little sofa, with cushions to curl up on. Just over it could be a shelf full of books so one could reach them easily. There could be a fur rug before the fire and hangings and pictures on the walls to cover up the cracks."

F COMPREHENSION

Write the answers.

1. Why did Sara like the attic?
2. When Sara and Erma were looking out the window, the story says, "The things happening in the world below seemed almost unreal." Why would those events seem unreal?
3. Why do you think Sara imagined what the attic could be like?
4. When Sara described what the attic could be like, why did Erma see what Sara described?
5. Why do you think Sara's mood changed after Erma left?

G WRITING

How would you like to change the room you're in right now?

Look carefully at the room you're in right now, whether it's your classroom, your bedroom, or some other place. Then imagine how you would change the room. Write an essay that describes the changes you would make. Try to answer the following questions:

• What does the room look like now?
• What changes would you make?

Make your essay at least sixty words long.

Ⓐ WORD LISTS

1
Word Practice
1. corral
2. coral
3. palace
4. place
5. rouse

2
New Vocabulary
1. inclined
2. horrid
3. shuffle

Ⓑ VOCABULARY DEFINITIONS

1. **inclined**—When you are *inclined* to do something, you have a tendency to do it. A person who has a tendency to talk loudly is *inclined* to talk loudly.
   - What's another way of saying *She had a tendency to wake early*?

2. **horrid**—Something that is *horrid* is horrible or disgusting.
   - What's another way of saying *The bully had a disgusting grin*?
3. **shuffle**—When you *shuffle,* you walk slowly and drag your feet.
   - What's another way of saying *The tired girl walked slowly across the room*?

Chapter 6
Melvin

Focus Question: How did Sara make friends with Melvin?

Sara was still sitting on the footstool when her attention was attracted by a slight sound near her. She lifted her head to see where it came from. If she had been a nervous child, she would have left her seat in a great hurry when she identified the source of the sound. A large male rat was sitting on his hind quarters and sniffing the air in an interested manner. Some of Erma's crumbs had dropped onto the floor, and their scent had drawn him out of his hole.

The rat looked so much like a gray-whiskered dwarf that Sara was rather fascinated. He looked at her with his bright eyes as if he were asking a question. A strange thought came into Sara's mind.

"It must be rather hard to be a rat," she observed. "Nobody likes you. People jump and run away and scream out, 'Oh, a horrid rat!' I shouldn't like people to scream and jump and say, 'Oh, a horrid Sara!' the moment they saw me. It's so different to be a sparrow. But nobody asked this rat if he wanted to be a rat when he was made. Nobody said, 'Wouldn't you rather be a sparrow?'"

She had sat so quietly that the rat had begun to gather courage. He was very much afraid of her, but perhaps his heart told him she was not a thing that pounced.

The rat was very hungry. He had a wife and a large family in the wall, and they had not eaten for several days. He had left the children crying bitterly and felt he would take a risk for a few crumbs, so he cautiously dropped onto his feet.

"Come on," said Sara, "I'm not a trap. You can have them, poor thing! Prisoners in the Bastille used to make friends with rats. Suppose I make friends with you?" ◆

How it is that animals understand things I do not know, but it is certain that they do understand. Perhaps there is a language that is not made of words, and everything in the world understands it. But whatever the reason, the rat knew from that moment that he was safe, even though he was a rat. He knew that this young girl sitting on the red footstool would not jump up and terrify him with wild, sharp noises or throw heavy objects at him.

He was really a very nice rat and did not mean the least harm. When he had stood on his hind legs and sniffed the air, with his bright eyes fixed on Sara, he had hoped she would understand this. When something inside him told him that Sara would not hurt him, he went softly toward the crumbs and began to eat them. As he ate, he glanced every now and then

at Sara, just as the sparrows had done, and his expression touched her heart.

Sara sat and watched him without making any movement. One crumb was much larger than the others—in fact, it could scarcely be called a crumb. The rat wanted that piece very much, but it lay quite near the footstool, and he was still rather timid.

"I believe he wants it to carry to his family in the wall," Sara thought. "If I do not stir at all, perhaps he will come and get it."

Sara scarcely allowed herself to breathe, she was so deeply interested. The rat shuffled a little nearer and ate a few more crumbs; then he stopped and sniffed delicately. He gave a side glance at Sara and darted at the piece of bun just as the sparrow had earlier. The instant he had the bun, he fled back to the wall, slipped down a crack, and was gone. ★

"I knew he wanted it for his children," said Sara. "I do believe I could make friends with him."

A week or so afterward, Erma was able to sneak up to the attic again. She tapped on the door with the tips of her fingers, but Sara did not answer. There was, indeed, such a silence in the room that Erma wondered if Sara was asleep. Then, to her surprise, she heard Sara utter a low little laugh and speak softly to someone.

"There," Erma heard her say. "Take it and go home, Melvin. Go home to your wife."

Then Sara opened the door, and when she did so, she found Erma standing there with alarmed eyes.

"Who . . . who are you talking to, Sara?" Erma gasped.

Sara looked as if something pleased and amused her. Then she answered, "You must promise not to be frightened, not to scream the least bit, or I can't tell you."

Erma felt almost inclined to scream on the spot, but she managed to control herself. She looked all round the attic and saw no one. And yet Sara had certainly been speaking to someone. She thought of ghosts.

"Is it—something that will frighten me?" Erma asked timidly.

"Some people are afraid of them," said Sara. "I was at first—but I am not now."

"Was it—a ghost?" asked Erma nervously.

"No," said Sara, laughing. "It was my rat."

Erma made one bound and landed in the middle of the dingy little bed. She tucked her feet under her nightgown and her red shawl. She did not scream, but she gasped with fright.

"Oh! Oh!" she cried under her breath. "A rat! A rat!"

"I was afraid you would be frightened," said Sara. "But you needn't be. I am making him tame. He actually knows me and comes out when I call him. Are you too frightened to want to see him?"

Erma did not answer.

D FIGURATIVE LANGUAGE

Write the answers.

Odysseus was like an eagle.

1. Name two things that are the same in that statement.
2. How could those two things be the same?
3. Name two ways those two things are different.

The mesa is like a table.

4. Name two things that are the same in that statement.
5. How could those two things be the same?
6. Name two ways those two things are different.

E VOCABULARY REVIEW

awed

dramatic

skeptical

discard

forlorn

wardrobe

frail

inherit

outcast

For each item, write the correct word.

1. Speech or gestures that create emotion are ▉▉▉.
2. When you are suspicious about something, you are ▉▉▉ about that thing.
3. Somebody who is thrown out of a group is an ▉▉▉.
4. When you are amazed by something, you are ▉▉▉ by that thing.
5. Someone who is sad and lonely is ▉▉▉.
6. When you throw away something, you ▉▉▉ that thing.

F COMPREHENSION

Write the answers.
1. How did Sara make friends with Melvin?
2. Why do you think Sara made friends with Melvin?
3. What did Sara mean when she said, "Nobody asked this rat if he wanted to be a rat when he was made"?
4. How did Erma feel when Sara told her about the rat?
5. How do you feel about rats? Explain your answer.

G WRITING

How well do you think people and animals communicate?

Write an essay that explains what you think. Try to answer the following questions:

- How well do different animals understand what people say or want?
- How well do people understand what animals say or want?
- How could people and animals communicate better?

Make your essay at least sixty words long.

43

A WORD LISTS

1
Hard Words
1. impudent
2. challenging
3. jostled
4. absurd
5. devour
6. simile

2
Word Practice
1. unchildish
2. enraged
3. breathlessly
4. apologize

3
New Vocabulary
1. challenging
2. impudent
3. smarting
4. absurd

B VOCABULARY DEFINITIONS

1. **challenging**—*Challenging* is another word for *difficult.*
   • What's another way of saying *Learning another language is difficult*?

2. **impudent**—Somebody who is *impudent* is rude and bold.
   • What's another way of saying *His remark was rude and bold*?

3. **smarting**—When something is *smarting,* it is painful or stinging.
   • What's another way of saying *Her cheek was stinging from the blow she received*?

4. **absurd**—*Absurd* is another word for *ridiculous.*
   • What's another way of saying *The captain made ridiculous demands*?

Chapter 7
The Princess

Focus Question: Why did Sara pretend to be a princess?

Erma was so alarmed by Sara's rat that she huddled on the bed and tucked up her feet. But the sight of Sara's calmness as she told the story of Melvin's first appearance began to rouse Erma's curiosity. She leaned forward over the edge of the bed and watched Sara kneel down by the hole in the wall. "He—he won't run out quickly and jump on the bed, will he?" Erma said.

"No," answered Sara. "He's as polite as we are. He is just like a person. Now watch!"

Sara began to make a low, whistling sound—so low and coaxing that it could only have been heard in entire stillness. She did it several times. Erma thought Sara looked as if she were working a spell. At last, a gray-whiskered, bright-eyed head peeped out of the hole. Sara had some crumbs in her hand. She dropped them, and Melvin came quietly forth and ate them. He then took a large piece and carried it back to his home.

"You see," said Sara, "that piece is for his wife and children. He is very nice. He only eats the little bits. After he goes back I can always hear his family squeaking for joy. There are three kinds of squeaks. One kind is the children's, and one is his wife's, and one is Melvin's own."

Erma began to laugh.

"Oh, Sara," she said. "You are strange—but you are nice.

"I know I am strange," admitted Sara cheerfully, "and I try to be nice." She rubbed her forehead with her hand, and a puzzled tender look came into her face. "My father always laughed at me," she said, "but I liked it. He thought I was strange, but he liked me to make up things. I . . . I can't help making up things. If I didn't, I don't believe I could live." She paused and glanced round the attic. "I'm sure I couldn't live here," she added in a low voice.

Erma was interested, as she always was. "When you talk about things," she said, "they seem to become real. You talk about Melvin as if he were a person."

"He is a person," said Sara. "He gets hungry and frightened, just as we do, and he is married and has children. How do we know he doesn't think things, just as we do? His eyes look as if he were a person. That's why I gave him a name."

Sara sat down on the floor.

"Besides," she continued, "he is a Bastille rat sent to be my friend. I can always get a bit of bread the cook has thrown away, and it is quite enough to support him."

Erma asked eagerly, "Do you always pretend the attic is the Bastille?"

"Nearly always," answered Sara. "Sometimes I try to pretend it is another kind of place, but the Bastille is generally easiest—particularly when it is cold."

Erma had almost forgotten that she was like an escaped prisoner herself. She could not remain in the Bastille all night, so she sneaked downstairs again and crept back into her deserted bed.

That was the last time Sara ever saw Erma, for the very next day, Erma's father came and took her to another school. ◆

Sara was crushed. She had lost her best friend.

Because she needed to lift her spirits, Sara began to pretend she was a princess. She went about the house with an expression on her face that annoyed Miss Minchin. It seemed as if Sara scarcely heard the insulting things said to her or, if she heard them, did not care for them at all.

One day, Miss Minchin found Sara's odd, unchildish eyes fixed on her with something like a proud smile in them. She did not know that Sara was saying to herself, "You don't know that you are looking at a princess. If I chose to, I could wave my hand and order you to prison. I only spare you because I am a princess and you are a poor, stupid thing who doesn't know any better."

These thoughts pleased Sara, and she found comfort in them.

"A princess must be polite," she said to herself. So when the servants were rude and ordered her about, Sara would hold her head high and reply to them in a way that made them stare at her.

"I am a princess in rags and tatters," she would think, "but I am a princess inside.

It would be easy to be a princess if I wore a crown, but it is more challenging to be one all the time when no one knows it."

Once when such thoughts were passing through her mind, the look in Sara's eyes so enraged Miss Minchin that she flew at Sara and slapped her. This occurred in the schoolroom.

Sara awakened from her dream, started a little, and then broke into a laugh.

"What are you laughing at, you bold, impudent child!" exclaimed Miss Minchin. ★

It took Sara a few seconds to remember she was a princess. Her cheek was red and smarting from the blow she had received.

"I was thinking," she said.

"Apologize," said Miss Minchin.

"I will apologize for laughing, if it was rude," said Sara, "but I won't apologize for thinking."

"What were you thinking?" demanded Miss Minchin. "How dare you think!"

All the girls looked up from their books to listen. It always interested them when Miss Minchin flew at Sara because Sara always said something strange and never seemed frightened. She was not frightened now, though her cheek was scarlet and her eyes were as bright as stars.

"I was thinking," she answered gravely and quite politely, "that you did not know what you were doing."

"That I did not know what I was doing!" Miss Minchin gasped.

"Yes," said Sara, "and I was thinking what would happen if I were a princess and you slapped me—what I would do to you. If I were a princess, you would never dare to hit me. I was thinking how surprised and frightened you would be if you suddenly found out."

Sara had the imagined picture so clearly before her eyes that her speech had an effect on Miss Minchin. It almost seemed for the moment to Miss Minchin's narrow mind that there must be some real power behind this brave girl.

"Go to your room this instant!" cried Miss Minchin breathlessly. "Leave the schoolroom. Attend to your lessons, young ladies."

Sara made a little bow.

"Excuse me for laughing, if it was impolite," she said and walked out of the room, leaving Miss Minchin in a rage and the girls whispering to each other over their books.

"I shouldn't be at all surprised if she did turn out to be a princess," said one of them. "Suppose she should!"

D SIMILES

Write the answers to items 1–6.

Here are some examples of figurative language:
- Her eyes were like emeralds.
- His feet were like lead.
- The mesa is like a table.

All those examples are called *similes.* Similes tell how two things are the same. Many similes contain the word *like.*

In the next column are some more similes. Complete the items for each simile.

The ship's sails were like a swan's wings.
1. What two things are the same in that simile?
2. How could those two things be the same?
3. Name two ways those things are different.

The lights of the ship were like two great eyes.
4. What two things are the same in that simile?
5. How could those things be the same?
6. Name two ways those things are different.

E COMPREHENSION

Write the answers.
1. In what ways is Melvin like a person?
2. Why did Sara pretend to be a princess?
3. How did Sara's behavior change when she pretended she was a princess?
4. What did Sara mean when she said, "I am a princess in rags and tatters"?
5. Why is it easier to be a princess if you wear a crown than if you wear rags?

F WRITING

Sara pretended to be a princess. What kind of person would you like to be?

Write an essay that explains what you would like to be. Try to answer the following questions:
- What kind of person would you like to be?
- Why are you interested in that kind of person?
- What do you think that person's life is like?
- How is that person's life different from yours?

Make your essay at least sixty words long.

Ⓐ WORD LISTS

1
Word Practice
1. tunic
2. tonic
3. simile
4. sized
5. seized
6. desperate

2
New Vocabulary
1. shock
2. bedraggled
3. jostled

Ⓑ VOCABULARY REVIEW

1. **shock**—A thick bunch of hair or other material is sometimes called a *shock.*
   - What's another way of saying *She had a thick bunch of blond hair*?
2. **bedraggled**—When something is *bedraggled,* it is muddy and limp.
   - What's another way of saying *The bird's feathers were muddy and limp*?

3. **jostled**—When you are *jostled,* you are pushed and shoved.
   - What's another way of saying *The boy was pushed and shoved by the crowd*?

Chapter 8
The Beggar Girl

Focus Question: Why did Sara decide to help the beggar girl?

After Sara was sent to her room that afternoon, she had a chance to prove whether she really was a princess. It was a dreadful afternoon. For several days, it had rained continuously, and the streets were chilly and sloppy. There was mud everywhere—sticky London mud—and over everything was a layer of fog and drizzle. Of course, there were several long and tiresome errands to be done—there always were on days like this—and Sara was sent out again and again, until her shabby clothes were soaked. The old feathers on her hat were bedraggled, and her worn-out shoes were so wet they could not hold any more water. She had also been deprived of her dinner because Miss Minchin wished to punish her.

Sara was so cold and hungry and tired as she ran her errands that her little face had a pinched look. Now and then some kindhearted person passing her in the crowded streets glanced at her with sympathy. But Sara did not notice them. She hurried on, trying to comfort herself in that strange way of hers—by pretending. But this time pretending was harder than she had ever found it, and once or twice she thought it almost made her colder and hungrier. But she kept on.

"Suppose I had dry clothes on," she thought. "Suppose I had good shoes and a long, thick coat and stockings and a whole umbrella. And suppose . . . suppose, just when I was near a baker's shop that sells hot buns, I should find a six-penny piece that belonged to nobody. Suppose, if I did, I should go into the shop and buy six of the hottest buns and should eat them all without stopping."

Then an odd thing happened to Sara. She had to cross the street, and the mud was so dreadful that she almost had to wade through it. She picked her way as carefully as she could, looking down at her feet to do so. As she was looking down, she saw something shining in the gutter. A piece of silver—a tiny piece trodden upon by many feet, but still with enough spirit left to shine a little. Not quite a six-penny piece, but the next thing to it—a four-penny piece! In one second, it was in her cold little hand.

"Oh," she gasped. "It is true!" ◆

And then she looked straight before her at the shop directly facing her. It was a baker's shop. A cheerful, stout, motherly woman with rosy cheeks was just putting into the window a tray of delicious hot buns—large, plump, shiny buns, with raisins in them.

It almost made Sara feel faint for a few seconds—the sight of the buns and the delightful odors of warm bread floating up through the baker's cellar window.

Sara knew she could use the little piece of money. It had been lying in the mud for some time, and its owner was completely lost in the streams of passing people who crowded and jostled each other all through the day.

"But I'll go and ask the baker woman if she has lost a piece of money," she said to herself, rather faintly.

So she crossed the pavement and put her wet foot on the step of the shop. As she did so, she saw something that made her stop.

It was a little girl who was not much more than a bundle of rags. Her small, bare, red, and muddy feet peeped out of rags. Above the rags appeared a shock of tangled hair and a dirty face with big, hollow, hungry eyes.

Sara knew they were hungry eyes the moment she saw them, and she felt a sudden sympathy. She said to herself, "She is hungrier than I am."

The beggar girl stared up at Sara and shuffled herself aside a little to give Sara more room. She was used to giving room to everybody. The girl knew that if a police officer saw her, he would tell her to "move on."

Sara clutched her little four-penny piece and hesitated a few seconds. Then she spoke to the girl.

"Are you hungry?" she asked.

The girl shuffled herself and her rags a little more.

"Sure," she said in a hoarse voice. "Sure."

"Haven't you had any dinner?" said Sara.

"No dinner," more hoarsely still and with more shuffling, "nor breakfast—nor supper—nor nothing."

"Since when?" asked Sara.

"Dunno. Never got nothing today—nowhere. I've begged and begged."

Just to look at her made Sara more hungry and faint. But those strange thoughts were at work in her brain, and she was talking to herself, though she was sick at heart.

"If I'm a princess," Sara was saying, "I have to act like a princess. A princess always shares if she meets somebody poorer and hungrier. She always shares. Buns are a penny each. If it had only been a sixpenny piece! I could have eaten six. It won't be enough for either of us, but it will be better than nothing."

"Wait a minute," Sara said to the beggar girl. Then Sara went into the shop, which was warm and smelled delightful. The woman was just going to put more hot buns in the window. ★

"If you please," said Sara, "have you lost a silver four-penny piece?" And she held out the little piece of money.

The woman looked at it and at her—at her intense little face and bedraggled, once-fine clothes.

"Bless us, no," she answered. "Did you find it?"

"In the gutter," said Sara.

"Keep it then," said the woman. "It may have been there a week, and goodness knows who lost it. You could never find out."

"I know that," said Sara, "but I thought I'd ask you."

"Not many would," said the woman, looking puzzled and interested and good-natured all at once. "Do you want to buy

something?" she added as she saw Sara glance toward the buns.

"Four buns, if you please," said Sara, "those at a penny each."

The woman went to the window and put some in a paper bag. Sara noticed that she put in six.

"I said four, if you please," she explained. "I have only the four-penny piece."

"I'll throw in two more," said the woman, with her good-natured look. "I dare say you can eat them sometime. Aren't you hungry?"

A mist of tears rose before Sara's eyes.

"Yes," she answered. "I am very hungry, and I am much obliged to you for your kindness, and," she was going to add, "there is a child outside who is hungrier than I am." But just at that moment, two or three customers came in at once and each one seemed in a hurry, so Sara could only thank the woman again and go out.

The girl was still huddled up on the corner of the steps. She looked frightful in her wet and dirty rags, and she was staring straight before her with a look of suffering. Sara saw her suddenly draw the back of her roughened, dirty hand across her eyes to rub away the tears that forced their way from under her lids.

Sara opened the paper bag and took out one of the hot buns, which had already warmed her cold hands a little.

"See," she said, putting the bun on the girl's ragged lap, "that is nice and hot. Eat it, and you will not be so hungry."

The child stared up at her; then she snatched up the bun and began to cram it into her mouth with great wolfish bites.

"Oh, my! Oh, my!" Sara heard her say hoarsely, in wild delight.

Sara took out three more buns and put them down.

"She is hungrier than I am," Sara said to herself. "She's starving." But her hand trembled when she put down the fourth bun. "I'm not starving," Sara said—and she put down the fifth.

The little starving beggar girl was still snatching and devouring when Sara turned away. The girl was too hungry to give any thanks.

"Goodbye," said Sara.

⒟ VOCABULARY REVIEW

awed
outcast
distinguished
skeptical
smarting
inclined
absurd
impudent

For each item, write the correct word.
1. An outstanding person is a ▆▆▆ person.
2. Something that is ridiculous is ▆▆▆.
3. Something that is stinging is ▆▆▆.
4. Somebody who is rude and bold is ▆▆▆.
5. When you have a tendency to do something, you are ▆▆▆ to do that thing.

E SIMILES

Write the answers.

The miner's hands looked like lumps of coal.

1. What two things are the same in that simile?
2. How could those things be the same?
3. Name two ways those things are different.

The sun was like a bloodstain.

4. What two things are the same in that simile?
5. How could those things be the same?
6. Name two ways those things are different.

F COMPREHENSION

Write the answers.

1. Why do you think pretending was so hard for Sara in this chapter?
2. Describe the beggar girl's appearance.
3. Why did Sara decide to help the beggar girl?
4. How were Sara and the beggar girl alike?
5. How were Sara and the beggar girl different?

G WRITING

Do you think Sara did the right thing when she gave most of the buns to the beggar girl?

Write an essay that explains what you think. Try to answer the following questions:

- What reasons did Sara have for giving the buns to the beggar girl?
- What reasons did Sara have for keeping the buns for herself?
- What else could Sara have done with the buns?
- What would you have done?
- What was the right thing to do?

Make your essay at least sixty words long.

Ⓐ WORD LISTS

1

Hard Words
1. luxurious
2. vague
3. luscious
4. pantry
5. exaggeration
6. Lascar

2

New Vocabulary
1. ponder
2. stroller
3. liver
4. tropical
5. luxurious
6. grate

Ⓑ VOCABULARY DEFINITIONS

1. **ponder**—When you *ponder* something, you think about it.
   - What's another way of saying *She thought about her future*?
2. **stroller**—A *stroller* is a small carriage for babies and young children.
   - What is a stroller?
3. **liver**—Your *liver* is an organ in your body that keeps your blood healthy.
   - What does your liver do?
4. **tropical**—Warm areas of the earth where plants grow year-round are called *tropical.* Plants that come from these areas are called *tropical* plants.
   - What happens to plants in tropical areas?

5. **luxurious**—When something is *luxurious,* it is fine and elegant.
   - What's another way of saying *His apartment was fine and elegant*?
6. **grate**—A *grate* is a frame of iron bars designed to hold wood in a fireplace or a stove.
   - What are grates designed to do?

Chapter 9
The Indian Gentleman

Focus Question: How were Sara and the Indian Gentleman alike?

As Sara left the bakery and reached the other side of the street, she looked back. The beggar girl held the last bun in her hands and had stopped in the middle of a bite to watch Sara. Sara gave her a little nod, and the girl, after another stare, nodded her shaggy head in response. Until Sara was out of sight, the beggar girl did not take another bite.

At that moment, the baker woman glanced out of her shop window and exclaimed, "That young girl has given her buns to a beggar! It wasn't because she didn't want them, either. I'd like to know why she did it."

The woman stood behind her window for a few moments and pondered. Then her curiosity got the better of her. She went to the door and spoke to the beggar child.

"Who gave you those buns?" she asked the child.

The child nodded her head toward Sara's vanishing figure.

"What did she say?" inquired the woman.

"Asked me if I was hungry," replied the hoarse voice.

"What did you say?"

"Said I was."

"And then she came in and got buns and came out and gave them to you, did she?"

The girl nodded.

"How many?"

"Five."

The woman thought it over. "That left just one for herself," she said in a low voice. "And she could have eaten all six—I saw it in her eyes."

The baker woman looked after Sara's faraway figure and felt more disturbed in her usually comfortable mind than she had felt for many a day.

"I wish she hadn't gone so quick," she said. "Perhaps I should have given her a dozen."

Then she turned to the girl.

"Are you still hungry?" she asked.

"I'm always hungry," the girl replied, "but it ain't so bad as it was."

"Come in here," said the woman, and she held open the shop door.

The child got up and shuffled in. To be invited into a warm place full of bread seemed an incredible thing. She did not know what was going to happen.

"Get yourself warm," said the woman, pointing to a fire in a tiny back room. "And, look here—when you're desperate for a bite of bread, you can come here and ask for it." ◆

Meanwhile, Sara found some comfort in her remaining bun. It was hot, and it was a great deal better than nothing. She broke off small pieces and ate them slowly to make it last longer.

"Suppose it was a magic bun," she said, "and a bite was as much as a whole dinner. I would be overeating if I went on like this."

It was dark when she reached the square in front of Miss Minchin's school. The lamps were lit, and there was light in most of the windows. Sara enjoyed catching glimpses of the brightly lit rooms before the shutters were closed. She liked to imagine things about people who sat before the fires in the houses or who bent over books at the tables.

There was, for instance, the Large Family that lived a few doors from Miss Minchin's school. She called these people the Large Family not because they were large but because there were so many of them. There were eight children in the Large Family and a stout, rosy mother and a stout, rosy father and a stout, rosy grandmother and any number of servants. The eight children were always being taken out for a walk or going for a ride in strollers, or they were flying to the door in the evening to kiss their father and dance around him and drag off his overcoat and look for presents in his pockets, or they were crowding about the windows and pushing each other and laughing. In fact, they were always doing something that seemed enjoyable.

Next door to the Large Family lived the Maiden Lady, who had a cat, two parrots, and a spaniel. But Sara was not very fond of her because she did nothing in particular but talk to the parrots and walk with the spaniel.

The most interesting person of all lived next door to Miss Minchin. Sara called him the Indian Gentleman. He was an elderly gentleman. According to rumors, he had lived in India and was immensely rich and had something the matter with his liver. It had even been rumored that he had no liver at all and was quite ill. At any rate, he was very pale, and he did not look happy. When he went out to his carriage, he was almost always wrapped in shawls and overcoats, as if he were cold. He had a servant from India who looked even colder, and he had a monkey who looked colder than both of them. Sara had seen the monkey sitting on a table in the sun. The monkey always had such a mournful expression that Sara sympathized with it deeply. She would sometimes say to herself, "The monkey is thinking all the time of coconut trees and of swinging by his tail under a tropical sun. He might have had a family, too, poor thing." ★

Sara called the Indian servant the Lascar. He looked mournful, too, but he was evidently very faithful to his master.

"Perhaps he saved his master's life," she thought. "They look as if they might have had all sorts of adventures. I wish I could speak to the Lascar. I remember a little of the language I spoke in India."

One day, Sara actually did speak to the Lascar. He was quite surprised to hear the sound of his own language. He was waiting for his master to come out to the carriage, and Sara, who was going on an errand as usual, stopped and spoke a few words. She had a special gift for languages and remembered enough of the Lascar's language to make herself understood.

When the Indian Gentleman came out, the Lascar spoke to him, and the Indian Gentleman turned and looked at Sara curiously. Afterward, the Lascar always greeted Sara by bowing to her.

Occasionally, Sara and the Lascar exchanged a few words. She learned that many of the rumors were true. It was true that the Indian Gentleman was very rich. It was true that he was ill. It was true that he had no wife nor children. And it was true England's weather did not agree with the monkey.

"The Indian Gentleman must be as lonely as I am," thought Sara. "Being rich does not seem to make him happy."

That evening, as Sara passed the windows, the Lascar was closing the shutters, and she caught a glimpse of the room inside. There was a bright fire glowing in the grate, and the Indian Gentleman was sitting before it in a luxurious chair. The room was richly furnished and looked delightfully comfortable, but the Indian Gentleman sat with his head resting on his hand and looked as lonely and unhappy as ever.

"Poor man!" said Sara, "I wonder what you are 'supposing'?"

D EXAGGERATION

Write the answers to items 1–8.

Exaggeration is another type of figurative language. When you exaggerate, you stretch the truth. You say that something is bigger or faster or longer than it really is.

Here's an example of exaggeration: *Frank worked for a year that afternoon.*

1. How long does the statement say Frank worked?
2. Could Frank really have worked that long in the afternoon?
3. What part of the statement stretches the truth?
4. Use accurate language to tell what the exaggeration means.

Here's another example of exaggeration: *Camila ran a thousand miles an hour.*

5. How fast does the statement say Camila ran?
6. Could Camila really have run that fast?
7. What part of the statement stretches the truth?
8. Use accurate language to tell what the exaggeration means.

E VOCABULARY REVIEW

jostled

bedraggled

crimson

impudent

challenging

shuffle

For each item, write the correct word.
1. When you are pushed and shoved, you are ▉▉▉▉.
2. Things that are muddy and limp are ▉▉▉▉.
3. Somebody who is rude and bold is ▉▉▉▉.

F COMPREHENSION

Write the answers.
1. What do you think will happen to the beggar girl?
2. How did Sara use her imagination to make the bun last longer?
3. Do you think Sara would like to belong to the Large Family? Why or why not?
4. Describe the Indian Gentleman.
5. How were Sara and the Indian Gentleman alike?

G WRITING

The story described three houses on the square—the Large Family's, the Maiden Lady's, and the Indian Gentleman's.

Write an essay that describes three houses or apartments in your neighborhood. Try to answer the following questions:

- What do the houses or apartments look like from the outside?
- Who lives in the houses or apartments?
- What kinds of things do those people do?
- How are the people different from each other?
- How are they the same?

Make your essay at least sixty words long.

A WORD LISTS

1
Word Practice
1. directed
2. decided
3. exaggeration
4. respectable
5. concealed

2
New Vocabulary
1. vent
2. vague
3. luscious

B VOCABULARY DEFINITIONS

1. **vent**—When you *vent* your emotions, you let them show. When you vent your anger, you let your anger show.
   • Name something you might do to vent your frustration.
2. **vague**—When something is *vague,* it is unclear. An unclear comment is a vague comment.
   • What's another way of saying *an unclear sight*?

3. **luscious**—When something is *luscious,* it is delicious. Delicious fruit is luscious fruit.
   • What's another way of saying *a delicious dessert*?

Chapter 10
A Friend

Focus Question: Who do you think Sara's friend is?

When the Indian Gentleman's shutters were closed, Sara walked slowly back to the boarding school. She met Miss Minchin in the hall.

"Where have you wasted your time?" said Miss Minchin. "You have been out for hours!"

"It was so wet and muddy," Sara answered. "It was hard to walk because my shoes slipped about so."

"Make no excuses," said Miss Minchin, "and tell no lies." She then told Sara to go downstairs to the kitchen.

"Why didn't you stay out all night?" said the cook in a mocking tone.

"Here are the things you wanted," said Sara and laid her purchases on the table.

The cook looked over them, grumbling. She was in a very bad temper indeed. She had just been scolded by Miss Minchin, and it was always safe and easy to vent her own resentment on Sara.

"May I have something to eat?" Sara asked rather faintly.

"Dinner is over and done with," was the answer. "Did you expect me to keep it hot for you?"

Sara was silent a second.

"I had no dinner," she said, and her voice was quite low. She made it low because she was afraid it would tremble.

"There's some bread in the pantry," said the cook. "That's all you'll get at this time of day."

Sara went and found the bread. It was old and hard and dry. The cook was in too bad a mood to give her anything to eat except the bread.

It was extremely hard for the child to climb the three long flights of stairs leading to her garret. She often found them long and steep when she was tired, but tonight it seemed as if she would never reach the top. Several times a lump of sorrow rose in her throat, and she had to stop and rest.

"I can't pretend anything more this night," she said wearily to herself. "I'm sure I can't. I'll eat my bread and drink some water and then go to sleep, and perhaps a dream will come and pretend for me."

When she reached the top landing, there were tears in her eyes, and she did not feel like a princess—only like a tired, hungry, lonely child.

"If my father had lived," she said, "they would not have treated me like this. If my father had lived, he would have taken care of me."

Then she turned the handle and opened the attic door.

Inside the attic, Sara saw something she could not believe. For the first few moments, she thought something strange had happened to her mind—that she was dreaming while still awake.

"Oh!" she exclaimed breathlessly. "Oh! It isn't true! I know, I know it isn't true!" But as she talked, she slipped into the room and closed the door and locked it. Then she stood with her back against it, staring straight before her. ◆

The grate below the stove—which had been empty and rusty and cold when she had left it—held a glowing, blazing fire. On the stove above was a little brass kettle, hissing and boiling. Spread upon the floor was a warm, thick rug, and before the fire was a chair with cushions on it. By the chair was a small table covered with a white cloth, and upon it were spread small dishes, a cup and saucer, and a teapot. On the bed were new, warm coverings, a silk robe, and some books. The little, cold, miserable room had been changed into Fairyland. It was actually warm and glowing.

"It is bewitched!" said Sara. "Or I am bewitched. I only think I see all this, but if I can only keep on imagining, I don't care—I don't care."

She was afraid to move for fear the images would melt away. She stood with her back against the door and looked and looked. Soon she began to feel warm, and then she moved forward.

"A fire that I only thought I saw surely wouldn't feel warm," she said. "It feels real—real."

She went to it and knelt before it. She touched the chair, the table. She looked at the dishes—one had toast on it, another had muffins. There was something hot and tasty in another dish—something delicious.

The teapot had tea in it, ready for the boiling water from the little kettle.

"It is real," said Sara. "The fire is real enough to warm me; I can sit in the chair; the things are real enough to eat."

It was like a fairy story come true—it was heavenly. She went to the bed and touched the blankets and the wrap. They were real, too. She opened one book. On the first page, somebody had written a note. It said, "To the girl in the attic." ★

Suddenly, Sara put her face down on the robe and burst into tears.

"I don't know who it is," she said, "but somebody cares about me a little—somebody is my friend."

Somehow that thought warmed her more than the fire. She had never had a friend since Erma left, and she had not been warm since those happy, luxurious days when she had everything. Those days seemed such a long way off—so far away as to be only dreams.

She really cried more at the strange thought of having a friend—even an unknown one—than she had cried over many of her worst troubles. But these tears seemed different from the others, for when she had wiped them away, she did not feel sad.

Then Sara experienced the delicious comfort of taking off the damp clothes and putting on the soft warm robe before the glowing fire. She slipped her cold feet into the luscious little wool-lined slippers she found near her chair. And then she experienced hot tea and tasty dishes, the cushioned chair, and the books!

Once Sara was certain that the things were real, she enjoyed them completely. She had lived such a life of imagining that she was willing to accept any wonderful thing that happened. After she was quite warm and had eaten her supper and enjoyed herself for an hour or so, it no longer surprised her that such magical surroundings should be hers. Although she wondered who had given her these gifts, she could not stretch her imagination far enough to come up with an answer. She did not know anybody who could have done it.

"There is nobody," she said to herself, "nobody. Still, I have a friend—I have a friend."

D EXAGGERATION

Write the answers to items 1–8.

Exaggeration is another type of figurative language. When you exaggerate, you stretch the truth. You say that something is bigger or faster or longer than it really is.

Here's an example of exaggeration: *She aged five years in a week.*

1. How much does the statement say she aged in a week?
2. Could she really have aged that much in a week?
3. What part of the statement stretches the truth?
4. Use accurate language to tell what the exaggeration means.

Here's another example: *The basketball player was about a hundred feet tall.*

5. About how tall does that statement say he was?
6. Could he really be that tall?
7. What part of the statement stretches the truth?
8. Use accurate language to tell what the exaggeration means.

E VOCABULARY REVIEW

tropical
ponder
jostled
strollers
luxurious
liver
grate

For each item, write the correct word.
1. When you think about something, you ▬▬ it.
2. Warm parts of the earth where plants grow year-round are ▬▬.
3. Something that is fine and elegant is ▬▬.
4. When you are pushed and shoved, you are ▬▬.

F OUTLINING

Complete the following outline for *Sara Crewe.* Copy each main idea; then write three supporting details for each main idea. Use complete sentences.

1. Miss Minchin was mean to Sara.
2. Sara had a strong imagination.
3. Sara performed a good deed near a bakery shop.

G COMPREHENSION

Write the answers.
1. Who do you think Sara's friend is? Explain your answer.
2. As Sara climbed the stairs, why did she have such a hard time pretending?
3. Tell what Sara's room looked like when she opened the door.
4. Why did Sara cry after she read the note in the new book?
5. How do you think Miss Minchin will react when she discovers Sara's new belongings? Explain your answer.

H WRITING

Pretend Sara decides to write a thank-you note to her secret friend.

Write Sara's thank-you note. Try to answer the following questions:
• What gifts had Sara received?
• How is she using those gifts?
• How does she feel about those gifts?
• What else does she want to tell her secret friend?

Make your thank-you note at least sixty words long.

A WORD LISTS

1

Hard Words
1. incident
2. agitated
3. miscalculation
4. caress
5. Carmichael
6. metaphor

2

New Vocabulary
1. parcel
2. incident
3. scant

B VOCABULARY DEFINITIONS

1. **parcel**—A *parcel* is a package.
   - What's another way of saying *She received a package*?
2. **incident**—An *incident* is an event.
   - What's another way of saying *There were five important events in her life*?

3. **scant**—If there is not enough of something, that thing is *scant.* If the food is *scant,* there is not enough food.
   - What's another way of saying *There is not enough rain*?

Chapter 11
The Parcels

Focus Question: Why was Miss Minchin afraid of the parcels?

Sara's unknown friend continued to be kind. When Sara went to her garret the next night, she found that the stranger had been again at work and had done even more than before. The fire and the supper were again there and beside them a number of other things. A piece of heavy cloth covered the battered mantel, and on it some ornaments had been placed. All the bare, ugly things that could be covered with draperies had been concealed and made to look quite pretty. Some odd materials in rich colors had been fastened against the walls with sharp, fine tacks—so sharp that they could be pressed into the wood without hammering. A long, old wooden box was covered with a rug, and some cushions lay on it, so it looked like a sofa.

Sara simply sat down and looked, and looked again.

"It is exactly like a fairy tale come true," she said. "There isn't the least difference. I feel as if I might wish for anything—diamonds and bags of gold—and they would appear! That couldn't be any stranger than this. Is this my garret? Am I the same cold, ragged, damp Sara? And to think how I used to pretend and pretend and wish there were fairies! The one thing I always wanted was to see a fairy story come true. I am living in a fairy story!"

It was like a fairy story, and best of all, it continued. Almost every day, something new was done to the garret. Some new comfort or ornament appeared in it when Sara opened her door at night. In a short time, it was a bright little room, full of all sorts of luxurious things. And the magician had taken care that Sara should not be hungry and that she should have as many books as she could read. When she left the room in the morning, the remains of her supper were on the table; when she returned in the evening, the magician had removed them and left another nice little meal.

Downstairs, Miss Minchin was as cruel and insulting as ever, Miss Amelia was as nasty, and the servants were as rude. Sara was sent on errands and scolded and ordered around, but somehow it seemed as if she could bear it all. The delightful sense of romance and mystery lifted her above the cook's temper. The comforts she enjoyed were making her stronger. If she came home from her errands wet and tired, she knew she would soon be warm, after she had climbed the stairs. In a few weeks, Sara began to look less thin. A little color came into her cheeks, and her eyes no longer seemed too big for her face. ◆

And then another wonderful thing happened. A man came to the door and left

TO THE GIRL
IN THE
ATTIC

TO THE GIRL
IN THE
ATTIC

several parcels. All were addressed in large letters to "The Girl in the Attic." Sara was sent to open the door, and she took the parcels in. She laid the two largest parcels on the hall table and was looking at the address when Miss Minchin came down the stairs.

"Take the parcels upstairs to the young lady to whom they belong," she said. "Don't stand there staring at them."

"They belong to me," answered Sara quietly.

"To you!" exclaimed Miss Minchin. "What do you mean?"

"I don't know where they came from," said Sara, "but they're addressed to me."

Miss Minchin came to her side and looked at them with an excited expression.

"What is in them?" she demanded.

"I don't know," said Sara.

"Open them!" she demanded still more excitedly.

Sara did as she was told. They contained pretty and comfortable clothing—shoes, stockings, gloves, a warm coat, and even an umbrella. On the pocket of the coat was a note that said, "This coat is to be worn every day. It will be replaced by others when necessary." ★

Miss Minchin was quite irritated. This was an incident which suggested strange things to her. Could she have made a mistake after all? Did Sara have some powerful friend in the background? It would not be very pleasant if there should be such a friend. The friend might learn all the truth about the thin, shabby clothes, the scant food, the hard work. Miss Minchin felt strange indeed, and uncertain, and she gave a side-glance at Sara.

"Well," Miss Minchin said in a voice she had never used since the day Sara lost her father. "Well, someone is very kind to you. As you have the things and are to have new ones when they are worn out, you may as well go and put them on and look respectable. And after you are dressed, you may come downstairs and learn your lessons in the schoolroom."

About half an hour afterward, Sara shocked the entire schoolroom of pupils by appearing in a set of new clothes. She scarcely seemed to be the same Sara. She was neatly dressed in a pretty gown of warm browns and reds, and even her stockings and slippers were nice and dainty.

"Perhaps someone has left her a fortune," one of the girls whispered. "I always thought something would happen to her."

D SIMILES

Write the answers to items 1–4.

Here's how to write a simile. First make an accurate statement, such as *Her eyes were blue.* Then name something that could be as blue as her eyes.

Here's a simile that tells what her eyes were like: *Her eyes were like a cloudless sky.*

Write a simile for this accurate statement: *The man ran fast.*

1. First name something that is fast.
2. Now write a simile that tells how the man ran. Use the word *like* in your simile.

Write a simile for this accurate statement: *The woman was very strong.*

3. First name something that is strong.
4. Now write a simile that tells how strong the woman was. Use the word *like* in your simile.

E EXAGGERATION

Write the answers.
The rain lasted forever.

1. How long does the statement say the rain lasted?
2. Write an accurate statement that tells how long the rain lasted.

Tatsu had a mountain of food on his plate.

3. How much food does the statement say Tatsu had?
4. Write an accurate statement that tells how much food Tatsu had.

F VOCABULARY REVIEW

jostled
luscious
ponder
vent
bedraggled
vague
tropical

For each item, write the correct word.
1. When something is not clear, it is ▆▆▆▆.
2. When something is delicious, it is ▆▆▆▆.
3. When you let your emotions show, you ▆▆▆▆ your emotions.
4. Things that are muddy and limp are ▆▆▆▆.

 COMPREHENSION

Write the answers.

1. Why was Miss Minchin afraid of the parcels?
2. Tell how Sara's room continued to change.
3. What did Sara mean when she said, "I am living in a fairy story"?
4. Why was Sara able to bear Miss Minchin and the others now?
5. Why do you think Miss Minchin let Sara come back to the schoolroom?

H WRITING

Pretend Miss Minchin has to write a letter to Sara's friend explaining what has happened to Sara.

Write Miss Minchin's letter. Think about the following questions before you begin.

- How does Miss Minchin want to appear to Sara's friend?
- How will Miss Minchin explain why Sara lives in the attic?
- How will Miss Minchin explain Sara's jobs at the school?
- What is Miss Minchin hoping will happen with Sara?

Make your letter at least sixty words long.

Ⓐ WORD LISTS

1
Word Practice
1. elfish
2. scene
3. metaphor
4. desert
5. sense
6. dessert

2
New Vocabulary
1. caress
2. agitated
3. miscalculation
4. devoted

Ⓑ VOCABULARY DEFINITIONS

1. **caress**—When you *caress* people or animals, you lightly stroke them.
   - What's another way of saying *The girl lightly stroked her dog*?
2. **agitated**—When you are *agitated*, you are excited and nervous.
   - What's another way of saying *an excited and nervous voice*?

3. **miscalculation**—A *miscalculation* is an error or a mistake.
   - What's another way of saying *He did not know about his mistake*?
4. **devoted**—Someone who is *devoted* is loyal.
   - What's another way of saying *She had a loyal servant*?

Chapter 12
The Monkey

Focus Question: How did the monkey get into Sara's room?

On the night Sara received the parcels, she carried out a plan she had been thinking about for some time. She wrote this note to her unknown friend:

> *I want to thank you for being so kind to me—so beautifully kind—and making everything like a fairy story. I am so grateful to you, and I am so happy! I used to be so lonely and cold and hungry, and now, just think what you have done for me! Thank you—thank you—thank you!*
> *The Girl in the Attic*

The next morning, she left this note on the little table. It was taken away with the other things, so she felt sure the magician had received it.

A few nights later, a very odd thing happened. She found something in the room that she certainly would never have expected. When she came in as usual, she saw something small and dark in her chair—an odd, tiny figure, which turned a small and weird-looking face toward her.

"Why, it's the monkey!" Sara cried. "It is the Indian Gentleman's monkey!"

It was the monkey, sitting up and looking forlorn. Very soon, Sara found out how he had gotten into her room. The skylight was open, and it was easy to guess that he had crept out of his master's garret window, which was only a few feet away. The monkey had probably been attracted by the light in Sara's attic and had crept in. And there he was.

When Sara went up to the monkey, he actually put out his elfish little hands, caught her dress, and jumped into her arms.

"Oh, you poor little thing!" said Sara, caressing him. "I can't help liking you, but you have such a forlorn look on your little face."

The monkey sat and looked at Sara while she talked. He seemed much interested in her remarks, judging by his eyes and his forehead and the way he moved his head up and down. He examined her quite seriously. He felt the material of her dress, touched her hands, climbed up and examined her ears, and then sat on her shoulder holding a lock of her hair, looking mournful but not at all agitated. Upon the whole, the monkey seemed pleased with Sara.

"I must take you back," she said to the monkey, "though I'm sorry to have to do it. Oh, you would be good company!"

She lifted the monkey from her shoulder, set him on her knee, and gave him a bit of cake. He sat and nibbled it. Then he put his head on one side, looked at her, wrinkled his forehead, and nibbled again.

"But you must go home," said Sara at last, and she took the monkey in her arms to carry him downstairs. Evidently, he did not want to leave the room, for as they reached the door, he clung to her neck and gave a little scream of anger.

"You mustn't be an ungrateful monkey," said Sara. "You ought to be fond of your own family. I am sure your master is good to you." ◆

Nobody saw Sara on her way out, and very soon she was standing on the Indian Gentleman's front steps. The Lascar opened the door for her.

"I found your monkey in my room," she said in Indian. "I think he got in through the window."

The man began a rapid outpouring of thanks, but he was interrupted by an agitated and hollow voice that came through the open door of the nearest room. The instant he heard it, the Lascar disappeared and left Sara in the front hall, still holding the monkey.

It was not many moments, however, before the Lascar came back bringing a message. His master had told him to bring Sara into the library. The master was very ill, but he wished to see Sara.

Sara followed the Lascar. When she entered the room, the Indian Gentleman was lying on an easy chair, propped up with pillows. He looked frightfully ill. His pale face was thin, and his eyes were hollow. He gave Sara a rather curious look.

"You live next door?" he asked.

"Yes," answered Sara. "I live at Miss Minchin's."

"She keeps a boarding school?"

"Yes," said Sara.

"And you are one of her pupils?"

Sara hesitated a moment.

"I don't know exactly what I am," she replied.

"Why not?" asked the Indian Gentleman.

The monkey gave a tiny squeak, and Sara stroked him.

"At first," she said, "I was a pupil, but now . . ."

"What do you mean by 'at first'?" asked the Indian Gentleman.

"When I was first taken there by my father."

"Well, what has happened since then?" said the gentleman, staring at her with a puzzled expression.

"My father died," said Sara. "He lost all his money, and there was none left for me, and there was no one to take care of me or pay Miss Minchin, so . . ."

"So you were sent up into the garret and neglected and made into a half-starved little servant!" added the Indian Gentleman. "That's about it, isn't it?"

The color deepened on Sara's cheeks.

"There was no one to take care of me and no money," she said. "I belong to nobody."

"How did your father lose his money?" asked the gentleman.

The color in Sara's cheeks grew even deeper, and she fixed her odd eyes on the pale face. ★

"He did not lose it himself," she said. "He had a friend he was fond of, and it was his friend who took his money. I don't know how. I don't understand. He trusted his friend too much."

She saw the gentleman start as if he had been suddenly frightened. Then he spoke nervously and excitedly: "That's an old story," he said. "It happens every day, but sometimes those who are blamed—those who do the wrong—don't intend it and are not so bad. It may happen through a mistake—a miscalculation."

"That's possible," said Sara, "but the suffering is just as bad for the others. It killed my father."

The Indian Gentleman pushed aside some of the gorgeous wraps that covered him.

"Come a little nearer, and let me look at you," he said.

His voice sounded very strange; it had a more nervous and excited tone than before. Sara thought he was half afraid to look at her. She came and stood nearer, with the monkey still clinging to her and watching his master anxiously over his shoulder.

The Indian Gentleman's hollow, restless eyes fixed themselves on her.

"Yes," he said at last. "Yes, I can see it. Tell me your father's name."

"His name was Ralph Crewe," said Sara. "Captain Crewe. Perhaps," a sudden thought flashed upon her, "perhaps you may have heard of him? He died in India."

The Indian Gentleman sank back onto his pillows. He looked very weak and seemed out of breath.

"Yes," he said. "I knew him. I was his friend. I meant no harm. If he had only lived, he would have known. It turned out well after all. He was a fine young fellow. I was fond of him. I will make it right. Call . . . call my servant."

Sara thought the Indian Gentleman was going to die. But there was no need to call the Lascar. He must have been waiting at the door. He was in the room and by his master's side in an instant. He seemed to know what to do. He lifted the drooping head and gave the gentleman something in a small glass. The gentleman lay panting for a few minutes, and then he spoke in an exhausted but eager voice, addressing the Lascar in Indian, "Go for Carmichael," he said. "Tell him to come here at once. Tell him I have found the child!"

D SIMILES

Write the answers for items 1–4.

Here's how to make a simile. First make an accurate statement, such as *His beard was rough.* Then name something that could be as rough as his beard.

Here's a simile that tells what his beard was like: *His beard was like sandpaper.*

Write a simile for this accurate statement: *The city was crowded and busy.*
1. Name something that is busy.
2. Write a simile that tells what the city was like. Use the word *like* in your simile.

Write a simile for this accurate statement: *The monster's voice was very deep.*
3. Name something that sounds deep.
4. Write a simile that tells how deep the monster's voice was.

E VOCABULARY REVIEW

| luscious |
| incident |
| impudent |
| tropical |
| scant |
| vague |
| absurd |
| parcels |

For each item, write the correct word.
1. Packages are ▮▮▮.
2. An event is an ▮▮▮.
3. If there is not enough of something, that thing is ▮▮▮.
4. Somebody who is rude and bold is ▮▮▮.
5. If something is not clear, it is ▮▮▮.

F COMPREHENSION

Write the answers.

1. How did the monkey get into Sara's room?
2. Why do you think the monkey had such a forlorn look?
3. Pretend you are Sara. Tell the Indian Gentleman why you are living in the attic.
4. What was the Indian Gentleman's connection to Sara's father?
5. What do you think the Indian Gentleman intends to do for Sara?

G WRITING

What do you think the Indian Gentleman's story is?

Write a story about the Indian Gentleman's experiences with Captain Crewe and Sara. Try to answer the following questions:

- What was the Indian Gentleman's connection with Captain Crewe?
- What had the Indian Gentleman done with Captain Crewe's money?
- How had the Indian Gentleman tried to find Sara?
- What was the Indian Gentleman's connection with Sara's friend?

Make your story at least sixty words long.

A WORD LIST

1

Word Practice

1. desert
2. dessert
3. dingy

B VOCABULARY REVIEW

miscalculation

caress

incident

vague

devoted

scant

jostled

agitated

For each item, say the correct word.
1. When you lightly stroke an object, you ▇▇▇ that object.
2. An error or mistake is a ▇▇▇.
3. When you are nervous and excited, you are ▇▇▇.
4. Someone who is loyal is ▇▇▇.
5. If there is not enough of something, that thing is ▇▇▇.

Chapter 13
Mr. Carrisford

Focus Question: How did Sara's life change after she met Mr. Carrisford?

Mr. Carmichael arrived in just a few minutes. It turned out that he was the father of the Large Family across the street. Shortly after he arrived, Sara went home and was allowed to take the monkey with her. She certainly did not sleep very much that night, though the monkey behaved beautifully and did not disturb her in the least. It was not the monkey that kept her awake. It was her thoughts and her wondering what the Indian Gentleman had meant when he said, "Tell him I have found the child."

"What child?" Sara kept asking herself. "I was the only child there. But how had he found me, and why did he want to find me? And what is he going to do, now that I am found? Is it something about my father? Do I belong to somebody? Is he one of my relations? Is something going to happen?"

She found out the answers to these questions the very next morning—and it seemed that she had been living in a story even more than she had imagined. Early that morning, Mr. Carmichael came to the boarding house and had an interview with Miss Minchin. He was a lawyer and had charge of the affairs of Mr. Carrisford—which was the real name of the Indian Gentleman. Mr. Carmichael had come over to explain something curious about Sara to Miss Minchin.

Mr. Carmichael had a kind and fatherly feeling for children. After seeing Miss Minchin alone, he went across the square and brought his wife because she could talk to Sara and explain the story in the best way. Mrs. Carmichael talked to Sara for a long time.

Sara learned that she would no longer be a poor little servant and outcast and that a great change had come in her life. All the lost fortune had come back to her and a great deal more. It was Mr. Carrisford who had been her father's friend and had made the investments that had seemed to lose Captain Crewe's money. But it so happened that after Captain Crewe's death, one of the investments had taken a sudden turn. It proved to be such a success that it more than doubled the captain's lost fortune, as well as making a fortune for Mr. Carrisford.

But Mr. Carrisford had been very unhappy. He had truly admired his handsome and generous young friend. The knowledge that he had caused Captain Crewe's death weighed on him always and broke both his health and his spirit. Worst of all, when he first thought that he and Captain Crewe were ruined, he had lost courage and gone away. And so Mr. Carrisford had not even known where the young captain's daughter had been sent to school. When he wanted to find her, he could discover no trace of her. Knowing that she was poor and friendless somewhere had made him more miserable than ever. ◆

When Mr. Carrisford had taken the house next to Miss Minchin's, he was so ill that he had given up the search. His troubles and the climate of India had brought him almost to death's door. Indeed, he had not expected to live more than a few months. Then one day the Lascar told him about Sara's speaking an Indian language. Mr. Carrisford gradually began to take a sort of interest in the forlorn child, although he had only caught a glimpse of her once or twice. He did not connect her with the child of his friend, perhaps because he was too sick to think much about anything.

But the Lascar had learned something of Sara's unhappy life and the garret where she lived. One evening when Sara had gone, the Lascar actually crept out of his own garret window and looked into hers, which was very easy to do because it was only a few feet away. The Lascar told his master what he had seen, and Mr. Carrisford told him to take gifts into the wretched little room.

The Lascar watched Sara coming in and out of the boarding house until he knew exactly when she was absent from her room and when she returned to it, and so he was able to calculate the best times for his work. Generally, he worked in the dusk of the evening. He would cross the few feet of roof from garret window to garret window without any trouble at all. Once or twice, when he had seen her go out on errands, he had dared to go over in the daytime.

The Lascar's pleasure in the work and

his reports of the results had added to Mr. Carrisford's interest. The planning gave Mr. Carrisford something to think of and almost made him forget his weariness and pain. At last, when Sara brought home the monkey, Mr. Carrisford had felt a wish to see her. When he observed her likeness to her father, he concluded that she was Captain Crewe's child.

"And now, my dear," said good Mrs. Carmichael after she finished her tale, "all your troubles are over. You are to come home with me and be taken care of as if you were one of my own little girls. We are pleased to have you with us until everything is settled and Mr. Carrisford is better. The excitement of last night has made him very weak, but we really think he will get well now that such a load is taken from his mind. When he is stronger, I am sure he will be as kind to you as your own father would have been. He has a good heart, and he is fond of children—and he has no family at all. But we must make you happy and rosy, and you must learn to play and run about, as my girls do." ★

"As your girls do?" said Sara. "I wonder if I could. I used to watch them and wonder what it was like. Will I feel as if I belong to somebody?"

"Ah, my love, yes—yes!" said Mrs. Carmichael. "Dear me, yes!" And her motherly blue eyes grew quite moist, and she suddenly took Sara in her arms and kissed her.

That very night, before Sara went to bed, she met the entire Large Family, and they liked her very much. All the older children knew something of her life story. She had been born in India; after her father died, had been poor and lonely and unhappy; she had lived in a garret and had been treated unkindly; now she was to be rich and happy again. The children were sorry for her, and yet they were delighted and curious. The girls wished to be with her constantly, and the little boys wished to be told about India.

"I shall certainly wake up," Sara kept saying to herself. "This must be a dream. But, oh! How happy it is!"

Sara finally went to bed, in a bright, pretty room not far from Mr. and Mrs. Carmichael's. Mrs. Carmichael kissed her and patted her and tucked her in. But Sara was still not sure whether her dream would end and whether she would wake up in the garret in the morning.

"Charles, dear," Mrs. Carmichael said to her husband when she went downstairs, "we must get that lonely look out of her eyes! It isn't a child's look at all. I couldn't bear to see it in one of my own children. What the poor girl must have had to bear in that dreadful woman's house! Surely, she will forget it in time."

Although the lonely look passed away from Sara's face, she never quite forgot the garret at Miss Minchin's. Indeed, she always liked to remember the wonderful night when she was too tired to 'suppose' she was a princess. On that night, she had crept upstairs, cold and wet, and found Fairyland waiting for her when she opened the door. No story was more popular in the Large Family than that one.

Mr. Carrisford recovered, and Sara went to live with him. No child could have been better taken care of than she was. It seemed to Mr. Carrisford that he could not do enough to make Sara happy and to repay her for the past, and the Lascar was her devoted servant.

D METAPHORS

Write the answers for items 1–6.

A metaphor is like a simile except it doesn't use the word *like.*

Here's an accurate statement: *The woman was very smart.* Here's a metaphor: *The woman was a walking encyclopedia.*

1. What two things are the same in that metaphor?
2. How could they be the same?

Here's another metaphor: *The man was a rattlesnake.*

3. What two things are the same in that metaphor?
4. How could they be the same?

Here's another metaphor: *Miss Minchin was a jailer.*

5. What two things are the same in that metaphor?
6. How could they be the same?

E MAIN IDEA

Write the main idea and three supporting details for the following paragraph.

Sara took off the damp clothes and put on the soft, warm robe before the glowing fire. She slipped her cold feet into the little wool-lined slippers she found near the chair. Then she made herself comfortable.

F COMPREHENSION

Write the answers.
1. How did Sara's life change after she met Mr. Carrisford?
2. Why had Captain Crewe made money after all?
3. Why was Mr. Carrisford unhappy about what had happened to Captain Crewe?
4. Explain how all the gifts appeared in Sara's garret.
5. What do you think Miss Minchin will do about Sara now?

G WRITING

In this chapter, Mr. Carmichael had a conversation with Miss Minchin about Sara.

Write what you think they said. Think about the following questions before writing the conversation:
- What will Mr. Carmichael tell Miss Minchin about Sara's fortune?
- How will Miss Minchin try to explain what has happened to Sara?
- How will Mr. Carmichael react to Miss Minchin's explanation?

Make your conversation at least sixty words long.

A WORD LISTS

1

Word Practice
1. desolate
2. quail
3. fiery
4. metaphor
5. grief

2

New Vocabulary
1. ex-
2. proposal
3. drab
4. suitable

B VOCABULARY DEFINITIONS

1. **ex-**—The prefix *ex-* means "former." An ex-husband is a former husband.
   • What's an *ex-student*?
2. **proposal**—A *proposal* is an offer or a plan to do something.
   • What's another way of saying *She told the teacher about her plan*?

3. **drab**—*Drab* is another word for *dreary.*
   • What's another way of saying *She lived in a dreary room*?
4. **suitable**—When something is *suitable*, it is appropriate.
   • What's another way of saying *His clothes were appropriate for work*?

Chapter 14
The Bakery Shop

Focus Question: What was Sara's plan for the bakery shop?

Sara and Mr. Carrisford became great friends, and they used to spend hours reading and talking together. Sara would sit next to Mr. Carrisford in her big chair, with a book on her knee and her soft, dark hair tumbling over her warm cheeks. She had a habit of looking up at him suddenly with a bright smile, and then he would often say to her, "Are you happy, Sara?"

"Yes," she would say, "there doesn't seem to be anything left to suppose."

There was a little joke between them that he was a magician and could do anything he liked. Scarcely a day passed in which he did not do something different for her. Sometimes she found new flowers in her room, sometimes a little gift tucked into some odd corner, sometimes a new book on her pillow.

The younger children of the Large Family often came to see Sara. She was as fond of the Large Family as they were of her. She soon felt as if she were a member of it. The companionship of the healthy, happy children was good for her. All of them looked up to her—particularly after they discovered that she not only knew stories of every kind but that she could help with lessons and speak French and German and talk with the Lascar in his language.

It was a rather painful experience for Miss Minchin to watch her ex-pupil's fortunes. Miss Minchin felt she had made a serious mistake from a business point of view. She even tried to suggest that Sara's education should be continued under her care, and she made an appeal to Sara herself.

"I have always been fond of you," Miss Minchin said.

Sara fixed her eyes upon Miss Minchin and gave her one of her odd looks.

"Have you always been fond of me?" Sara asked.

"Yes," said Miss Minchin. "Amelia and I have always said you were the cleverest child we had with us, and I am sure we could make you happy."

Sara thought of the garret and the day Miss Minchin had slapped her cheek. Then she thought of that other day, that dreadful, desolate day when she had been told she belonged to nobody, that she had no home and no friends. She kept her eyes fixed on Miss Minchin's face.

"You know why I would not stay with you," Sara said.

And it seems likely that Miss Minchin did know, for after that simple answer, she did not say anything more. She merely sent Mr. Carrisford a bill for the expense of Sara's education and support, and she made it quite large. Because Mr. Carrisford thought Sara would like the bill to be paid, it was paid.

When Mr. Carmichael paid the bill, he had a brief interview with Miss Minchin in which he expressed his opinion with much clearness and force. It is quite certain Miss Minchin did not enjoy the conversation. ◆

One night, after Sara had been with Mr. Carrisford for about a month, he saw her staring at the fire.

"What are you supposing, Sara?" he asked. Sara looked up with a bright color on her cheeks.

"I was supposing," she said. "I was remembering a hungry day."

"But there were a great many hungry days," said Mr. Carrisford with a rather sad tone in his voice. "Which hungry day was it?"

"I forgot you didn't know," said Sara. "It was the same day I later found the things in my garret."

Then she told him the story of the bakery shop and the four-penny piece and the child who was hungrier than she. As she told the story, Mr. Carrisford found it necessary to shade his eyes with his hand and look down at the floor.

"I was supposing a kind of plan," said Sara when she had finished. "I was thinking I would like to do something."

"What is it?" said her guardian in a low tone. "You may do anything you like, Sara."

"I was wondering," said Sara. "You say I have a great deal of money, and I was wondering if I could go to see the baker woman and tell her that if, when hungry children—particularly on those dreadful days—come and sit on the bakery steps or look in at the window, she could just call them in and give them something to eat. She could send the bills to me, and I would pay them. Could I do that?"

"You shall do it tomorrow morning," said Mr. Carrisford.

"Thank you," said Sara. "You see, I know what it is to be hungry, and it is very hard when one can't even pretend it away."

"Yes, yes, my dear," said Mr. Carrisford. "Yes, it must be."

The next morning a carriage drew up before the door of the bakery shop. A gentleman and a girl got out just as the baker woman was putting a tray of steaming hot buns into the window. When Sara entered the shop, the woman turned and looked at her. For a moment, she looked at Sara very hard indeed, and then her good-natured face lit up.

"I'm sure I remember you, miss," she said. "And yet . . ."

"Yes," said Sara, "once you gave me six buns for a four-penny piece, and . . ."

"And you gave five of them to a beggar child," said the woman. "I've always remembered it. I couldn't place you at first. I beg your pardon, sir, but there's not many young people that notice a hungry face in that way, and I've thought of it many a time. Excuse the liberty, miss, but you look rosier and better than you did that day."

"I am better, thank you," said Sara, "and . . . and I am happier, and I have come to ask you to do something for me." ★

"Me, miss?" exclaimed the woman. "Why, bless you, yes, miss! What can I do?"

And then Sara made her little proposal, and the woman listened to it with an astonished face.

"Why, bless me!" she said when she had heard it all. "Yes, miss, it'll be a pleasure for me to do it. I am a working woman myself and can't afford to do much on my own. But if you'll excuse me, I'm bound to say I've given many a bit of bread away since that wet afternoon, just thinking of you. And how wet and cold you were, and how you looked . . ."

Mr. Carrisford smiled, and Sara smiled a little, too, as she said, "The beggar girl looked so hungry. She was hungrier than I was."

"She was starving," said the woman. "Many times she's told me of it since—how she sat there in the wet and felt as if a wolf was tearing at her poor young insides."

"Oh, have you seen her since then?" exclaimed Sara. "Do you know where she is?"

"Do I know?" said the woman. "Why, she's in that back room now, miss, and has been for a month, and a decent, well-meaning girl she's going to turn out, and such a help to me in the shop and in the kitchen as you'd scarcely believe, knowing how she's lived."

The bakery woman stepped to the door of the little back parlor and called. The next minute, a girl came out and followed the woman behind the counter. It was the beggar girl, clean and neatly clothed, and looking as if she had not been hungry for a long time. She looked shy, but she had a nice face, and the wild look had gone from her eyes. She knew Sara in an instant and stood and looked at her as if she could never look enough.

"You see," said the woman, "I told her to come here when she was hungry, and when she'd come, I'd give her odd jobs to do, and I found she was willing, and somehow I got to like her. So now I've given her a place and a home, and she helps me and behaves as well as a girl can. Her name is Anne—she has no other."

The two children stood and looked at each other a few moments. In Sara's mind, a new thought was growing.

"I'm glad you have a good home," she said. "Perhaps the baker woman will let you give the buns and bread to the children. Perhaps you would like to do it—because you know what it is to be hungry, too."

"Yes, miss," said the girl.

And somehow Sara felt the girl understood her, though she said nothing more and only stood still and looked. The girl continued to stare as Sara left the shop, got into the carriage, and drove away.

D METAPHORS

Write the answers for items 1–6.

A metaphor is like a simile except that it doesn't use the word *like.*

Here's an accurate statement: *Gray clouds covered the sky.* Here's a metaphor: *The clouds were a gray ceiling.*

1. What two things are the same in that metaphor?
2. How could they be the same?

Here's another metaphor: *Sara's attic room was a nest in a tree.*

3. What two things are the same in that metaphor?
4. How could they be the same?

Here's another metaphor: *The boxer's arms were lightning bolts.*

5. What two things are the same in that metaphor?
6. How could they be the same?

E COMPREHENSION

Write the answers.
1. Why do you think Sara had a joke that Mr. Carrisford was a magician?
2. Why do you think Miss Minchin tried to make up with Sara?
3. What was Sara's plan for the bakery shop?
4. Why did Sara want to help hungry children?
5. Sara used her money to help hungry children. If you had a lot of money, whom would you help? Why?

F WRITING

What do you think Sara learned from her experiences?

Write an essay that explains what you think Sara learned. Try to answer the following questions:
- What did Sara learn about Miss Minchin?
- What did Sara learn about suffering?
- What did Sara learn about using her imagination?
- What did Sara learn about animals?

Make your essay at least sixty words long.

51

A WORD LISTS

1

Word Practice
1. Longfellow
2. hastens
3. efface
4. curlew
5. neigh

2

New Vocabulary
1. curlew
2. efface
3. hostler
4. nevermore
5. steed

B VOCABULARY DEFINITIONS

1. **curlew**—A *curlew* is a brown sea bird with long legs and a long, curving bill. The picture shows a curlew.
   • Describe a curlew.
2. **efface**—When you *efface* something, you erase it.
   • What's another way of saying *Time had erased all the writing on the wall*?

3. **hostler**—A *hostler* is a person who takes care of horses or mules.
   • What is a person who takes care of horses called?
4. **nevermore**—*Nevermore* means "never again."
   • What's another way of saying *He left home, never again to return*?
5. **steed**—*Steed* is another word for *horse*.
   • What's another way of saying *The rider galloped away on her trusty horse*?

The Tide Rises, the Tide Falls
by Henry Wadsworth Longfellow

The tide rises, the tide falls,
The twilight darkens, the curlew calls;
Along the sea-sands damp and brown
The traveler hastens toward the town,
   And the tide rises, the tide falls.

Darkness settles on roofs and walls,
But the sea, the sea in the darkness calls;
The little waves, with their soft white hands,
Efface the footprints in the sands,
   And the tide rises, the tide falls.

The morning breaks; the steeds in their stalls
Stamp and neigh, as the hostler calls;
The day returns, but nevermore
Returns the traveler to the shore,
   And the tide rises, the tide falls.

Ⓓ METAPHORS

Write the answers for items 1–5.

Some metaphors do not name the two things that are the same. Here's an example: *The ship plowed through the water.* That metaphor says the ship was like something that plowed.

1. What object could plow things?
2. Use accurate language to tell what could be the same about a tractor's action and a ship's action.

Here's another metaphor: *Her voice twittered and chirped.*

3. What was her voice like?
4. What could that thing be?
5. Use accurate language to tell how her voice and that thing's voice could be the same.

Ⓔ COMPREHENSION

Write the answers.

1. In the poem, how is the sea different from the traveler?
2. Which line does the poet keep repeating? Why?
3. How does the poet make the waves seem like people?
4. How is the sea like night and day?
5. Do you think the poem is still true? Explain your answer.

Ⓕ WRITING

"The Tide Rises, the Tide Falls" tells about the sea.

Write a poem that tells about another place, such as a mountain, a river, a forest, or a town. Think about the following questions before writing your poem.

- What does your place look like?
- What sounds do you hear there?
- What smells and tastes come from there?
- What do people do in that place?
- What does that place mean to you?

Make your poem at least ten lines long. Your lines do not have to rhyme.

A WORD LISTS

1

Hard Words
1. Guy de Maupassant
2. Matilda Loisel
3. franc
4. humiliating

2

New Vocabulary
1. pertain
2. franc
3. humiliating
4. satin

B VOCABULARY DEFINITIONS

1. **pertain**—Information that *pertains* to something relates to that thing.
   Here's another way of saying *a plan that relates to the new school: a plan pertaining to the new school.*
   • What's another way of saying *She gathered information that relates to her goals?*
2. **franc**—A *franc* used to be the basic unit of money in France.
   • What is a franc?

3. **humiliating**—When something is *humiliating,* it is quite embarrassing.
   • What's another way of saying *It was quite embarrassing to wear the torn shirt?*
4. **satin**—*Satin* is a smooth and shiny fabric.
   • What is satin?

Guy de Maupassant

The next story is titled "The Necklace." It was written by a French writer named Guy de Maupassant, who lived from 1850 to 1893. He grew up in a small town in France and moved to Paris, the capital of France, after he finished high school.

Maupassant soon began to write short stories about life in Paris. Few people read his work until 1880, when he published his most famous story, "Ball of Fat." He kept writing stories, novels, and plays until his early death in 1893. Altogether, he wrote more than three hundred short stories.

Like O. Henry, Maupassant often ended his stories with a surprise. "The Necklace" is about a young couple who live in Paris in the late 1800s.

D **READING**

THE NECKLACE

*by Guy de Maupassant**
Part 1

Focus Question: Why did Matilda want a necklace?

Matilda Loisel was a pretty and charming woman, but she was very poor. She had no fortune and no expectations of ever getting one. She was married to a clerk who worked for the government.

Matilda suffered endlessly. She suffered from the poverty of her apartment, from the wretched look of the walls, from the worn-out chair, and from the ugliness of the curtains. All those things tortured her and made her angry.

When she sat down to dinner, she looked at the worn tablecloth and tried to imagine what it would be like to use shining silverware and golden plates. In her mind, she could almost taste the pink flesh of a trout or the delicate wings of a quail.

In contrast, her husband was satisfied with what they had. It annoyed Matilda to see him looking into the soup bowl and saying, "Ah, stew! There's nothing I like better than that."

Matilda had no fancy dresses or jewels. But these were the only things she really loved.

Matilda had a friend, Mrs. Forester, who was rich. But Matilda did not like to visit Mrs. Forester anymore because she

suffered so much when she returned to her drab apartment.

But one evening, Matilda's husband returned home with a triumphant look on his face. He was holding a large envelope in his hand.

He said, "Here is something for you."

Matilda tore open the envelope and pulled out a printed card, which said:

"The Governor requests the honor of Mr. and Mrs. Loisel's company at the grand ball on Monday evening, January 18."

Instead of being delighted, Matilda threw the invitation onto the table and murmured, "What do you want me to do with that?"

"But, Matilda, I thought you would be glad. You never go out, and this is such a fine opportunity. I had an awful time getting the invitation. Everyone wants to go. It is a very fancy affair, and they are not giving many invitations to clerks. All the most important people will be there."

Matilda looked at her husband with an irritated eye and said impatiently, "And what do you want me to wear?"

Her husband had not thought of that. He stammered, "Why, the dress you go to the theater in. I think it's very nice."

He stopped talking because his wife

---

* *Adapted for young readers*

was crying. Two great tears descended slowly from the corners of her eyes toward the corners of her mouth.

Mr. Loisel stuttered, "What's the matter? What's the matter?"

Matilda conquered her grief and wiped her wet cheeks. In a calm voice, she said, "I have no dress; therefore, I can't go to this ball. Give your invitation to a friend whose wife is dressed better than I am."

Mr. Loisel was in despair. He said, "Come, let us see, Matilda. How much would a suitable dress cost? You could use it for other occasions."

Matilda calculated for several seconds.

Finally, she said, "I don't know exactly, but I think I could manage it with four hundred francs."

Her husband grew a little pale, but he said, "All right. I will give you four hundred francs. Find the prettiest dress you can." ◆

• • •

The day of the ball drew near. Al-though Matilda had her new dress, she seemed sad and uneasy. Her husband said to her one evening, "What is the matter? You've been acting so oddly these last three days."

She answered, "It annoys me not to have a single jewel, not a single stone, nothing to put on. I would almost rather not go at all."

Her husband said, "You might wear natural flowers. It's very stylish this time of the year. For ten francs, you can get two or three magnificent roses."

Matilda was not convinced.

"No," she said, "there is nothing more humiliating than looking poor among other women who are rich."

Suddenly, her husband cried out, "Why don't you go see your rich friend Mrs. Forester and ask her to lend you some jewels?"

Matilda uttered a cry of joy. "I never thought of that!" she said.

The next day she went to her friend

and explained her problem.

Mrs. Forester went to a closet and took out a large jewel box. She brought it back, opened it, and said to Matilda, "Choose whatever you want, my dear."

Matilda examined some bracelets, then a pearl necklace, then a gold cross. She tried on the jewels in front of the mirror, hesitated, and could not make up her mind.

Finally, Matilda said, "Do you have anything else?"

"Why, yes, look through these," Mrs. Forester said, pointing to other boxes.

In a black satin box, Matilda discovered a superb necklace of diamonds. Her heart began to beat quickly. Her hands trembled as she took the necklace from the box. She fastened it around her throat and was very pleased when she looked at herself in the mirror. ★

Then she asked, "Can you lend me this one?"

"Why, yes, certainly."

Matilda hugged and kissed her friend before she left with her treasure.

The day of the ball arrived. Matilda was a big success. She was prettier than anyone—elegant, gracious, smiling, and sparkling with joy. All the men looked at her and asked her name. All the government officials wanted to dance with her. Even the governor noticed her.

She danced with pleasure and forgot all about her poverty. She was in a cloud of happiness.

After midnight, she left the ball with her husband. Mr. Loisel threw a coat around Matilda's shoulders. Her modest coat contrasted with the elegant dress. It embarrassed Matilda, and she wanted to leave quickly because other women were wrapping themselves in costly furs.

Her husband held her back.

"Wait a bit," he said. "You will catch cold outside. I will call a cab."

But Matilda did not listen to him, and she rapidly descended the stairs. When they were in the street, they did not find a cab. They looked for one, shouting after the cabs they saw passing by in the distance.

Matilda and her husband went toward the river, shivering with cold. At last they found an old cab near the docks. The cab took them to their door, and then they climbed the stairs to their apartment. The wonderful evening was all over for Matilda. As for her husband, he remembered that he must be at work at nine o'clock in the morning.

Matilda removed her coat in front of the mirror. She wanted to see her beautiful dress once more. Suddenly she uttered a cry. She no longer had the necklace around her neck!

E METAPHORS

Write the answers for items 1–5.

Some metaphors do not name the two things that are the same. Here's an example: *The images melted away.* That metaphor says the images were like something that melts.

1. What object could melt?
2. Use accurate language to tell what could be the same about ice and the images.

Here's another example: *The river twisted and squirmed through the valley.*

3. What was the river like?
4. What could that thing be?
5. Use accurate language to tell how the river and that thing could be the same.

F VOCABULARY REVIEW

scant

agitated

devoted

caress

suitable

ex-

drab

proposal

For each item, write the correct word.
1. Another word for *dreary* is ▬▬.
2. Something that is appropriate is ▬▬.
3. A prefix that means "former" is ▬▬.
4. An offer or a plan to do something is a ▬▬.
5. Someone who is loyal is ▬▬.

G COMPREHENSION

Write the answers.
1. Why did Matilda suffer so much?
2. At first, why didn't Matilda want to go to the ball?
3. Why did Matilda want a necklace?
4. Why do you think Matilda chose the diamond necklace?
5. What would you do if you lost a friend's diamond necklace?

H WRITING

How is Matilda like Sara Crewe? How is she different?

Write an essay that compares Matilda and Sara Crewe. Try to answer the following questions:

• In what ways are Matilda and Sara Crewe alike?
• In what ways are they different?
• What kinds of things did Sara and Matilda imagine?

Make your essay at least sixty words long.

A WORD LISTS

1
Hard Words
1. anguish
2. unravel
3. rheumatism

2
Word Practice
1. route
2. headquarters
3. grocer
4. Ulysses

3
New Vocabulary
1. lobby
2. clasp
3. anguish
4. endure
5. rheumatism
6. unravel

B VOCABULARY DEFINITIONS

1. **lobby**—A *lobby* is a waiting room at the entrance of hotels and other large buildings.
   - What is a lobby?
2. **clasp**—A *clasp* is a hook that holds objects together. Some necklaces have a clasp at the back.
   - What does a clasp do?
3. **anguish**—When you feel *anguish*, you feel extreme pain or sorrow.
   - What's another way of saying *Her cry was filled with extreme sorrow*?
4. **endure**—When you *endure* a painful experience, you survive that experience.
   - What's another way of saying *They could hardly survive the heat*?

5. **rheumatism**—*Rheumatism* is a disease that affects people's muscles and joints. People with *rheumatism* have trouble moving their joints.
   - What does rheumatism affect?
6. **unravel**—When you *unravel* a garment, you pull apart its threads.
   - What's another way of saying *She pulled apart the threads of her sweater*?

THE NECKLACE
Part 2

Focus Question: What did Matilda learn about the necklace?

Matilda stood in front of the mirror in horror. Her husband, who had already taken off his shoes, said, "What is the matter with you?"

She turned madly towards him. "I have . . . I've lost Mrs. Forester's necklace!"

He stood up. "What? Impossible!"

And they looked in the folds of her dress, in the folds of her coat, in her pockets—everywhere. They did not find it.

He said, "Are you sure you had it on when you left the ball?"

"Yes, I felt it in the lobby."

"But if you had lost it in the street, we should have heard it fall. It must be in the cab."

"Yes. Probably. Did you take the cab's number?"

"No. And you, did you notice the number?"

"No."

They looked, thunderstruck, at one another. At last, Mr. Loisel put his shoes back on.

"I shall go back on foot," he said, "over the whole route we took, to see if I can find the necklace."

And he went out. Matilda sat and waited. She did not even have the strength to go to bed.

Matilda's husband returned around seven o'clock in the morning. He had found nothing.

Then Mr. Loisel went to the police headquarters, to the newspaper offices, to the cab companies—everywhere.

Matilda waited all day, in a condition of mad fear.

Mr. Loisel returned that night with a pale face. He had discovered nothing.

"You must write to your friend," he said. "Tell her you have broken the clasp of her necklace and are having it mended. That will give us more time to look around."◆

● ● ●

But by the end of the week, they had lost all hope.

Mr. Loisel, who had aged five years in that one week, finally said, "We must consider how to replace the necklace."

The next day they took the box that had contained the necklace and went to the jeweler whose name was on the box. The jeweler checked his records.

"I did not sell that necklace," the jeweler said. "Somebody must have used one of my boxes."

They went from jeweler to jeweler, searching for a necklace like the other one. Matilda and her husband were both sick with anguish.

They finally found a string of diamonds that seemed exactly like the one Matilda had lost. It was worth forty thousand francs. The jeweler said they could have it for thirty-six thousand francs.

They begged the jeweler not to sell it for the next three days. And they made a bargain that the jeweler would buy the necklace back if they found the other one within a month.

Mr. Loisel had only eighteen thousand francs, which his father had left him. He had to borrow the rest, asking a thousand francs from one person, five hundred from another, and so on. He took out loans without knowing if he could ever pay them back. He was frightened by how much he owed and by the misery he would have to endure. At last, he went to get the new necklace, putting thirty-six thousand francs on the counter.

Matilda gave the new necklace to Mrs. Forester. Speaking in a chilly voice, Mrs. Forester said, "You should have returned it sooner. I might have needed it."

Mrs. Forester did not open the case, as Matilda had feared. If Mrs. Forester had detected the change, what would she have thought? What would she have said? Would she have thought Matilda was a thief?

• • •

Matilda began to find out about the horrible existence of true poverty. But she took her fate bravely. The dreadful debt had to be paid. And she resolved that she would help pay it. The Loisels left their apartment and moved into a garret.

Matilda worked as a maid, and she came to know what heavy work was. She washed the dishes, using her rosy nails on the greasy pots and pans. She washed the dirty linens, shirts, and dishcloths. She car-ried the trash down to the street every morning and carried the groceries upstairs, stopping to catch her breath at every landing. Dressed like a peasant, she went to the grocer with her basket on her arm. She bargained with the grocer, franc by franc. ★

Mr. Loisel worked in the evening, sometimes until midnight. Each month, the Loisels had to pay some debts and renew others. This life lasted ten years. At the end of ten years they had paid everything— everything.

Matilda looked old now. She had become a woman of poverty—strong and hard and rough. She talked to herself loudly while washing the floor with great swishes of water. Sometimes, when her husband was at the office, she sat down near the window and thought of that gay evening long ago. She thought of the ball where she had been so beautiful and so happy.

What would have happened if she had not lost that necklace? Who knows? Who knows? How strange life is!

• • •

One Sunday, Matilda took a walk to refresh herself from a hard week's work. She suddenly saw a woman leading a child. It was Mrs. Forester. She still looked young and beautiful and charming.

Matilda felt moved. Should she speak to Mrs. Forester? Yes, certainly. Now that Matilda had paid for the necklace, she would tell Mrs. Forester all about it. Why not?

She went up to her former friend.

"Hello, Mrs. Forester," she said.

Mrs. Forester did not recognize Matilda at all and stammered, "But . . . Madame . . . I do not know . . . you must be mistaken."

"No. I am Matilda Loisel."

Matilda's friend uttered a cry.

"Oh, my poor Matilda! You have changed so much!"

"Yes, I have had many hard days since I last saw you—and all because of you!"

"Of me! How so?"

"Do you remember that diamond necklace you loaned me to wear at the ball?"

"Yes. Well?"

"Well, I lost it."

"What do you mean? You brought it back."

"I brought you another one just like it. And we have been paying for it for ten years. It was not easy for us, because we had nothing. But at last it is over, and I am very glad."

Mrs. Forester's face seemed frozen.

"You say you purchased a necklace of diamonds to replace mine?"

"Yes. You never noticed it, then. They were very much alike."

And Matilda smiled with joy.

Mrs. Forester was deeply moved, and she took Matilda's two hands.

"Oh, my poor Matilda! Why, my necklace was fake! It was worth less than five hundred francs!"

D VOCABULARY REVIEW

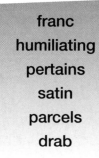

franc

humiliating

pertains

satin

parcels

drab

For each item, write the correct word.
1. Information that relates to something ▰▰▰ to that thing.
2. Another word for *dreary* is ▰▰▰.
3. Something that is quite embarrassing is ▰▰▰.

E SIMILES

Write the answers about the similes.
The party was like a dream.
1. What two things are the same in that simile?
2. How could those things be the same?
3. Name two ways those things are different.
Her face was like a star.
4. What two things are the same in that simile?
5. How could those things be the same?
6. Name two ways those things are different.

F METAPHORS

Write the answers about the metaphors.
Felix was a real motor mouth.
1. What two things are the same in that metaphor?
2. How could they be the same?
In the pool, the athlete was a fish.
3. What two things are the same in that metaphor?
4. How could they be the same?
The express train flashed right through town.
5. What was the train like?
6. Use accurate language to tell how an express train and that thing could be the same.

G COMPREHENSION

Write the answers.
1. What did Matilda learn about the necklace?
2. Why did Matilda lie to Mrs. Forester about having broken the clasp of the necklace?
3. What do you think would have happened if Matilda had told Mrs. Forester the truth right after Matilda lost the necklace?
4. What do you think Matilda learned in this story?
5. What do you think Matilda will do if Mrs. Forester gives her back the expensive necklace?

H WRITING

Matilda suffered because she assumed Mrs. Forester's necklace was made of real diamonds.

Write a story about someone who assumes something is true and then discovers it's not true. For example, a woman could assume that a man is her friend and then discover that he's not. Think about the following questions before you write your story:
- Who is the main character?
- What does the main character assume to be true?
- What does the main character do based on that assumption?
- How does the character discover that his or her assumption was wrong?
- What happens next?

Make your story at least sixty words long.

Ⓐ WORD LISTS

1
Word Practice
1. busy
2. busied
3. Telemachus
4. lyre

2
New Vocabulary
1. appeal
2. diversion
3. spurn
4. croon

Ⓑ VOCABULARY DEFINITIONS

1. **appeal**—When you *appeal,* you make an earnest request. If you *appeal* to somebody's sympathy, you make an earnest request for that person's sympathy.
   - What are you doing when you make an earnest request for somebody's sympathy?
2. **diversion**—A *diversion* is something that pulls your attention away from something else.
   - What is a diversion?

3. **spurn**—When you *spurn* something, you reject it.
   - What's another way of saying *Michael rejected their offer*?
4. **croon**—When you *croon,* you sing softly.
   - What's another way of saying *She softly sang a lullaby*?

Mystery Yarn

by Robert McCloskey
Part 1

Focus Question: Why did Uncle Telemachus and the
sheriff decide to have a contest?

One fall afternoon Homer was whistling a little tune and raking up leaves from Uncle Ulysses' front lawn and trying to decide whether to ask for his pay in cash or in doughnuts from Uncle Ulysses' Lunch Room.

He'd just finished raking the leaves into a neat pile at the curb and was about to go find a match when the sheriff turned the corner in his car.

"Hi Sheriff! Do you have a match?" shouted Homer.

"Sure thing, Homer," said the sheriff as his car jerked to a stop. "That's a right smart pile o' leaves you got there. Lurning beaves, I mean burning leaves sure smell nice don't they?" he said as he struck a match on his seat and lit the pile.

"Yep, Sheriff, and burning leaves always make me think of football and school," said Homer.

"And the county fair," added the sheriff. "That'll be along in a couple weeks. I'm gonna exhibit my chickens again this year, my white leghorns took a blue ribbon last fall. Well, I'll be seeing you, Homer," added the sheriff. Then he flicked a bit of ash off his sleeve, because he had his best Sunday suit on, climbed into his car, and drove to the end of the block. Homer watched while the sheriff got out of his car, straightened his tie and started up Miss Terwilliger's front steps.

Miss Terwilliger, as any one from Centerburg can tell you, is one of the town's best known and best loved citizens. She runs knitting classes and in years past has taught almost every woman in Centerburg how to knit. She is a familiar sight on Sundays, holidays, and at social functions, dressed in a robin's-egg-blue dress which she had knit years ago when she first started her knitting classes. In fact, Sundays and holidays did not seem complete without Miss Terwilliger in her robin's-egg-blue dress. You might think that a dress so old would look worn and out of style, but not Miss Terwilliger's. After church or after a party she changes to a house dress of simple cotton print and carefully hangs her favorite blue knit in a closet to save it for the next occasion. The matter of style doesn't bother Miss Terwilliger. If short skirts are the latest thing, she merely unravels a few inches from the bottom and the dress looks like the latest thing. Of course Miss Terwilliger saves the robin's-egg-blue yarn that she removes for, as she has so often remarked, "Longer skirts will be in style again in a year or two and then I'll have the right yarn to knit a few inches back onto the bottom of the skirt."

Miss Terwilliger is a *very* clever woman, and besides being an accomplished knitter, she is a wonderful cook. Her fried chicken is famous for miles around Centerburg. It is only natural for such a woman to have many admirers, and two special ones, the sheriff and Homer's uncle Telemachus. As long as Homer could remember the sheriff had gone every Thursday, and Uncle Telemachus had gone every Sunday, to call on Miss Terwilliger and eat a chicken dinner. And it was no secret that both the sheriff and Uncle Telemachus wanted to marry Miss Terwilliger. She liked them both but somehow she just couldn't seem to make up her mind. ◆

Homer remembered that he had another job for this afternoon so he poked the fire some more to make it burn faster.

When the fire was out Homer put away the rake and hurried off to Uncle Telemachus' house.

Homer's Uncle Telly lived all by himself in a trim little house near the railroad. Homer's mother always said, "It's a shame that Uncle Telly had to live alone because he would make an ideal husband for some fine woman like Miss 'T'." Aunt Aggy would always answer, "But I don't know how any fine woman could put up with his carryings on!"

By "carryings on" Aunt Aggy meant Uncle Telly's hobby of collecting string. Yes, Uncle Telly was a string saver and he had saved string for years and years. He had quite a lot of it too. And every Thursday afternoon he would take all of the pieces of string that he had collected during the week and wind them on his huge ball out in the garage.

That was one of Homer's jobs on Thursdays, helping Uncle Telly wind string, because Uncle Telly had had a bit of rheumatism of late. You see, the ball of string was getting too large to wind without a lot of stooping and reaching.

Uncle Telly greeted Homer at the door, "Hello, Homer, we've got a lot to wind today!"

"That's good, Uncle Telly, I brought a few pieces from home too!"

They went out to the garage and as Uncle Telly looked at his ball of string he said with pride, "Another quarter inch and it'll be six feet across . . . biggest ball of string in the world."

"Well, I don't know, Uncle Telly," said Homer, "Freddy's been helping the sheriff wind his string down at the jail, and he says the sheriff's ball of string is just about six feet across too."

"Humph! I've heard tell that the sheriff winds his string loose, so's the ball looks bigger. Mine's wound *tight*," said Uncle Telly poking the ball, "and it's a lot longer than the sheriff's ball of string'll ever be."

"Yep! I guess you're right," said Homer, and he began winding the string while Uncle Telly tied the pieces together in double knots.

"Wind it tight," reminded Uncle Telly, "don't let anybody say that my string isn't wound right! I'll have none of this loose, sloppy, sheriff kind of winding on my ball o' string!"

Just as Homer and Uncle Telly were about finished there was a knock on the garage door and when Uncle Telly opened the door there stood the sheriff and Judge Shank.

"Good day, Telemachus!" said the judge.

"Howdy, Telly," said the sheriff, trying to peer over Uncle Telly's shoulder and see the ball of string.

"Howdy, Judge," said Uncle Telly, and scowling at the sheriff he said, "I didn't expect *you'd* be calling on *me* on a Thursday afternoon." ★

"Ahem, Telemachus," said the judge, "I just happened to stop in the knitting shop to drive my wife home when I met the sheriff. As you know Telly,—er Telemachus, it is necessary to cut down expenses at the fair this year, and we cannot afford to have the trotting races that we have always had. The sheriff, who like myself is on the fair board, and who, like yourself, is a string saver has suggested that he, and you, Telemachus, enter into an event that could be held on the race track, and provide the diversion that the trotting races have . . ."

"Yep!" interrupted the sheriff, "I challenge you to unroll your string around the race track, just to prove once and for all that I've got more string than you have."

"Er, yes, to put it bluntly, that is the situation, Telemachus. I appeal to your sense of county pride. Do not spurn the offer. And then, of course, the winner will receive a prize . . ."

"I'll *do* it, by Zeus!" said Uncle Telly. "We'll see who's got the most string, Sheriff! Your ball might be just as big as mine but it ain't wound tight." And to prove his point Uncle Telly gave his ball a kick and almost lost his balance.

"Very well, gentlemen," said the judge, "I shall . . ."

"Wait a minute, Judge," interrupted Uncle Telly, "I mean, I'll do it on one condition." (Uncle Telly was noted for driving a hard bargain and Homer wondered just what it would be.) "If I win this here contest, the sheriff has to promise to spend his Thursday afternoons out of town and give Miss Terwilliger a chance to make up her mind to marry me."

"Well," said the sheriff, "in that case, if *I* win you'll have to leave town on Sundays, and give Miss Terwilliger a chance to make up her mind to marry *me*!"

"It's a deal," said Uncle Telly, and he and the sheriff shook hands for the first time in years (just to clinch the bargain of course).

"Very well, gentlemen," crooned the judge, "I shall judge this contest, and at our earliest convenience we will draw up a set of rules pertaining . . . Good day, Telemachus."

"G'by Telly," said the sheriff, "sorry I can't stay but I got an appointment."

Uncle Telly slammed the door on the sheriff and went back to tying knots.

"We'll see!" he said, and pulled the next knot so hard that he broke the string.

"Golly, Uncle Telly," said Homer. "That's going to be a swell contest. I hope you win the prize."

"Uhumpf! Prize or no prize we'll see who's got the most," said Uncle Telly, "and Miss Terwilliger will get a chance to make up her mind. That woman certainly can cook!" sighed Uncle Telly with a dreamy look. Then he busied himself with his knots and said, "Now mind you, Homer, wind it tight."

D DEDUCTIONS

Write the answers for items 1 and 2.

Here's the evidence: *All living things need water. An antelope is a living thing.*

1. What's the conclusion about an antelope?

Here's the evidence: *Some birds cannot fly. An egret is a bird.*

2. What's the conclusion about an egret?

E METAPHORS

Write the answers about the metaphor. *The detective scratched and dug for clues.*

1. So, the detective was like something that ▮▮▮▮.
2. What could that something be?
3. Use accurate language to tell how the detective and that thing could be the same.

F VOCABULARY REVIEW

endure
drab
suitable
anguish
proposal
humiliating
pertains

For each item, write the correct word.
1. Something that is quite embarrassing is ▮▮▮▮.
2. Extreme pain or sorrow is ▮▮▮▮.
3. When you survive a painful experience, you ▮▮▮▮ that experience.
4. Information that relates to something ▮▮▮▮ to that thing.

G COMPREHENSION

Write the answers.

1. Why did Uncle Telemachus and the sheriff decide to have a contest?
2. How was Miss Terwilliger able to shorten or lengthen her robin's-egg-blue dress?
3. When Aunt Aggy talked about Uncle Telly, she said, "I don't know how any fine woman could put up with his carryings on." What did she mean?
4. Why do you think Uncle Telly collects string?
5. How do you think Miss Terwilliger will feel if she finds out about the bargain between the sheriff and Uncle Telly? Explain your answer.

H WRITING

Uncle Telly's hobby was collecting string. What hobby do you have or would you like to have?

Write an essay that describes your hobby and explains why you like that hobby. Try to answer the following questions:

- If you have a hobby, what is it?
- If you don't have a hobby, what hobby would you like to have?
- Why is the hobby interesting to you?
- What would you like to accomplish in your hobby?
- What other hobbies interest you? Why?

Make your essay at least sixty words long.

Ⓐ WORD LISTS

1

Hard Words

1. maneuver
2. plaid
3. diameter
4. unprecedented
5. mustache

2

Word Practice

1. edition
2. interruptions
3. frantically

3

New Vocabulary

1. maneuver
2. regard
3. diameter
4. contestant
5. unprecedented
6. plaid

Ⓑ VOCABULARY DEFINITIONS

1. **maneuver**—When you *maneuver,* you move skillfully.
   - What's another way of saying *She moved skillfully through traffic*?
2. **regard**—When you *regard,* you consider. If somebody is considered a winner, that person is *regarded* as a winner.
   - What's another way of saying *They considered their options*?
3. **diameter**—The *diameter* of a circle is the length of a straight line that goes through the center of the circle.
   - What do we call the length of a straight line that goes through the center of a circle?

4. **contestant**—A *contestant* is somebody who takes part in a contest.
   - What is a contestant?
5. **unprecedented**—Something that is *unprecedented* has never occurred before. An event that has never occurred before is an *unprecedented* event.
   - What's another way of saying *an agreement that has never occurred before*?
6. **plaid**—*Plaid* is a type of fabric covered with crisscrossing stripes.
   - What is plaid?

Mystery Yarn

Part 2

Focus Question: How do you think Miss Terwilliger felt about the string contest?

In the Friday night edition of the *Centerburg Bugle* Homer read a long article on the county fair, and a special announcement about the contest to determine the world's champion string saver, and then the rules that Judge Shank had drawn up.

"Each contestant may appoint an assistant to help with the maneuvering of his ball of string."

"The balls of string shall be unwound, i.e., rolled around the county fair race track in a counter clockwise direction, starting from the judge's booth in front of the main grandstand."

"The ball of string reaching around the race track the greatest number of times shall be regarded as the winning string, and that string's owner shall be declared winner of the prize and of the title of World's Champion String Saver. The string shall be unwound for two hours every afternoon of the week of the fair, starting at two o'clock."

Homer read the rules and noticed that nothing was mentioned about the gentleman's agreement between the sheriff and Uncle Telly, but that sort of news travels fast in a town the size of Centerburg, and

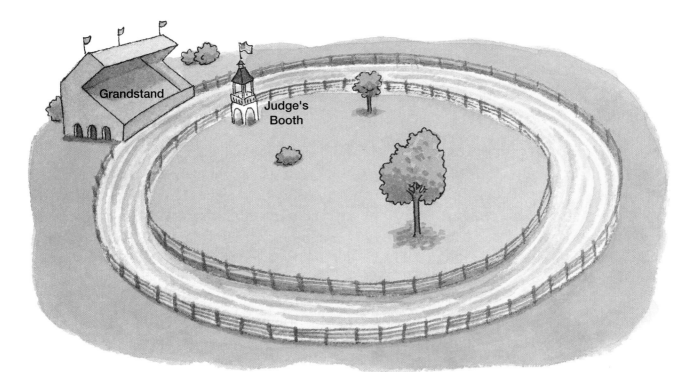

it wasn't long before practically everybody knew that the winner was *supposed* to have the hand of Miss Terwilliger in marriage.

Homer decided to go past Uncle Telly's house and see what he thought about the rules.

Homer couldn't help wondering what a woman who could cook fried chicken so well, and who was as *clever* as Miss Terwilliger would do if *she* heard about the agreement.

Homer found Uncle Telly trying to figure out how many miles of string were wound on his ball. He was multiplying 3.1416 by the diameter and after multiplying by several figures he asked Homer how many feet in a mile.

"Five thousand, two hundred and eighty," said Homer.

Then Uncle Telly multiplied by four. Then he turned to Homer and said, "I figure there's enough string to go around that race track a hundred times. Yep! Twenty-five miles of string! Just let the sheriff beat that if he can!" ◆

"Look, Uncle Telly, here comes the judge and the sheriff again, and look who's with them, *Miss Terwilliger!*"

Uncle Telly opened the door before the judge had a chance to knock, and the judge puffed in, followed by the sheriff and Miss Terwilliger.

"Ah, phuf! Ha, good day, Ha, Phuf! Telemachus, Haah! We have a new contestant for the title of World's Champion String Saver!" puffed the judge.

Miss Terwilliger blushed and giggled while Uncle Telly backed around to the other side of the room and raised his eyebrows at the sheriff in a way that asked, "Did *you* tell her about the agreement?" The sheriff shrugged his shoulders and wig-gled his mustache to show he was just as puzzled as Uncle Telly.

Miss Terwilliger (if she did know about the agreement) wasn't admitting it. "Isn't it *wonderful*," she said to Uncle Telemachus and the sheriff, "that we have *so* much in common?"

"Yes," she tittered, "I've been a savin' string for the past fifteen years! All of the colored yarn and odds and ends from knitting classes. I have a beautiful ball of yarn, all colors of the rainbow."

"Splendid!" said the judge, rubbing his hands together. "Simply splendid, Miss Terwilliger!"

"But Judge," interrupted Uncle Telly anxiously.

"Do you think," said the sheriff, nudging the judge, and winking frantically, "that a *woman* should enter into a sing of this thort, I mean, thing of this sort?"

"Splendid!" continued the judge, ignoring these interruptions. "The American female is beginning to find her rightful place in the business and public life of this nation. The sheriff and Telemachus and I deeply appreciate your public spirit, Miss Terwilliger, and I'm sure that the county fair will be an unprecedented success."

"Come, Judge," said Miss Terwilliger with a smile, "I must get back to my knitting shop. Good-by Sheriff, good-by Telemachus, I'll see *you* on Sunday."

After the judge and Miss Terwilliger were gone the sheriff and Uncle Telly each accused the other of telling about the agreement. They finally calmed down and decided that the judge had double crossed them with his fancy speech about "woman's rights." ★

"But Uncle Telly," said Homer, "there couldn't be *three* balls of string in the world as large as yours and the sheriff's."

"You're wrong, son!" said the sheriff with a sigh. "Her ball of string's *bigger* than mine! She's a clever woman, son, a *very* clever woman."

"If she wins," said Uncle Telly gloomily, "we'll be right back where we started from, waiting forever for her to make up her mind."

• • •

During the next week the whole county got excited about the contest to determine the world's champion string saver. Everybody started saving string for their favorite contestant. The ladies in Miss Terwilliger's knitting classes reported that Miss Terwilliger was knitting a brand new dress for the occasion. When Homer's mother heard this she called Aunt Aggy and said, "We should do something about Uncle Telly. You know how men are about clothes. They can hardly tell one dress or suit from another. The next day they dragged Uncle Telly down town and picked out a nice new and very becoming plaid suit for him. The sheriff said, "If they're going to make a shashion fow, I mean fashion show, out of this thing I can dress up, too!" He sent away special delivery to Chicago and ordered an expertly fashioned double-breasted Hollywood model suit.

On the day before the fair started, Homer went up to Miss Terwilliger's with the sheriff to see them take her ball of string out of the house. Mr. Olson, the carpenter, had to take out the side of the house

because the ball just wouldn't go through the door. When the moving men rolled it out and on to the truck, the sheriff said, "That's as purty a ball a string as I've ever seen. It's got a toman's woutch! I mean a woman's touch!"

Just then Uncle Telly walked up and agreed, "It's awful pretty, being all colors of the rainbow, but it ain't wound tight. It's so soft you can poke your fist right into it."

"Yes, but yarn stretches purty much," said the sheriff unhappily.

D DEDUCTIONS

Write the answers for items 1 and 2.
Here's the evidence: *No person can live forever. Lamar is a person.*
1. What's the conclusion about Lamar?
Here's the evidence: *Some Greek gods lived on Mount Olympus. Pan was a Greek god.*
2. What's the conclusion about Pan?

E METAPHORS

Write the answers about the metaphor. *Odysseus swooped down on the lazy suitors.*
1. So, Odysseus was like something that ▬▬.
2. What could that something be?
3. Use accurate language to tell how Odysseus and that thing could be the same.

F VOCABULARY REVIEW

endure
devoted
humiliating
diversion
spurn
appeal
proposal

For each item, write the correct word.
1. Something that is quite embarrassing is ▬▬.
2. When you reject something, you ▬▬ it.
3. Something that pulls your attention away from something else is a ▬▬.
4. When you make an earnest request, you ▬▬.

G COMPREHENSION

Write the answers.
1. How do you think Miss Terwilliger felt about the string contest?
2. What do you think Miss Terwilliger will do if she wins the contest?
3. How is Miss Terwilliger like Penelope in *The Odyssey*?
4. How is Miss Terwilliger's ball of string different from Uncle Telly's?
5. How is the judge's way of talking different from the sheriff's?

H WRITING

The judge uses a lot of big words when he talks.

Pretend the judge is presenting the string-saving award to someone. Write the speech the judge might make. Think about the following questions before you begin:
- How will the judge describe the person who won the contest?
- How will the judge explain the rules of the contest?
- How will the judge congratulate the winner?
- What words might the judge use to explain simple things?

Make your speech at least sixty words long.

56

A WORD LISTS

1
Hard Words
1. reception
2. parasol
3. bough
4. deduction
5. antelope
6. egret

2
Word Practice
1. Iliad
2. Athena
3. Ithaca
4. Penelope

3
New Vocabulary
1. best man
2. parasol
3. core
4. reception
5. undisputed

B VOCABULARY DEFINITIONS

1. **best man**—The *best man* is a person who assists the groom during a wedding.
   - What does a best man do?
2. **parasol**—A *parasol* is a light umbrella that people use to shade themselves.
   - What is a parasol?
3. **core**—*Core* is another word for *center.* The core of an apple is the center of the apple.
   - What's another way of saying *the center of the city*?

4. **reception**—A *reception* is a party that takes place after an important event. A party that takes place after a wedding is a wedding *reception*.
   - What do we call a party that takes place after a concert?
5. **undisputed**—If something is *undisputed,* there is no doubt about it. If there is no doubt that she won the race, she is the *undisputed* winner.
   - What do we call a fact that there is no doubt about?

Mystery Yarn
Part 3

Focus Question: Why did Miss Terwilliger wear her robin's-egg-blue dress on the last day of the contest?

The day the fair opened the grandstand was crowded and people stood halfway around the track when the contestants and their assistants started unrolling their string. Miss Terwilliger's new pink dress and the sheriff's and Uncle Telly's new suits caused much favorable comment from the ladies present. The men were more interested in the string, but as Homer's mother said, "They can hardly tell one dress or suit from another." Miss Terwilliger and the sheriff and Uncle Telly were hot and tired after the first two times around the track and so were their assistants. So the judge had some of the regular county fair employees roll the balls while the contestants rode around the track alongside in the sheriff's car.

After the first afternoon's unrolling, Miss Terwilliger's ball measured 5'9"; the sheriff's measured 5'8¾"; Uncle Telly's 5'8". Uncle Telly and the sheriff were very uneasy. At the end of the second day the sheriff's and Miss Terwilliger's 5'; Uncle Telly's 4'11¹⁵⁄₁₆". Uncle Telly felt a little better, and so did the sheriff.

The measurements at the end of the next to the last day of the fair were Uncle Telly and the sheriff running 16½", and Miss Terwilliger only 12⅝", and each contestant's ball of string had unrolled around the track ninety-nine times.

Uncle Telly and the sheriff were feeling pretty confident now, and each one was sure of winning the title of world's champion string saver *and* the hand of the clever Miss Terwilliger.◆

On the last day of the contest everybody in Center County was on hand early. The contestants were going to roll their balls of string around the track themselves. The sheriff and Uncle Telly were all dressed up for the occasion but Miss Terwilliger was not wearing her new knit dress. The ladies noticed right away that she was wearing the old robin's-egg-blue one that she had saved all these years. She started off carrying her ball in a gay little basket and a parasol to protect her from the autumn sun. She marched right off at 2:00 with her string trailing behind her.

Most everybody knew that Miss Terwilliger's ball was 3⅜" less across than the sheriff's or Uncle Telly's and they admired her confidence and her spirit, but they all knew that she couldn't win.

Uncle T. and the sheriff, each feeling confident, were taking it slow. They watched each other like hawks, and they unwound their string right up against the fence and checked up on each other's knots. They hadn't even gotten a quarter of the way around when Miss Terwilliger was at the half-way mark.

Homer could see her walking right along wearing her robin's-egg-blue dress with the pink trim at the bottom, carrying her basket and the parasol to protect her from the autumn sun. The sheriff and Telly were half-way around still checking every knot and stretching their string as tight as they dared against the fence.

Now Miss Terwilliger was three-quarters of the way around, still walking right along wearing her robin's-egg-blue blouse with the pink skirt, carrying her basket and the parasol to protect her from the autumn sun.

Uncle Telly shouted at the three-quarters mark, "I've won! The sheriff wound his string around a walnut! Mine's solid to the core!"

Everybody started shouting "Hurrah for Telly! Hurrah for Telly the world's champion string saver!" And after the noise had died down people heard another shout, "I've won!" And then they noticed for the first time that Miss Terwilliger was standing right down in front of the grandstand wearing her dress with the robin's-egg-blue trim at the neck and sleeves, holding her basket and the parasol to protect her from the autumn sun. ★

The judge puffed down to where Miss Terwilliger was and held up the end of her string and shouted, "I pronounce you the winner of the title of String Saving Champion of the World!"

Then everybody started cheering for Miss Terwilliger.

Uncle Ulysses and the sheriff trudged up and congratulated Miss Terwilliger, and told her how glad they were that she had won the championship. Everyone could see though that they were unhappy about having to wait forever for her to make up her mind—especially Uncle Telly.

Practically every woman who was there that day knew how the clever Miss Terwilliger had won the championship. They enjoyed it immensely and laughed among themselves, but they didn't give away the secret because they thought, "all's fair in love," and besides a woman ought to be allowed to make up her own mind.

There *might* have been a few *very*

observing men, who like Homer, knew how she won. But they didn't say anything either, or, maybe they just didn't get around to mentioning it before Miss Terwilliger finally decided to marry Uncle Telly the following week. It was a grand wedding with the sheriff as best man.

Uncle Telemachus and his new wife left for Niagara Falls, while the guests at the reception were still drinking punch and eating wedding cake, and doughnuts—not to mention fried chicken.

"That was a wandy dedding, I mean a dandy wedding!" said the sheriff to Homer while polishing off a chicken breast. He looked at the wishbone and sighed. Then after a minute he brightened and said, "But they've asked me to dinner every Thursday night!"

"You know, Homer," said the sheriff with a smile, "they'll be a very cappy houple, I mean, happy couple, going through life savin' string together."

"Yep," said Homer, "I guess they're the undisputed champions now."

"Guess you're right, Homer, nobody'll *ever* get so much string saved on one ball as they have . . . Heck, I think I'll start savin' paper bags or bottle caps!"

D DEDUCTIONS

Complete each deduction.

Here's the evidence: *Every bird has feathers. A heron is a bird.*

1. What's the conclusion about a heron?

Here's the evidence: *Some poems rhyme.* Paradise Lost *is a poem.*

2. What's the conclusion about *Paradise Lost*?

E INFERENCE

Write the answers for items 1–6.

You have to answer different types of questions about the passages you read. Some questions are answered by words in the passage. Other questions are *not* answered by words in the passage. You have to figure out the answer by making a deduction.

The following passage includes both types of questions.

Ecology

Ecology is the study of how the life of one living thing affects the lives of other living things. The more we study ecology, the more we discover that the life of a beetle in a faraway place may affect the lives of birds near us. The lives of these birds may affect the lives of trees, or even the lives of people. We are finding that a change in any living thing affects many other living things.

1. What does a change in any living thing affect?
2. Is that question answered by **words** or by a **deduction?**
3. If mice change, what might happen to cats?
4. **Words** or **deduction?**
5. Could a change in a cow's life affect the life of a rose?
6. **Words** or **deduction?**

F VOCABULARY REVIEW

diversion
appeal
regard
spurn
endure
unprecedented
anguish
plaid
maneuver
croon

For each item, write the correct word.

1. When you consider something, you ____ it.
2. Something that has never occurred before is ____.
3. When you move skillfully, you ____.
4. When you make an earnest request, you ____.
5. When you reject something, you ____ it.
6. When you survive an experience, you ____ it.
7. A word that means "extreme pain" is ____.

G COMPREHENSION

Write the answers.

1. Why did Miss Terwilliger wear her robin's-egg-blue dress on the last day of the contest?
2. How did Miss Terwilliger's appearance change as she walked around the racetrack?
3. Why didn't most of the men at the contest understand how Miss Terwilliger had won?
4. The women thought, "All's fair in love." What does that phrase mean?
5. Do you think Miss Terwilliger won the contest by cheating? Explain your answer.

H WRITING

"Mystery Yarn" makes fun of the differences between men and women.

Write an essay that explains some of the differences between men and women in the story. Think about the following questions:

- What was different about how the men and the women behaved?
- What was different about the things each group noticed?
- How did the men think Miss Terwilliger should make up her mind?
- How did Miss Terwilliger actually make up her mind?

Make your essay at least sixty words long.

Ⓐ WORD LISTS

1
Hard Words
1. heron
2. trio
3. Sylvia
4. wilderness
5. gallant
6. pigeon

2
Word Practice
1. Circe
2. Calypso
3. Scylla

3
New Vocabulary
1. heron
2. foster parent
3. huckleberry
4. bough
5. gallant
6. trio
7. game

Ⓑ VOCABULARY DEFINITIONS

1. **heron**—*Herons* are birds that wade through water and eat frogs and fish. Herons usually have tall, thin legs and a long, S-shaped neck. The picture shows a *white heron.*
   • Describe a heron.
2. **foster parent**—A *foster parent* is somebody who brings up a child but is not the child's real parent.
   • What do we call somebody who brings up a child but is not the child's real parent?
3. **huckleberry**—A *huckleberry* is a small purple or black berry that grows on bushes.
   • What is a huckleberry?
4. **bough**—A *bough* of a tree is a branch of the tree.
   • What is a branch of a tree?
5. **gallant**—Somebody who is *gallant* is brave and noble.
   • What's another way of saying *He was a noble warrior*?
6. **trio**—A *trio* is a group of three.
   • What's another way of saying *A group of three went to the river*?
7. **game**—Wild animals that are hunted are called *game.*
   • What do we call wild animals that are hunted?

READING

A White Heron

by Sarah Orne Jewett *
Part 1

Focus Question: How did Sylvia feel about
living on her foster mother's farm?

The woods were filled with shadows one June evening, but a bright sunset still glimmered faintly among the trunks of the trees. A girl named Sylvia was driving a cow from the pasture to her home. Sylvia had spent more than an hour looking for the cow and had finally found her hiding behind a huckleberry bush.

Sylvia and the cow were going away from the sunset and into the dark woods. But they were familiar with the path, and the darkness did not bother them.

Sylvia wondered what her foster mother, Mrs. Tilley, would say because they were so late. But Mrs. Tilley knew how difficult it was to find the cow. She had chased the beast many times herself. As she waited, she was only thankful that Sylvia could help her. Sylvia seemed to love the out-of-doors, and Mrs. Tilley thought that being outdoors was a good change for an orphan girl who had grown up in a town.

The companions followed the shady road. The cow took slow steps, and the girl took very fast ones. The cow stopped at the brook to drink, and Sylvia stood still and waited. She let her bare feet cool themselves in the water while the great twilight moths struck softly against her. She waded on through the brook as the cow moved away, and she listened to the waterbirds with pleasure.

There was a stirring in the great boughs overhead. They were full of little birds that seemed to be wide awake and going about their business. Sylvia began to feel sleepy as she walked along. However, it was not much farther to the house, and the air was soft and sweet.

She was not often in the woods so late as this. The darkness made her feel as if she were a part of the gray shadows and the moving leaves. She was thinking how long it seemed since she had first come to her foster mother's farm a year ago. Sylvia wondered if everything was still going on in the noisy town just the same as when she had lived there. ◆

It seemed to Sylvia that she had never been alive at all before she came to live at her foster mother's farm. It was a beautiful place to live, and she never wished to go back to the town. The thought of the children who used to chase and frighten her made her hurry along the path to escape from the shadows of the trees.

_____
* *Adapted for young readers*

Suddenly, she was horror-struck to hear a clear whistle not very far away. It was not a bird's whistle. It sounded more like a boy's. Sylvia stepped aside into the bushes, but she was too late. The whistler had discovered her, and he called out in a cheerful voice, "Hello, little girl, how far is it to the road?"

Trembling, Sylvia answered quietly, "A long distance."

She did not dare to look at the tall young man, who carried a gun over his shoulder. But Sylvia came out of the bushes and again followed the cow, while the young man walked alongside her.

"I have been hunting for some birds," the stranger said kindly, "and I have lost my way. Don't be afraid," he added gallantly. "Speak up and tell me what your name is and whether you think I can spend the night at your house and go out hunting early in the morning." ★

Sylvia was more alarmed than before. Would her foster mother blame her for this? She hung her head, but she managed to answer "Sylvia" when her companion again asked her name.

Mrs. Tilley was standing in the doorway when the trio came into view. The cow gave a loud moo as if to explain the situation.

Mrs. Tilley said, "Yes, you'd better speak up for yourself, you naughty old cow! Where'd she hide herself this time, Sylvia?" But Sylvia kept silent.

The young man stood his gun beside the door and dropped a heavy gamebag next to it. Then he said good evening to Mrs. Tilley. He repeated his story and asked if he could have a night's lodging.

"Put me anywhere you like," he said. "I must be off early in the morning, before day, but I am very hungry indeed. Could you give me some milk?"

"Dear sakes, yes," said Mrs. Tilley. "You might do better if you went out to the main road, but you're welcome to what we've got. I'll milk the cow right now, and you make yourself at home. Now step round and set a plate for the gentleman, Sylvia!"

Sylvia promptly stepped. She was glad to have something to do, and she was hungry herself.

D INFERENCE

Write the answers for items 1–8.

You have to answer different types of questions about the passages you read. Some questions are answered by words in the passage. Other questions are *not* answered by words in the passage. You have to figure out the answer by making a deduction.

The following passage includes both types of questions.

More about Ecology

Two hundred years ago, many people were not concerned with ecology. They believed there was no end to the different types of wildlife, so they killed wild animals by the hundreds of thousands. When we look back on these killings, we may feel shocked. But for the people who lived two hundred years ago, wild animals seemed to be as plentiful as weeds.

Because of these killings, more than a hundred types of animals have become extinct since 1800. An animal is extinct when there are no more animals of that type.

One type of extinct animal is the passenger pigeon. At one time, these birds were so plentiful that flocks of them used to blacken the sky. Now the passenger pigeon is gone forever. Think of that. You will never get to see a living passenger pigeon or any of the other animals that have become extinct. The only place you can see those animals is in a museum, where they are stuffed and mounted.

1. Are house cats extinct?
2. Is that question answered by **words** or a **deduction?**
3. What extinct animal is mentioned in the passage?
4. **Words** or **deduction?**
5. How many types of animals have become extinct since 1800?
6. **Words** or **deduction?**
7. The dodo bird is extinct. How many animals of that type are alive today?
8. **Words** or **deduction?**

Write the answers about the deductions.

E DEDUCTIONS

Oliver believed that if he studied, he would pass the test. Oliver studied for the test.

1. So, what did Oliver believe would happen?

Nadia believed that if you ate an apple a day you would stay healthy. Nadia ate an apple every day.

2. So, what did Nadia believe would happen?

VOCABULARY REVIEW

| unprecedented |
| maneuver |
| devoted |
| spurn |
| endured |
| regard |

For each item, write the correct word.
1. When you move skillfully, you ▬▬.
2. When you consider something, you ▬▬ it.
3. Something that has never occurred before is ▬▬.

G COMPREHENSION

Write the answers.
1. How did Sylvia feel about living on her foster mother's farm?
2. Why didn't Sylvia like the town?
3. Why do you think Sylvia didn't dare to look at the young man?
4. How do you think Sylvia feels about hunting? Explain your answer.
5. What do you think will happen in the next part of the story?

H WRITING

Where would you rather live, on a farm or in a town?

Write an essay that explains your answer. Try to answer the following questions:
• What are the advantages of living on a farm?
• What are the disadvantages of living on a farm?
• What are the advantages of living in a town?
• What are the disadvantages of living in a town?
• Where would you rather live? Why?
Make your essay at least sixty words long.

58

A WORD LISTS

1

Word Practice
1. sympathetic
2. unsuspecting
3. Phacia
4. Demeter
5. pigeon
6. Bastille

2

New Vocabulary
1. New England
2. landmark
3. wilderness
4. rare

B VOCABULARY DEFINITIONS

1. **New England**—The northeastern part of the United States is called *New England.*
   - What is the northeastern part of the United States called?
2. **landmark**—A *landmark* is an easily recognized feature of a landscape. A large hotel may be a landmark in a particular city. A cliff may be a landmark along a river.
   - What are some other landmarks?
3. **wilderness**—A *wilderness* is a wild place with no signs of people.
   - What do we call a wild place with no signs of people?
4. **rare**—When something is *rare,* it is hard to find. A book that is hard to find is a rare book.
   - What's another way of saying *a bird that is hard to find*?

A White Heron
Part 2

Focus Question: Why was the young man looking for the white heron?

The young man was surprised to find such a clean and comfortable house in this New England wilderness. When the three people sat down to dinner, he listened eagerly to the old woman. From time to time, he looked at Sylvia's pale face and shining black eyes. He insisted that this was the best supper he had eaten for a month. Afterward, the new friends sat down on the front step to watch the moon rise.

Mrs. Tilley began to tell the young man about her family. She said that a son in California was all the family she had left. "Dan, my boy, was a great hunter," she explained sadly. "I always had ducks or gray squirrels while he was at home. He's been a great wanderer, though, and he doesn't write letters. I don't blame him. I'd have seen the world myself if I could have."

Mrs. Tilley frowned and glanced first at the young man and then at Sylvia. Before he could ask about her, she explained, "It gets lonesome out here with nobody to care for or talk to, so I took Sylvia in. She was in a sad state when I found her in town. But she took to living out here like a duck takes to water."

She laughed and continued, "Sylvia's a lot like Dan. There isn't a foot of ground she doesn't know, and the wild creatures think of her as one of themselves. She'll tame squirrels to come and feed right out of her hands, and all sorts of birds. Last winter, she got the jaybirds to feeding here, and I believe she'd have thrown her own meals to them if I hadn't kept watch. I tell her that she can bring around any creatures but crows."

"So Sylvia knows all about birds, does she?" the young man exclaimed as he looked round at the girl. Sylvia looked very quiet and sleepy as she sat in the moonlight. "I am making a collection of birds myself," the young man said. "I have been at it ever since I was a boy."

Mrs. Tilley smiled. ◆

He continued, "There are two or three rare birds I have been hunting for the last five years. I intend to get them if they can be found."

"Do you cage them?" asked Mrs. Tilley.

"Oh, no, I shoot them, and then they're stuffed and preserved, dozens and dozens of them," said the young man. "I caught a glimpse of a heron a few miles from here on Saturday, and I have followed it in this direction. Herons have never been found in this area at all. A white heron, it is."

He turned again to look at Sylvia with the hope of discovering that she knew about the rare bird.

But Sylvia was watching a hop toad in the narrow footpath.

"You would know the heron if you saw it," the stranger continued eagerly. "An odd tall white bird with soft feathers and long thin legs. It would have a nest made of sticks in the top of a high tree, something like a hawk's nest."

Sylvia's heart gave a wild beat. She knew that strange white bird. She had once stood near the bird in some bright green swamp grass at the other side of the woods. The grass was in an open place where the sunshine always seemed strangely yellow and hot and where tall, nodding bushes grew. Not far beyond that place were the salt marshes, and beyond those was the sea. Sylvia wondered and dreamed about the sea, but she had never seen it. Sometimes, she could hear its great voice above the noise of the woods.

"I can't think of anything I should like better than finding that heron's nest," the handsome stranger was saying. "I would give a hundred dollars to anybody who could show me the nest," he added, "and I will spend my whole vacation hunting for it if that's necessary."

Mrs. Tilley paid attention to all he said, but Sylvia just watched the toad.

That night, Sylvia thought of all the things she could buy for a hundred dollars.

The next day, the young sportsman went into the woods, and Sylvia kept him company. She had lost her fear of the young man. He turned out to be kind and sympathetic. He told her many things about the birds and what they knew and where they lived and what they did. ★

Sylvia only felt afraid of the young man when he shot down an unsuspecting bird from its bough. Sylvia would have liked the young man vastly better without his gun; she could not understand why he killed the very birds he seemed to like so much. But as the day went on, Sylvia still watched the young man with admiration. She had never seen anybody so charming and delightful.

The two companions crossed the woodlands with silent care. They stopped to listen to a bird's song, then advanced again. They spoke to each other rarely and in whispers. The young man went first, and Sylvia followed a few steps behind. Her eyes were dark with excitement.

The young man did not find the white heron that day. Sylvia did not lead the young man anywhere; she only followed, and she never spoke first. At last, evening began to fall. Sylvia and the young man came to the pasture and began to lead the cow home. Sylvia smiled with pleasure when they came to the place where she had heard the young man's whistle and had been afraid only the night before.

● ● ●

Half a mile from Sylvia's home, at the farthest edge of the woods, a great pine tree stood, the last of its kind. No one knew why it was still standing. The woodchoppers who had cut down the other pine trees were dead and gone. A whole forest of smaller trees—pines and oaks and maples—had grown since then. But the proud branches of this old pine towered above all the other trees and made a landmark that could be seen from miles and miles away.

Sylvia knew the tree well. She had always believed that whoever climbed to the top of it could see the ocean. She had often laid her hand on the great rough trunk and looked up at the top branches. The wind always stirred these branches, no matter how hot and still it was below.

That evening, she thought of the tree with a new excitement. If she climbed it at daybreak, she could see all around. She could easily discover where the white heron came from and mark the place and find the hidden nest.

D DEDUCTIONS

Complete each deduction.
All planets orbit around a sun. Neptune is a planet.
1. What's the conclusion about Neptune?

Some plants bloom at night. A crocus is a plant.
2. What's the conclusion about a crocus?

E INFERENCE

Read the following passage and answer the questions.
Endangered Species

Once a type, or species, of animal becomes extinct, it is gone forever. More than one hundred species of animals have become extinct since the year 1800. In addition to these animals, several hundred species are endangered. An endangered species is one that is nearly extinct.

Sumatran tigers are an endangered species. They used to roam across most of Indonesia. Now they survive only on Sumatra, an island off the coast of Indonesia. The Alaskan brown bear, the African elephant, the bald eagle, and the sea turtle are other endangered species.

The list of endangered and extinct species will continue to grow until people make the world a better place for all living things. Tigers may not get along well with people, but if we kill them all, we won't ever be able to get them back. Once an animal is extinct, it is extinct forever.

1. What is another word for *type*?
2. Is that question answered by **words** or by a **deduction?**
3. The bald eagle is an endangered species. Could it become extinct?
4. **Words** or **deduction?**
5. Name four endangered species.
6. **Words** or **deduction?**
7. The dodo bird is extinct. Can you have a dodo bird for a pet?
8. **Words** or **deduction?**

🅕 OUTLINING

Complete the following outline for "The Necklace." Copy each main idea; then write three supporting details for each main idea. Use complete sentences.

1. Matilda was a big success at the ball.
2. The Loisels had a hard life for ten years.
3. Ten years later, Matilda talked with Mrs. Forester.

🅖 VOCABULARY REVIEW

appeal
game
reception
gallant
bough
pertains
diversion
heron
trio
undisputed
core

For each item, write the correct word.
1. A party that takes place after an important event is a ▮▮▮▮.
2. Somebody who is brave and noble is ▮▮▮▮.
3. A group of three is a ▮▮▮▮.
4. If there is no doubt about something, that thing is ▮▮▮▮.
5. A branch of a tree is a ▮▮▮▮ of the tree.
6. Something that pulls your attention away from something else is a ▮▮▮▮.
7. When you make an earnest request, you ▮▮▮▮.
8. Information that relates to something ▮▮▮▮ to that thing.

H COMPREHENSION

Write the answers.
1. Why was the young man looking for the white heron?
2. Why did the wild creatures think of Sylvia as one of them?
3. Why do you think the young man killed the birds he seemed to like?
4. Why was Sylvia tempted to help the young man find the heron?
5. Do you think Sylvia should help the young man find the heron? Why or why not?

I WRITING

What would you rather look at, a stuffed bird in a museum or a live bird in the woods?

Write an essay that explains what you would rather look at. Try to answer the following questions:
- What are the advantages of looking at stuffed birds in a museum? The disadvantages?
- What are the advantages of looking at live birds in the woods? The disadvantages?
- Which type of bird would you rather see? Why?

Make your essay at least sixty words long.

A WORD LISTS

1
Word Practice
1. Greenwich Village
2. Persephone
3. pigeon
4. extinct
5. Hades
6. Cerberus

2
New Vocabulary
1. pine pitch
2. birch
3. hemlock
4. crest
5. slender
6. reveal

B VOCABULARY DEFINITIONS

1. **pine pitch**—*Pine pitch* is a sticky material that comes from under the bark of pine trees.
   • What is pine pitch?
2. **birch**—A *birch* is a type of tree that loses its leaves in the fall.
   • What is a birch?
3. **hemlock**—A *hemlock* is a type of tree that stays green all year long.
   • How are hemlocks different from birches?

4. **crest**—A *crest* is a tuft of feathers on top of a bird's head.
   • What is a crest?
5. **slender**—*Slender* is another word for *slim.*
   • What's another way of saying *He had a slim waist*?
6. **reveal**—When you *reveal* something, you take it out of hiding and show it or tell about it.
   • What's another way of saying *She told about her secret*?

A White Heron
Part 3

Focus Question: What did Sylvia learn about the white heron?

All night, the door of the little house stood open, and the birds came and sang on the front step. The young sportsman and Mrs. Tilley were sound asleep, but Sylvia's great plan kept her wide awake and watching. She forgot to think of sleep. The short summer night seemed as long as the winter darkness. At last, when she thought morning was near, Sylvia stole out of the house. She followed the pasture path through the woods, hurrying toward the open ground beyond.

Sylvia finally came to the huge tree in the pale moonlight. The tree reached up, up, almost to the sky itself.

First, Sylvia mounted the white oak tree that grew alongside. Her bare feet and fingers pinched and held like a bird's claws. She was soon almost lost among the dark branches and the green leaves heavy and wet with dew. A bird fluttered from its nest, and a red squirrel ran to and fro. Sylvia felt her way easily. She had often climbed here. She knew that one of the oak's upper branches rubbed against the pine tree, just where its lower branches began. When she had made the dangerous pass from one tree to the other, the great climb would really begin.

She crept out along the swaying oak limb at last and took the daring step across into the old pine tree. It was harder than she had imagined. She had to reach far and hold tightly. The sharp dry twigs caught and scratched her like angry claws, and the pine pitch made her thin little fingers clumsy and stiff. Still, she went from bough to bough round the tree's great trunk, higher and higher upward. The sparrows and robins in the woods below were just beginning to wake up, yet it seemed much lighter in the pine tree. Sylvia knew she must hurry.

As Sylvia climbed, the tree seemed to reach farther and farther upward. It was like a great mast for the earth. The birds must have been amazed that morning as they watched this determined girl creeping and climbing from branch to branch. The tree stood still and held away the winds while the dawn grew bright in the east.

Finally, Sylvia passed the last thorny bough and stood, trembling and tired, high in the treetop. To the creatures on the ground, her face was like a pale star.

Sylvia looked toward the east. There was the sea with the sun dawning over it. Two hawks flew toward the eastern horizon with slow-moving wings. How low they looked in the air from that height! Their feathers were as soft as moths. They seemed only a little way from the tree, and

Sylvia almost felt as if she too could go flying away among the clouds.

To the west, the woodlands and farms reached miles and miles into the distance.

Here and there were church steeples and white villages. Truly, it was a vast and awesome world. ◆

The birds sang louder and louder. At last, the bright sun came up. The purple and rose-colored clouds began to fade away. Sylvia could see the white sails of ships at sea.

But where was the white heron's nest? Was this wonderful sight of the world the only reward for having climbed so high?

Sylvia looked down again, toward the green marsh set among the shining birches and dark hemlocks. There, where she had seen the white heron once, she saw him again!

A white spot of him, like a single floating feather, came up from the dead hemlock and grew larger. He rose and came close at last. He flew by the pine tree with a steady sweep of wing. His long legs stretched out behind him. Sylvia did not dare to move a toe or a finger. The heron perched on a pine bough not far from hers. Then he called back to his mate in the nest and began to plume his feathers.

Sylvia gave a long sigh a minute later when the solemn heron flew away. She knew his secret now. The wild, light, slender bird floated and wavered. Then he went back like an arrow to his home in the green hemlock trees.

Sylvia made her way down again, not daring to look at the ground. She was ready to cry because her fingers ached and her feet kept slipping. She wondered over and over again what the stranger would say to her and what he would think when she told him how to find his way straight to the herons' nest.

• • •

"Sylvia! Sylvia!" called Mrs. Tilley again and again, but nobody answered. The small bed was empty, and Sylvia had disappeared. ★

The young man was awakened by Mrs. Tilley's call. He hurried to dress himself. From the moment he had come to the cottage, he had suspected that the girl had at least seen the white heron and knew where it dwelled. He was determined to make her reveal her secret.

At last, he saw Sylvia coming down the path. Her worn old shirt was torn and tattered and smeared with pine pitch. Mrs. Tilley ran out to question her, and the young man followed. The moment had come for Sylvia to tell the secret of the white heron.

But Sylvia did not speak. Mrs. Tilley kept asking, "Where have you been? Why did you leave the house during the night?" But Sylvia did not tell where she had been or what she had seen. The young man looked straight into her eyes and asked if she had seen the white heron, but she simply bent her head and refused to answer.

Even as she stood there, she wondered what it was that suddenly prevented her from speaking. Why was she giving up the money to save the life of a bird? But she knew why she couldn't betray the heron. The murmur of the pine's green branches was still in her ears. She remembered how the white heron came flying through the golden air and how she and the great white bird had watched the sea and the morning together. Sylvia could not speak. She could not tell the heron's secret and give its life away.

• • •

The young man went away later in the day. For a long time afterwards, Sylvia heard the echo of his whistle haunting the pasture path when she came home with the cow. During these haunting moments, she wondered if the heron was a better friend than the hunter might have been. Who can tell?

D SARCASM

Write the answers for items 1–4.

Sometimes people say the opposite of what they really mean. But they give evidence that they don't mean what they say. When people speak in this way, they are using **sarcasm.**

Here's an example of sarcasm: *A man says, "I just love going to work. I love to sit there all day long and do boring things. I love to sit at my desk when I could be outside playing golf with nobody telling me what to do."*

1. How does the man say he feels about work?
2. The man gives evidence that contradicts what he says. Name something he says about work that contradicts the idea that he loves it.

Here's another example of sarcasm: *A woman says, "My, wasn't that a good television show. There's nothing I like more than watching two people argue about unimportant things. The show was almost as exciting as waiting for a bus in the rain."*

3. The woman says something that she later contradicts. What is that?
4. Name one piece of evidence that contradicts her statement.

E INFERENCE

Read the following passage and answer the questions.

Photosynthesis

Plants and animals need food to survive, but they get their food in different ways. Animals must hunt for their food. Animals that eat plants must hunt for those plants. Animals that eat meat must hunt and kill other animals and eat their meat.

Green plants are different. They don't have to hunt for food because they manufacture their own food. The leaves of green plants convert three ingredients—sunlight, water, and carbon dioxide—into food for the entire plant. This process is called *photosynthesis.*

1. Name the three ingredients used by leaves to manufacture food for the entire plant.
2. Is that question answered by **words** or by a **deduction?**
3. What do we call the process by which a plant manufactures its own food?
4. **Words** or **deduction?**
5. Does a giraffe hunt for food or manufacture food?
6. **Words** or **deduction?**
7. Does an elm tree hunt for food or manufacture food?
8. **Words** or **deduction?**

F COMPREHENSION

Write the answers.

1. What did Sylvia learn about the white heron?
2. The story says the pine tree "was like a great mast for the earth." Explain what that simile means.
3. How do you think Sylvia felt about the heron when she looked at him?
4. Why did Sylvia decide to keep the heron's secret?
5. Do you think the heron was a better friend than the hunter might have been? Explain your answer.

G WRITING

The story described what the world looked like to Sylvia from the top of the pine tree.

Describe what the world looks like from where you're sitting right now. Look all around you and tell what you see. Try to answer the following questions:

- What do you see in front of you?
- What colors, shapes, and sizes do the objects have?
- What kind of light is in the air?
- What objects are moving? What are their movements like?
- How does the sight make you feel?

Make your description at least sixty words long.

Ⓐ WORD LISTS

1

Word Practice
1. prevailing
2. awesome
3. plough
4. ploughboy

2

New Vocabulary
1. doth
2. hath
3. anon
4. ploughboy

Ⓑ VOCABULARY DEFINITIONS

1. **doth**—*Doth* is an old word for *does*.
   - What's another way of saying *He does seem well*?
2. **hath**—*Hath* is an old word for *has*.
   - What's another way of saying *She has not spoken*?

3. **anon**—*Anon* is an old word for *again*.
   - What's another way of saying *I will take the test again*?
4. **ploughboy**—A *ploughboy* is a boy who helps a farmer plow fields.
   - What does a ploughboy do?

Written in March
by William Wordsworth

The cock is crowing,
The stream is flowing,
The small birds twitter,
The lake doth glitter,
The green field sleeps in the sun;
The oldest and youngest
Are at work with the strongest;
The cattle are grazing,
Their heads never raising;
There are forty feeding like one!

Like an army defeated
The snow hath retreated,
And now doth fare ill
On the top of the bare hill;
The ploughboy is whooping—anon—anon:
There's joy in the mountains;
There's life in the fountains;
Small clouds are sailing,
Blue sky prevailing;
The rain is over and gone!

D SARCASM

Write the answers for items 1–4.

Sometimes people say the opposite of what they really mean. But they give evidence that they don't mean what they say. When people speak in this way, they are using **sarcasm.**

Here's an example of sarcasm: *A father told his daughter, "Thanks for all your help, Rita. I really appreciated the way you looked on as I made your bed and picked up all your dirty clothes. I hope you're not all tired out."*

1. How does the father say he feels about Rita's help?
2. The father gives evidence that contradicts what he says. Tell something he says about Rita's help that contradicts the idea that he appreciates it.

Here's another example of sarcasm: *Odelia says, "Oh, I feel just great. My right leg is broken in two places, and I have a burn on my left hand. I'd like to have another accident as soon as possible."*

3. Odelia says something that she later contradicts. What is that?
4. Name one piece of evidence that contradicts her statement.

E INFERENCE

Read the following passage and answer the questions.

Herbivores and Carnivores

Different kinds of animals eat different things. Animals that eat plants are called *herbivores.* Animals that eat herbivores and other animals are called *carnivores.*

Herbivores could not survive without plants. If there were no plants, herbivores would have nothing to eat and would soon become extinct.

But carnivores need plants as much as herbivores do. If there were no plants, there soon wouldn't be any more herbivores for carnivores to eat. Carnivores would then have to eat each other. Before long, the carnivores would run out of food, and they would become extinct.

Herbivores feed directly on green plants. Carnivores feed indirectly on green plants because they feed on animals that feed on plants.

1. What are carnivores?
2. Is that question answered by **words** or by a **deduction?**
3. What are herbivores?
4. **Words** or **deduction?**
5. Is a lion a carnivore or a herbivore?
6. **Words** or **deduction?**
7. Does a lion feed directly on green plants?
8. **Words** or **deduction?**

F VOCABULARY REVIEW

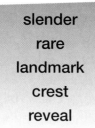

slender

rare

landmark

crest

reveal

For each item, write the correct word.
1. A tuft of feathers on top of a bird's head is a ▬▬.
2. Another word for *slim* is ▬▬.
3. When you take something out of hiding and show it or tell about it, you ▬▬ that thing.

G COMPREHENSION

Write the answers.
1. One line of the poem says, "The lake doth glitter." Why is the lake glittering?
2. Another line says, "The green field sleeps in the sun." Explain the metaphor in that line.
3. Two other lines say, "Like an army defeated/The snow hath retreated." How is the snow like a defeated army?
4. Why do you think the ploughboy is whooping anon and anon?
5. The last two lines say, "Blue sky prevailing;/The rain is over and gone!" Explain what those lines mean.

H WRITING

"Written in March" describes springtime in the country.

Write a poem that describes the current season in your neighborhood— winter, spring, summer, or fall. Think about the following questions before writing your poem:
• What sights do you see in your neighborhood during this season?
• What sounds do you hear during this season?
• What odors do you smell during this season?
• What other things do you feel or sense during this season?
• What is the weather like?
Make your poem at least ten lines long. Your lines do not have to rhyme.

Glossary

A

abroad When you go *abroad*, you travel outside your country.

absurd *Absurd* is another word for *ridiculous*.

accomplish When you *accomplish* something, you succeed in doing that thing.

accustomed When you are *accustomed* to something, you are used to that thing.

adorn When you *adorn* something, you decorate it.

advanced When something is *advanced*, it is ahead of other things.

affair When something is your *affair*, it is your business.

agitated When you are *agitated*, you are excited and nervous.

agreeable When something is *agreeable*, it is pleasing.

ancestors Your *ancestors* are your relatives who lived many generations ago.

anguish When you feel *anguish*, you feel extreme pain or sorrow.

anon *Anon* is an old word for *again*.

appeal When you *appeal*, you make an earnest request.

apt When you are *apt* to do something, you are likely to do it.

assemble When people *assemble*, they get together in a group.

awe When you are *awed* by something, you are amazed by that thing.

B

Bastille The *Bastille* was a prison in Paris, France, where French kings kept prisoners.

batter *Batter* is used to make doughnuts, pancakes, and similar foods.

bedraggled When something is *bedraggled*, it is muddy and limp.

bedstead A *bedstead* is the frame of a bed.

behold When you *behold* something, you observe it.

best man The *best man* is a person who assists the groom during a wedding.

bewildered Someone who is *bewildered* is very confused.

birch A *birch* is a type of tree that loses its leaves in the fall.

boar A *boar* is a wild pig.

bough A *bough* of a tree is a branch of the tree.

box social A *box social* is a fund-raising event where box lunches are sold to the highest bidder.

bricklebrit *Bricklebrit* is a nonsense word, like *abracadabra*, that people use to cast a spell.

bronze *Bronze* is made by mixing copper with other metals.

broth *Broth* is clear soup.

burro A *burro* is a small donkey.

C

calamity A *calamity* is a misfortune.

canvas *Canvas* is a strong cloth used for sails. Artists sometimes paint on canvas.

caress When you *caress* people or animals, you lightly stroke them.

carpenter A *carpenter* is a skilled person who makes things from wood.

cavern A *cavern* is a large cave.

cease When something *ceases*, it stops.

challenging *Challenging* is another word for *difficult*.

chauffeur A *chauffeur* is a person who is paid to drive a car for somebody else.

cherish When you *cherish* something, you value it.

chute A *chute* is a slide.

citizens *Citizens* are people who live in a place.

clasp A *clasp* is a hook that holds objects together. Some necklaces have a clasp at the back.

collapse When you *collapse*, you fall down suddenly.

commotion A *commotion* is a disturbance.

compose When you *compose* something, you make up that thing.

contempt When you show *contempt*, you show hatred or disrespect.

contestant A *contestant* is somebody who takes part in a contest.

coop A *coop* is a cage for small animals.

core *Core* is another word for *center*.

corral A *corral* is a fenced area for farm animals.

courteous *Courteous* is another word for *polite*.

craving When you have a *craving* for something, you have a great desire for that thing.

create a market When you *create a market*, you create a demand.

crest A *crest* is a tuft of feathers on top of a bird's head.

crimson *Crimson* is a deep red color.

croon When you *croon*, you sing softly.

cross *Cross* is another word for *irritated*.

curlew A *curlew* is a brown sea bird with long legs and a long, curving bill.

custom A *custom* is a way of behaving that everybody follows.

D

dainty When something is *dainty*, it is fine and delicate.

day of reckoning The *day of reckoning* is a time when people are repaid for their good deeds or their bad deeds.

decay When something *decays*, it rots.

decked out When you are *decked out*, you are dressed up.

deed A *deed* is an action.

delicacies *Delicacies* are the finest and richest foods.

demand The *demand* for a product tells how many people want to buy that product. When the demand is high, many people want to buy the product.

depart When you *depart* from a place, you leave that place.

dependable When something is *dependable*, it always works without failing.

deprive When you are *deprived* of something, that thing is taken away from you.

detained When you are *detained*, you are held against your will.

devoted Someone who is *devoted* is loyal.

devour When you *devour* something, you eat it quickly.

diameter The *diameter* of a circle is the length of a straight line that goes through the center of the circle.

disaster A *disaster* is a horrible event.

discard When you *discard* something, you throw it away.

distinguished A *distinguished* person is an outstanding person.

diversion A *diversion* is something that pulls your attention away from something else.

divine *Divine* is another word for *marvelous*.

doth *Doth* is an old word for *does*.

drab *Drab* is another word for *dreary*.

dramatic When speech or gestures are *dramatic*, they produce emotion.

draw straws When people *draw straws*, they pull pieces of straw out of a bundle. Whoever pulls out the shortest piece has to do a hard job.

dusky When something is *dusky*, it is like twilight.

E

easel An *easel* is a frame that an artist uses to hold a picture.

efface When you *efface* something, you erase it.

emerge When something *emerges* from a place, it comes out of that place.

encounter When you *encounter* something, you come into contact with that thing.

endure When you *endure* a painful experience, you survive that experience.

enlarge When you *enlarge* something, you make it bigger.

entice When you *entice* somebody, you tempt that person.

ex- The prefix *ex-* means "former."

excessive *Excessive* means "too much."

exchange When you *exchange* something, you trade it for something else.

exhausted When you are *exhausted*, you are very tired.

exquisite When something is *exquisite*, it is beautifully made.

F

fasting When you are *fasting*, you don't eat any food.

fawn A *fawn* is a young deer.

feeble When something is *feeble*, it is very weak.

flask A *flask* is a kind of bottle.

flee When you *flee*, you run away from danger.

fleece *Fleece* is the fur of a sheep.

for a spell *For a spell* is another way of saying "for a while."

forlorn When you are *forlorn*, you are sad and lonely.

foster parent A *foster parent* is somebody who brings up a child but is not the child's real parent.

frail Somebody who is *frail* is weak and delicate.

franc A *franc* used to be the basic unit of money in France.

frivolous *Frivolous* is another word for *foolish*.

fulfill When something is *fulfilled*, that thing comes true.

G

gadget A *gadget* is a device.

gallant Somebody who is *gallant* is brave and noble.

game Wild animals that are hunted are called *game*.

garret *Garret* is another word for *attic*.

gift One meaning of *gift* is "talent."

gnarled When something is *gnarled*, it is twisted and full of knots.

goblin A *goblin* is an ugly and wicked fairy.

gourd A *gourd* is a fruit with a hard shell. People sometimes use gourd shells as tools or containers.

grate A *grate* is a frame of iron bars designed to hold wood in a fireplace or stove.

gratify *Gratify* is another word for *satisfy*.

graze When animals *graze*, they eat plants that are growing in the ground.

grisly When something is *grisly*, it is horrible or disgusting.

H

hath *Hath* is an old word for *has*.

health hazard When something is a *health hazard*, it is dangerous to your health.

hemlock A *hemlock* is a type of tree that stays green all year long.

heron *Herons* are birds that wade through water and eat frogs and fish.

hideous When something is *hideous*, it is horrible or disgusting.

hinder When you *hinder* people, you get in their way or slow them down.

hire When you *hire* somebody, you give that person a job.

hoe A *hoe* is a tool that is used to break up dirt.

hold the wire *Hold the wire* is another way of saying "wait a minute" to somebody on the phone.

horrid When something is *horrid*, it is horrible or disgusting.

hostler A *hostler* is a person who takes care of horses or mules.

huckleberry A *huckleberry* is a small purple or black berry that grows on bushes.

humiliating When something is *humiliating*, it is quite embarrassing.

I

idiotic When something is *idiotic*, it is stupid.

idle When something is *idle*, it is still and not working.

illuminated When something is *illuminated*, it is lit up.

impudent Somebody who is *impudent* is rude and bold.

incident An *incident* is an event.

inclined When you are *inclined* to do something, you have a tendency to do it.

indignant When you are *indignant*, you are angry and insulted.

inherit When you *inherit* things, you receive them from somebody who has died.

in the midst When you're *in the midst* of something, you're in the middle of that thing.

in vain When you do something *in vain*, you do it without any success.

J

jostled When you are *jostled*, you are pushed and shoved.

juniper A *juniper* is a bush with strong-smelling berries.

L

landmark A *landmark* is an easily recognized feature of a landscape.

lasso A *lasso* is a rope that is used to catch horses and cattle.

launch When you *launch* a ship, you put it into water.

liberty *Liberty* is another word for *freedom*.

lice *Lice* are small insects that live in the hair of people and other animals.

liver Your *liver* is an organ in your body that keeps your blood healthy.

lobby A *lobby* is a waiting room at the entrance of a hotel or other large building.

lofty When something is *lofty*, it is very high.

loom A *loom* is a device used for weaving cloth.

lunatic asylum *Lunatic asylum* is an old term for a place where mentally ill people live.

lurk When someone *lurks*, that person hides somewhere for an evil purpose.

luscious When something is *luscious*, it is delicious.

lush When plants are *lush*, they are growing well and have lots of leaves.

luxurious When something is *luxurious*, it is fine and elegant.

M

maneuver When you *maneuver*, you move skillfully.

massive When something is *massive*, it is very large.

mast A *mast* is a large pole that holds up sails on a sailing ship.

melancholy When you are *melancholy*, you are sad.

merchandise When you *merchandise* a product, you carry out a plan for selling that product.

mesa A *mesa* is a large landform with steep sides and a flat top.

minstrel *Minstrels* are entertainers. In ancient Greece, minstrels told stories, sang songs, and played the lyre.

mirage A *mirage* is something that seems to be there but is really not there at all.

miscalculation A *miscalculation* is an error or a mistake.

mist *Mist* is fine rain.

morsel A *morsel* is a bit of food.

motive A person's *motive* for doing something is a person's reason for doing that thing.

mount When you *mount* something, you climb it.

N

neglect When you *neglect* something, you fail to take care of it.

nevermore *Nevermore* means "never again."

New England *New England* is the northeastern part of the United States.

noble A *noble* person is proud and brave.

nonetheless *Nonetheless* is another way of saying "in spite of that."

nourishment The ingredients of food that help your body work and grow are called *nourishment.*

O

obliged When you are *obliged* to do something, you are required to do it.

of your own accord When you do something *of your own accord*, you do it willingly.

one chance in ten In a group of ten people, if there's *one chance in ten* that somebody in the group will get sick, one of the people in the group will probably get sick.

orchard An *orchard* is a farm where fruit trees or nut trees are grown.

outcast An *outcast* is somebody who is thrown out of a group.

outrage An *outrage* is a great insult.

P

palette A *palette* is a thin board that artists use for mixing paint.

parasol A *parasol* is a light umbrella that people use to shade themselves.

parcel A *parcel* is a package.

peer When you *peer* at something, you stare at that thing.

peril A *peril* is a danger.

perish When something *perishes*, it dies.

persistent When something is *persistent*, it won't give up.

pertain Information that *pertains* to something relates to that thing.

pine pitch *Pine pitch* is a sticky material that comes from under the bark of pine trees.

pinochle *Pinochle* is a card game played with a special deck of cards.

plaid *Plaid* is a type of fabric covered with crisscrossing stripes.

plaza A *plaza* is an open area surrounded by walls or buildings.

ploughboy A *ploughboy* is a boy who helps a farmer plow fields.

pluck When you *pluck* a plant from the ground, you quickly remove it from the ground.

plume A *plume* is a large feather. People sometimes wear plumes on hats.

pneumonia *Pneumonia* is a disease that attacks the lungs.

pomegranate A *pomegranate* is a red fruit that contains many seeds.

ponder When you *ponder* something, you think about it.

pottery Dishes and pots made of clay are called *pottery.*

precious When something is *precious*, it has great value or costs a lot of money.

preen When a bird *preens* itself, it uses its beak to fluff its feathers.

proposal A *proposal* is an offer or a plan to do something.

prudent When you are *prudent*, you are wise and careful.

quiver A *quiver* is a container for arrows.

R

rare When something is *rare*, it is hard to find.

receipt *Receipt* is another word for *recipe.*

reception A *reception* is a party that takes place after an important event.

recollect *Recollect* is another word for *remember.*

regard When you *regard*, you consider.

rejoice When you *rejoice*, you feel great joy or delight.

remarkable When something is *remarkable*, it is uncommon or unusual.

reveal When you *reveal* something, you take it out of hiding and show it or tell about it.

revenge When you take *revenge* on someone, you get even with that person.

rheumatism *Rheumatism* is a disease that affects people's muscles and joints.

risk When you take a *risk*, you take a chance.

rodeo A *rodeo* is a show that includes bull riding and calf roping.

roost When birds *roost*, they sit on a branch or a perch.

rot When something *rots*, it becomes soft and falls apart.

ruins *Ruins* are the remains of old buildings.

S

satin *Satin* is a smooth and shiny fabric.

savage When something is *savage*, it is wild and cruel.

scant If there is not enough of something, that thing is *scant.*

scoff at When you *scoff at* something, you make fun of that thing.

sheltered When something is *sheltered*, it is protected.

shock A thick bunch of hair or other material is sometimes called a *shock.*

shriveled When something is *shriveled*, it is wrinkled and withered.

shuffle When you *shuffle*, you walk slowly and drag your feet.

skeptical When you are *skeptical* about something, you are suspicious of that thing.

skylight A *skylight* is a window in the roof of a house.

slay When you *slay* something, you kill it.

slender *Slender* is another word for *slim.*

smarting When something is *smarting*, it is painful or stinging.

smudge When you *smudge* something, you smear it.

sow the seeds of doom When you *sow the seeds of doom* for somebody, you plan how to punish that person.

splendor *Splendor* is another word for *beauty.*

sprouts *Sprouts* are young plants that are just starting to grow.

spurn When you *spurn* something, you reject it.

squash *Squash* is a vegetable that is like a pumpkin.

squat When something is *squat*, it is short and thick.

stalk When a hunter *stalks* an animal, the hunter follows the animal quietly.

steed *Steed* is another word for *horse.*

stroller A *stroller* is a small carriage for babies and young children.

studio A *studio* is a room where an artist works.

subscribe When you *subscribe* to a magazine, you pay money to the magazine and receive each issue in the mail.

subside When something *subsides*, it settles down.

suitable When something is *suitable*, it is appropriate.

suitor A man who wants to marry a particular woman is that woman's *suitor*.

sullen When you are *sullen*, you are gloomy and silent.

summon When you *summon* a person, you order that person to go somewhere.

superb When something is *superb*, it is truly great.

supple When something is *supple*, it is flexible and easy to bend.

surf The *surf* is the waves near a shore.

swagger When you *swagger*, you walk around with great confidence.

sympathize When you *sympathize* with someone, you understand that person's feelings.

T

tamper When you *tamper* with something, you meddle with that thing.

tar *Tar* is a hard black substance that turns into a sticky mass when it is heated.

tenant A *tenant* is a person who rents space in a building.

tether When you *tether* an animal, you tie it with a rope or a chain to an object.

threshold The *threshold* of a place is the entrance of that place.

translate When you tell a story in another language, you *translate* the story into that language.

trio A *trio* is a group of three.

triumphant *Triumphant* is another word for *victorious*.

tropical Warm areas of the earth where plants grow year-round are called *tropical*. Plants from these areas are called *tropical* plants.

twine When something *twines*, it wraps around something else.

twitch A *twitch* is a quick, nervous gesture.

U

undisputed If something is *undisputed*, there is no doubt about it.

unearthly When something is *unearthly*, it is unlike things you normally find on earth.

unkindly disposed When you are *unkindly disposed* toward something, you don't like it.

unprecedented Something that is *unprecedented* has never occurred before.

unravel When you *unravel* a garment, you pull apart its threads.

up and coming Something that is becoming popular is *up and coming*.

uproar An *uproar* is a loud commotion.

V

vacant *Vacant* is another word for *empty*.

vague When something is *vague*, it is unclear.

vent When you *vent* your emotions, you let them show.

victorious A *victorious* person is one who wins.

vow A *vow* is a promise.

wallow When something *wallows*, it struggles in mud or water.

wardrobe All the clothes you have are called your *wardrobe*.

wilderness A *wilderness* is a wild place with no signs of people.

wilt When plants *wilt*, they dry up and droop.

wrath *Wrath* is another word for *anger*.

wretch A *wretch* is a miserable person.

yucca *Yucca* is a plant that grows in the desert.